More Praise for *The Intuitive Compass*

"I was fortunate enough to meet Francis Cholle in 2009, introduce him into our company, and experience The Intuitive Compass in action. This game changing approach to rethinking your business allowed us to re-invent ourselves and break the mold of the past. Despite economic volatility we grew revenue streams profitably, increased our share of the market, and created new opportunities. We now have a successful, innovative team poised to leverage a sea of opportunities in the digital marketplace. I strongly recommend his work and urge you to engage The Intuitive Compass."

— Nick Matarazzo, CEO, Jumpstart Automotive Group

"The Intuitive Compass is helpful for better decision making. It is a very valuable model to succeed in the fast changing and complex environment of the new economy."

— Nicolas Kachaner, senior partner & managing director,
Boston Consulting Group

"The fast, aggressive competition of today requires enterprises to unleash and stimulate creative thinking (and feeling!) to win. Francis Cholle completely gets where the business is going and knows how to guide leaders to get there. The Initiative Compass makes it tangible, actionable and scalable."

— Eric Thoreux, chief marketing officer, Essilor Group Worldwide;
executive president, Sun and Readers division

"As a physician moving into the medical device industry after 20 years of practice in a University hospital, I was in dire need of a mentor. Francis guided my first steps in this new world and helped me understand how to use my emotion and instinct-dominated mind in a rational corporate environment. His original holistic approach and rich background were instrumental to making this transition successful."

— Christian Spaulding, M.D., worldwide vice president,
medical affairs, Cordis

"Francis Cholle's approach helped Firmenich enormously in re-engineering our focus on creativity with a unique new perspective. The Intuitive Compass makes tangible the intangible and by doing so it helps to inspire and lead creative teams to an optimal level of performance."

— Jerry Vittoria, president, fine fragrances, Firmenich North America

"With The Intuitive Compass, Francis Cholle presents a revolutionary new approach to unlock the incredible human potential for innovation and creation in any form. Cholle's insights are both compelling and clear and the results he has helped us achieve at Matrix are outstanding!"

— Colin Walsh, vice president / general manager, Matrix

"With The Intuitive Compass, Francis Cholle has developed a breakthrough model for sparking creative thinking and guiding better decision making. It is simple to comprehend and use while honoring the complexity of human nature. The best of any business should come into clearer view when following such an original framework."

— Roy Pea, David Jacks Professor of Education and Learning Sciences, Stanford University

"The current transformative and transitioning business climate mandates change for any company to survive and thrive. Francis Cholle's innovative, holistic approach to business in the 21st century enables companies to re-think, re-tool and re-invent, ensuring success."

— Deborah Burns, managing director, American Media International Ventures

"Francis Cholle is the Al Gore of Creativity, evangelizing an 'inconvenient truth' of an altogether different kind—that creativity is actually declining at an alarming rate. The Intuitive Compass is a sure path business leaders can use to guide them towards innovation, disruptive thinking, and the creative atmosphere necessary to succeed in today's disorienting business climate."

— Mike Lundgren, partner and director of innovation strategy, VML (Young & Rubicam)

"What strikes one the most after reading *The Intuitive Compass* is the lucid and effortless way it leads the reader's mind to look into his/her decision making system—prodding one to reflect that we recognize the role of the gut or intuition in our lives but rarely acknowledge the same in public spaces. The well articulated role of play and how it needs to flow into work, the benefits of sometimes circumventing reason to tap into our reservoir of creativity are not very 'comfortable' suggestions for minds trained to revere reason, logic and tangibles. I love the way the content pushes the reader out of his/her comfort zone to question, reflect, learn, and experience; the book caters to this whole process and at the same time doesn't favor/disfavor any view with force. Francis Cholle's book is a gift to the restless world."

— Brij Bakshi, director, Doordarshan

the *intuitive* compass

francis p. cholle

the *intuitive* compass

WHY THE BEST DECISIONS BALANCE REASON AND INSTINCT

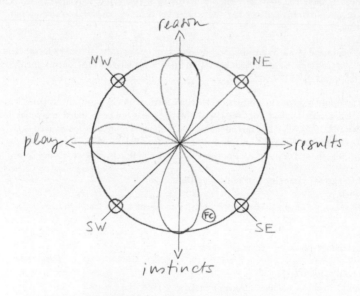

JOSSEY-BASS
A Wiley Imprint
www.josseybass.com

Published by Jossey-Bass
A Wiley Imprint
989 Market Street, San Francisco, CA 94103-1741—www.josseybass.com

Jossey-Bass books and products are available through most bookstores. To contact Jossey-Bass directly call our Customer Care Department within the U.S. at 800-956-7739, outside the U.S. at 317-572-3986, or fax 317-572-4002.

Wiley also publishes its books in a variety of electronic formats and by print-on-demand. Some material included with standard print versions of this book may not be included in e-books or in print-on-demand. If the version of this book that you purchased references media such as CD or DVD that was not included in your purchase, you may download this material at http://booksupport.wiley.com. For more information about Wiley products, visit www.wiley.com.

Library of Congress Cataloging-in-Publication Data
Cholle, Francis P.
   The intuitive compass : why the best decisions balance reason and instinct / Francis P. Cholle.
—1st ed.
      p. cm.
   Includes bibliographical references and index.
   ISBN 978-1-118-07754-2; ISBN 978-1-118-11907-5 (ebk) ; ISBN 978-1-118-11908-2 (ebk); ISBN 978-1-118-11909-9 (ebk)
   1. Intuition. 2. Problem solving. 3. Decision making. I. Title.
   BF315.5.C45 2012
   153.4′4—dc23

                                                                2011025364

Printed in the United States of America
FIRST EDITION
HB Printing   10 9 8 7 6 5 4 3 2 1

The intuitive mind is a sacred gift and the rational mind is a faithful servant. We have created a society that honors the servant and has forgotten the gift.
—ALBERT EINSTEIN

contents

A la que sabe

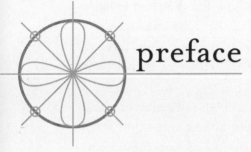 preface

*There are two ways to live your life — one is as though nothing is
a miracle, the other is as though everything is a miracle.*
—ALBERT EINSTEIN

In 2002 the head of training and career management at L'Oréal
USA, Bertrand de Laleu, asked me to design a global training
seminar for L'Oréal's executives on the management of creative
teams. This assignment is partly what led to the development of the
Intuitive Compass, although I was unaware of it at the time. Bertrand
and I had been introduced sometime before, and he knew I had a diverse
background and an interest in human development and creativity. In
addition, knowing that I have worked and lived in both Europe and
the United States, Bertrand felt I could understand the dynamics of
a French-born enterprise that had become the world's largest beauty
company. He did not know how much I could also appreciate the
challenges of bringing science and marketing together.

I was born into a scientific family — in fact, three generations of scientists. Among my grandparents, parents, aunts, uncles, cousins, and siblings there are medical doctors, mathematicians, biologists, chemists, engineers, surgeons, pharmacists, and physicists. This helped me understand the scientific mind and its quest for rational solutions. However, I didn't display any professional interest in the sciences and did not feel any inclination to follow in my family's footsteps. A familiar refrain from my father, an engineer, was "When are you going to do things like other people!?" I heard this all my life. You can imagine his relief when I was accepted at HEC, the leading business school in Europe, and when, a couple of years after graduation, I was hired to lead a prestigious publishing company in Paris. However, his relief was relatively short-lived.

Hazan Publishing, which was founded in 1946 and had an excellent reputation for the creation of fine art books, hired me at a time when they were in dire financial straits. My mission was to orchestrate its revival. Within three years Hazan doubled in size and was ranked as the most profitable publishing house in France. By the age of twenty-eight, I had become a significant shareholder in Hazan and was financially very successful in an industry that enabled me to leverage my business training as well as my personal interest in the arts. However, as much as I enjoyed the challenge of leading this publishing company's revival, I was frustrated by the responsibilities that came with being at the top of a company. I had tremendous energy and a lot of desire to be a part of making the company successful — and we had achieved that, to a great degree — but the way we were doing it was draining me, and probably my employees too. I felt that I was carrying the heavy weight of employees who didn't always want to take responsibility for their own decisions and professional growth. That was true, in part, but I was also contributing to their inability to become autonomous and empowered because of my partner's and my own need for control. I did not know any better.

In addition, my business partner and I had come to the realization that we had irreconcilable views about the leadership of the company and its strategic impact on the business. He was a high-profile French intellectual whose views were strongly inspired by communism born out of the French Resistance and a European political tradition. He would often say that he was uncomfortable leading a capitalistic organization. In his opinion it was organized exploitation. His leadership style was rather paternalistic and authoritarian. He was inclined to dominate work relationships with his exceptional intellect, and he paid little attention to how employees would feel. I, on the other hand, had the strong conviction that empowerment and a holistic approach to people's inspirations and differences in personality could result in more creativity, autonomy, and success—and, conversely, that his approach to leadership would keep the company stuck at best or bankrupt it at worst. These two facts were enough for me to make the decision to embark on new adventures. So I ended this first chapter of my professional life and moved to New York City to pursue new personal and business ventures.

I spent the next decade surrounded by artists and artistic groups, humanists, visionaries, creative entrepreneurs, and change agents. I studied acting at the Lee Strasberg Theater Institute and took music and singing lessons. I acted and sang opera professionally, and I directed off-Broadway theater performances. I studied clinical psychology and how the human voice influences the development of the psyche. I traveled broadly, participated in the art and culture of Lakota Native Americans, and explored shamanic traditions. After ten years of intense yoga practice in New York, I visited India to study Hinduism in an ashram set on the banks of the Ganges River high in the Himalayas, where I received professional certification to teach the art and science of yoga.

It is a truism that the one thing that doesn't change in life is change; we are constantly dealing with the unknown. A decade immersed in the performing arts and cultural studies gave me a new perspective on how the modern world deals with change. When directing or acting, I had to accept that great art is not about control. It is about having discipline in the preparation and surrendering during the performance.

Management, at least the way I had experienced it, is about controlling the environment to ensure flawless execution and reach the expected results. Management is a powerful means to reach one's ends, but my artistic journey made me realize that in the modern world, our fear of change and our inability to deal creatively with the unpredictability of change lead us to seek control over the process of life. This means that although management should be about stabilizing our environment to facilitate the natural creative process belying any human activity, we attempt to control the process to secure the results we want; we do everything we can to eliminate the unknown, but in doing so we work against the creative nature of life.

There was value in all I had been exposed to, and it made me want to redefine and expand my professional horizons in a way that would merge my varied interests in life and allow me to be of service to society. So when L'Oréal approached me about designing a seminar for them, it was an interesting opportunity that gave me the means with which to take a bold step toward putting my ideas into action with the highest level of leadership in the corporate world.

The seminar I designed for L'Oréal gave their marketing directors and the managers of their R&D departments tools to leverage their own creativity and implement innovative solutions at a time when innovation was on its way to the top of the list of mandates by the CEO. In addition to being my entrée into the field of business education, this seminar was also one of two catalysts that led to the development of the Intuitive Compass. The second catalyst was my increasing preoccupation with the lack of sustainable development in the modern world.

In 2004 I decided to share my time between Los Angeles and new York. Because my clients and speaking engagements take me across the United States and to Europe frequently, I fly in and out of Los Angeles on a regular basis. Often, as the plane takes off or lands at the LAX airport, I see an enormous cloud of pollution hovering over Santa Monica's beautiful coastline. Every time I see this huge scar in the sky, I cannot help but wonder: how did we get into this impossible situation? What can we do to turn things around?

Science has created so many fantastic inventions, from vaccinations and minimally invasive surgery to the space shuttle, nanotechnologies and the Internet. How can science be used to address the endemic problem of urban pollution? How can we approach progress in a more beneficial way? How can we prosper and thrive in a way that betters all of us and everything around us?

I became more and more preoccupied with these questions. Whenever we focus on a specific topic, information relevant to the question we hold active in our mind starts to come our way. Elements of answers arrive in an unexpected fashion. I started to think of everything I had been exposed to, and I began researching contemporary scientific discoveries for new answers, with the help of enlightening conversations with good friends, experts, and other wise minds. All of these experiences not only gave me new perspectives, but also inspired my pursuit of a new integrated and balanced approach to business and problem solving.

I recognized that the logical way we approach business management is largely supported by a worldview with a considerable focus on dominance of nature and life, which has led to great destruction and inefficiency. But I also realized from personal research and practical experience that it did not have to be this way.

So, spurred on by this unexpected assignment at L'Oréal, I began trying to find workable answers to help my clients (and, I hoped, many other people) think and behave differently in business and in life, in a way that would be simultaneously creative, humble, informed, and wise—and, as a result, both more prosperous and sustainable. I knew it would require us to look at the world in a radically new way and to develop a new understanding of how life unfolds.

The fact of the matter is that life and logic don't match. In modern times we have developed a highly sophisticated relationship with the part of life that is logical, and we are much less eloquent when it comes to the part of life that is not logical. This book is about establishing a productive relationship with the part of life that is not logical so we can find solutions beyond the boundaries of what we know. My experiences are not exhaustive, but my approach was built through cautious observations, research, and reflections. And I have seen its transformational impact on leaders and organizations such as Ralph Lauren, L'Oréal, Matrix, and many other small and midsize companies worldwide.

It is not an easy task to explain through words the part of life that is not logical, so I thank you in advance for your attention and patience. If you have puzzling questions racing through your mind as you read this book, please simply remember that creative answers and understanding may come in their own mysterious ways sooner than you think.

introduction: why we need the intuitive compass

The world has been doing business the same way for a long time. Although we have always been threatened by boom and bust financial cycles, political conflict, civil and regional wars, and destructive, unsustainable environmental practices, our logical and methodical approach to business has proceeded in spite of those things. But now, businesses, large and small, global and local, are facing an unprecedented level of complexity and unpredictability. The world's social and economic pyramid is crumbling and cracking everywhere we look. An entirely new economic landscape has emerged, characterized by fast-track technology, lower barriers to entry, new consumers with new behaviors, new emerging markets, a hard-to-predict future, and pressing sustainability issues. To be successful in this fast-evolving and complex context, we must take on these new challenges, but the same old business methods won't work. It demands a creative and agile business mindset as well as powerful innovative solutions.

We need a new way of doing business. We will not get far trying to solve twenty-first-century problems with twentieth-century (and older) thinking. To function well today requires a new kind of innovation and creativity. Yet at a time when we need to better understand and use our creative processes, research shows that creativity has in fact been significantly declining for more than two decades. Intelligence scores (IQ) and creativity scores (CQ) were both regularly growing until 1990. But since then, only IQ scores have been consistently getting better, whereas CQ scores have inched significantly downward.[1] It has become essential to look more deeply into how creativity can be accessed and trained to generate a successful future for businesses.

In recent years, neuroscience research has revealed three key facts that may change forever the way we think about and approach creativity:

- Instinct plays a leading role in complex decision making.[2]
- Eighty percent of our grey matter is dedicated to nonconscious thought.[3]
- Imaginative play is one of the most direct means of activating our creativity and problem-solving abilities.[4]

These three discoveries open up unprecedented opportunities for progress, creativity, and efficiency, if we only embrace the instinctual and unconscious aspects of the mind and the randomness and chaos of life.

The uncomfortable part of this is that we are not used to relying on instinct and the unconscious, and we are certainly not used to accepting randomness or chaos. We are used to seeing life and reality as linear and logical when they aren't. Success in modern times means making a leap from seeing the world as we think it operates to seeing how it really operates. In reality both life and the whole of the human mind operate in a way that is closer to chaos than to linear order.

This, however, does not mean our world is void of any order. But it is an order that cannot be fully understood by the logic of the human mind alone. As evolutionary biology, quantum physics, and fractal geometry all show, there is at the center of chaotic, random processes a self-organizing principle that will enable order to arise. In the midst of chaos, when all things fall apart (as we will see in the story that follows), the smart thing to do is to *assist* that self-organizing principle, not resist it, because it's stronger than any individual or group of individuals, no matter how big the group may be.

In my seminars at L'Oréal, SAP, and other companies, I often recount Edgar Allan Poe's "A Descent into the Maelstrom," a story that beautifully illustrates this aspect of chaos theory. It describes how three brothers go out on their fishing boat only to be caught in "the most terrible hurricane that ever came out of the heavens." The storm drives their boat into a powerful whirlpool, the maelstrom of the title. One brother is thrown overboard into the whirlpool and quickly carried under. Another brother goes mad with terror. But the third brother is suddenly struck by the awesome beauty of the maelstrom. With an inner calm he notices that some objects are being spun around at the top of the whirlpool rather than sucked into it. Unable to convey this to his mad brother, he submits himself to the sea, clings onto a barrel, and rides the maelstrom until it subsides and he is rescued. In the meantime the mad brother, because he fights the chaos rather than submitting to it, drowns when their boat spirals down to the depths. Although the experience turns the surviving brother's hair white and makes him look older than his age, it gives him a deep insight into the workings of nature, and an enduring serenity.

I always remind participants that Poe's story shows that the way each one of us chooses to handle confusion and chaos may have a huge impact on the final outcome for everybody. Each brother acted his own way and by doing so chose his own final outcome. In Poe's story, when the third brother decides, in spite of his fear, to give up the fight with the maelstrom, he actually facilitates the organizing principle (which is well hidden in the depth of the maelstrom, yet always present) and creatively lets things fall into place. In the world, this self-organizing principle creates all the marvels that have evolved in nature. In our minds, it brings reason, feeling, and instinct into balance, if only we have the wisdom to trust it and stop trying to override it.

The Intuitive Compass addresses the problem that we think of the world and organize ourselves like this as shown in Figure I.1.

FIGURE I.1

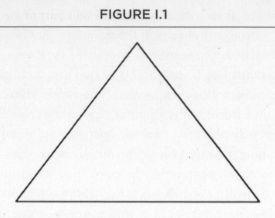

We attempt to interact with one another and arrange our institutions in hierarchical pyramids, because we have been taught that the world fundamentally operates according to physical laws that allow us to impose a predictable, stable order on our environment. We believe that our minds can and should operate in a hierarchical way, with reason directing feeling and instinct. But that thinking doesn't match up with reality.

Reality works more as shown in Figure I.2.

FIGURE I.2

This image represents a chaotic environment in which there is no sense of linear order or obvious hierarchy, all relationships are intertwined, and all parts are interdependent; therefore every part needs to be considered in relationship with the whole.

The hierarchical view of the world only tells part of the story. It is a reflection of the classical physics of the atom: a limited, finite, separate, stable entity that is always precisely identifiable in space and time. But in the 1920s physicists like Niels Bohr discovered that we cannot describe the reality of subatomic — or quantum — particles. These entities are not separate and stable but random and chaotic. Subatomic particles cannot be precisely identified in space and time except within certain probabilities, and they are entangled in mysterious ways that Albert Einstein called "spooky action at a distance."[5]

To describe reality fully, we need both classical Newtonian physics and quantum physics. Likewise, to understand how our unconscious and conscious minds work, we need to account for instinct and feeling as well as reason, for both chaotic thinking and linear thinking. As the second decade of the twenty-first century starts, even many scientists remain only dimly aware of the implications of quantum physics for the nature of reality, from the makeup of the physical world to the operations of our minds and their creative processes. That doesn't leave much hope for the rest of us.

Chaos and order can and do coexist. Figure I.3 represents a world where both logic and reason have their place and are not in contradiction with one another, although it may appear otherwise to our logical mind; it depicts a highly paradoxical world.

The good news is you don't need to fully understand the theory to understand how to be successful in our chaotic world. What you do need is *Intuitive Intelligence*.

WHAT IS INTUITIVE INTELLIGENCE?

Intuitive Intelligence is a set of skills I designed that uses intuition to get to the instinctual and nonconscious parts of our minds. It can be learned and developed, but because instinct does not operate in the same way as reason, Intuitive Intelligence requires unusual forms of learning and thinking. This is why understanding intuition is key.

Intuition doesn't seek "the truth" or even "sense." Intuition is completely open to non-sense. It dives down into the depths of the

FIGURE I.3

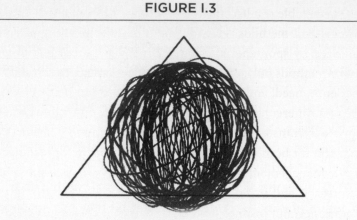

unconscious where reason and instinct collide in unexpected ways, and it latches onto hidden connections and contradictions. Then it brings this information—via an unusual sign, a rare sensation, an unexpected feeling, or a seemingly irrelevant fact—to the surface of consciousness to feed the rational mind and enable logic to work with paradox. Intuition empowers us to operate in the zone of ambiguity and change, the exact place where imagination and genius occur.

Intuitive Intelligence helps us survive in new and changing environments by incorporating intuition and instinct into our thought process and our business endeavors. The purpose of instinct is survival. Its ultimate mission is to ensure the sustainability of our species. It understands how to collaborate with and adapt to our ecosystems. This is its inherent wisdom. This is why Intuitive Intelligence is so needed today.

We access our Intuitive Intelligence via the Intuitive Compass. The Intuitive Compass helps make sense of chaos and leverage its power. It is an actionable model that applies Intuitive Intelligence in practical situations. It is based on fundamental dynamics of human performance: the tension between linear efficiency and random play, and the synergy between reason and instinct. Linear efficiency seeks an organized and predictable path that can be conveniently reproduced and leads to predictable results; efficiency is attained through well-thought-out systems and methods. Play, on the other end of the spectrum, is characterized by spontaneity and free flow; play cannot be limited to systems or methods only, and it often produces unexpected results. We all experience, need, and seek both efficiency and play in our lives, yet they are very different by nature, and it can be very difficult to create the appropriate circumstances for them to happen at once. A tension occurs when we aim for both linear efficiency and play, as in, for instance, the case of the management of creativity. This is why we need the synergy between reason and instinct; reason is a great instrument to optimize linear efficiency, but instinct — the part of us that allows us to adapt to life and constant change — is much better suited to engage with play. Both are necessary to achieve sustainable progress: reason, to break down problems, and instinct, to adapt in a way that sustains life.

As shown in Figure I.4, the four cardinal points of the Intuitive Compass are Reason in the north, Instinct in the south, Results in the east, and Play in the west. The horizontal and vertical figure eights each illustrate the dynamic and intertwined relationship between these pairs of opposite cardinal points. The Intuitive Compass is made of four quadrants that each represents a particular type of approach to business. In the northeast quadrant you will find people who are organized and result oriented, applying logical reasoning to get things done; in the southeast quadrant are people who are performance driven and rely heavily on their instinct to get results. Creative thinkers who use reason and logic for creative purposes (like architects, designers or strategic planners) will find themselves in the northwest quadrant, whereas the southwest quadrant represents people like artists, inventors, or researchers, who use play and rely on instinct to come up with new ideas and adapt to the often chaotic process of creativity and change.

The Intuitive Compass breaks down the functioning of the mind and the process of decision making. It helps us leverage the specific advantages of each of the four quadrants and create synergy among the four, which when they come together allow us to make optimum decisions.

FIGURE I.4

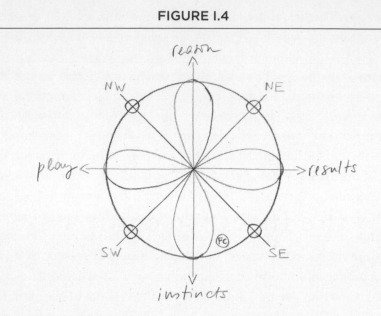

The Intuitive Compass is a proven model for successful adaptation to change, evolution, and disruption in business, education, and every other aspect of human endeavor. By using the Intuitive Compass, organizations and individuals can radically improve their approach to problem solving, optimize decision making, boost creativity, and successfully implement innovative and sustainable solutions.

This book analyzes in detail how the Intuitive Compass works and illustrates through real business cases how it can help us to redefine leadership, optimize cultures of innovation and change, rethink marketing strategies to reach new consumers who are now organized in powerful networks of influencers, and reinvent failing business models that are being challenged by lower barriers to entry due to fast-paced technology and global shifts in industrial locations.

the intuitive compass

Where do you fall on the Intuitive Compass? A great way to start understanding the Intuitive Compass is to actually use it. Take a few minutes to answer the following questionnaire; your answers will give you a snapshot of how you make decisions. As you will learn by reading this book, each person's Intuitive Compass is unique, revealing something about the person's approach to a specific topic (in this case, decision making) at a specific moment in time (today!).

For each question, rate yourself from 1 to 5 (1 is least, 5 is most) as it relates to how you approach decision making. When you are finished I will explain how to chart your answers on a diagram of the Intuitive Compass. At the end of the book, you will find guidelines to interpret what your Intuitive Compass tells you about your way of decision making and how you can apply what you will have read. I hope you will gain insights on how to optimize your decision-making process in the future.

For each question, rate yourself from 1 to 5 (1 is least, 5 is most) as it relates to how you approach decision making.

Questionnaire

1. How willing are you to review your creative options with an open mind while you are in the process of making a decision?

2. How willing are you to systematically gather facts and data surrounding your decisions?

3. How willing are you to evaluate the potential outcome of your decisions before you make them?

4. How organized are you in making the best use of the time you have to make decisions?

5. How willing are you to approach making a decision with a playful attitude — that is, not focusing on expected tangible results?

6. How committed are you to making proactive decisions when the decision-making process is challenging and it would be easier to avoid making a decision altogether?

7. How ready are you to question your own ideas and beliefs while making a decision?

8. How willing are you to be present in your emotions, regardless of whether they are pleasant or unpleasant, while you are in the process of making a decision?

9. How willing are you to organize your environment and resources to optimize your decision making?

10. How willing are you to openly explore new concepts and new perspectives while making a decision?

11. How committed are you to making the best decision possible?

12. How accepting are you of being confused while you are in the process of making a decision?

To calculate how you score in each quadrant:

For the northeast quadrant, using Table IC.1, add questions #2, 4, and 9 and divide the total by 3.

Table IC.1   Northeast Quadrant Score

Question number	Your Score
2	
4	
9	
Total	
Total Divided by 3	

For the southeast quadrant, using Table IC.2, add questions #3, 6, and 11 and divide the total by 3.

Table IC.2   Southeast Quadrant Score

Question Number	Your Score
3	
6	
11	
Total	
Total Divided by 3	

For the northwest quadrant, using Table IC.3, add questions #1, 7, and 10 and divide the total by 3.

Table IC.3   Northwest Quadrant Score

Question Number	Your Score
1	
7	
10	
Total	
Total Divided by 3	

For the southwest quadrant, using Table IC.4, add questions #5, 8, and 12 and divide the total by 3.

Table IC.4   Southwest Quadrant Score

Question Number	Your Score
5	
8	
12	
Total	
Total divided by 3	

YOUR INTUITIVE COMPASS

Mark a dot in each quadrant at the point on the line that is closest to your score for that quadrant and then draw lines to connect the dots in all quadrants. Refer to the sample in Figure IC.1, a completed compass for someone who scored 2 in the Northeast, 3 in the southeast, 4 in the southwest, and 3 in the northwest.

FIGURE IC.1 Example: the Intuitive Compass of someone who scored NE 2, SE 3, SW 4, NW 3

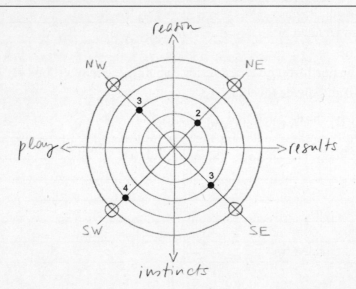

Use the sample compass in Figure IC.2 to plot your own score and
connect the dots.

FIGURE IC.2 Sample Intuitive Compass

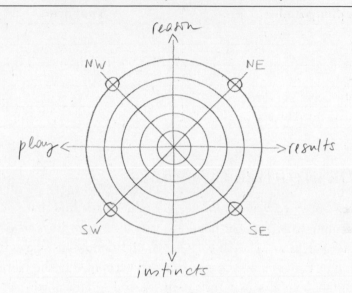

At this stage you do not have all the keys to interpret your results.
As you read through this book, you will begin to understand the
significance of your score in each quadrant as well as the significance
of the shape that you have created by connecting the dots that indicate
your score in each quadrant. At the end of the book there is a section
specifically dedicated to decoding your score.

Please visit www.theintuitivecompass.com to try out a longer questionnaire; in it, you'll find comments tailored to your combination of
results. You can also download on your iPhone, iPodTouch, or iPad the
application The Intuitive Compass App or visit www.facebook.com/
theintuitivecompass to take a quiz and compare results with friends.
Whenever you see the Web icon in the margins of the book, please go
to www.theintuitivecompass.com for additional information, tools, and
resources.

WEB

Part One

*Human Nature Beyond
the Conscious Mind*

1

the need for a new intelligence *or* the serious role of play

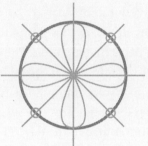

Play is the highest form of research.
—ALBERT EINSTEIN

P lay is magical. And profound. Not only is it essential to our growth and development when we are children and a source of joy throughout our lives, but it is also a largely untapped channel for innovative ideas in the work place.

Play is essential to the survival of organizations in a complex and fast-changing marketplace, as it is a key factor in creativity and agility. I have seen play help executives find new ideas and shape better teams, show more engagement and reach higher levels of efficiency. I have used play to help people become more creative, deal with challenging emotions like self-consciousness or even fear, and regain energy, enthusiasm, and hope when their company was going through difficult times. Play opens the doors to our deeper creative potential, helping us achieve change and implement innovative solutions.

FLYING BLIND: THE ABC GAME

The seminar has just started. Eighteen men and women, all rising executives at Estée Lauder Companies, one of the leading American high-end cosmetics companies, stand in an empty conference room with windows looking onto Central Park. The tables have been removed and the chairs pushed to the four corners of the room. I have asked the participants to take off their shoes and close their eyes, but I have not told them what will happen next. It's absolutely silent. This is how the ABC game begins.

I had been hired a few months earlier by the president of one of Estée Lauder Companies' divisions to work on reinventing the servicing model for fragrance in department stores. The client and I had agreed to organize a seminar to identify breakthrough solutions and create a sense of ownership of the project among the team members early on. I often start my seminars without any introduction or explanation of what will happen over the course of the day. The goal of the seminar is for the participants to enter a group creative process and come up with disruptive ideas. I intentionally introduce disruptive processes, such as diving directly into action from the very beginning of the seminar without having participants introduce themselves to each other, and without explaining the objectives or going through the schedule of the day. This is a way to put their tolerance for confusion to the test. Later on in the seminar, I will ask them to reflect individually and as a group on how they were able to navigate this lack of linearity and predictability and how this level of disruption helped them gain a new perspective on themselves and learn about the nature of the creative process and how to best manage it.

As with sports or music, to open up to creativity you need to relax, be present to your body, and let go of your mind. A playful activity not only comes in handy, there is no way around it. This is why the ABC game is important. I enjoy this part of the work and offer this exercise each time without fail. Once everyone has their shoes off and eyes closed, I tell them, "You are going to build the alphabet from A to Z. You need to follow the alphabetical order, one letter at a time, without any repeats. It is okay to participate by remaining silent, so long as the group completes the alphabet. But if two people speak at the same time, you must start all over again. That is the hard part." Everyone laughs. Then the room grows quiet again. The silence builds.

Some participants always try to outsmart the exercise using their mind to find a way to get to z more quickly and gain control over the experience rather than being receptive and trusting their perceptions. Made rigorously analytical by prior education and training, these highly successful executives want to circumvent the confusion they're in: eyes closed, in stocking feet, no way to predict who is going to speak next, no way to be sure of when to speak. The ambiguity is too much for some of them to bear emotionally. Sometimes they also feel a nervous need to be more productive. They think the exercise is an inefficient use of their time. They don't see the point of calmly and blindly observing their inner process.

Finally a voice is heard: "A." Silence in the room. Then another participant says, "B." Silence returns. We hear another voice say, "C." A while later, another participant dares a "D" and then, from somewhere in the group, another rushes to say "E." Unfortunately somebody else tries the same trick, and a second "E" tumbles out at the same time. The group has to start all over again.

Usually it takes a few trials and errors for the group to feel frustration. Then and only then I give them new instructions: "Try to breathe deep and calm down. Feel what's going on in the room around you—even if you cannot see anything—and allow yourselves to play."

The game starts again. As always, a participant tries again to beat the process and make the group reach "Z" faster. As always, it does not work. Back to "A."

There is no way to succeed at this game by forcing it. Everybody depends on each other. So everybody needs to give up individual control and allow a natural rhythm to emerge from the group dynamic. It takes concentration, self-confidence, trust, deep inner listening, and letting go. With proper guidance, most groups manage to get to "Z."

On good days, I ask the participants to do the exercise again with more distance between them, so that they are even more isolated from one another. Later in the seminar, when the group has made substantial progress, I sometimes ask them to block their ears with their index fingers. This way they can't anticipate when someone is going to speak by listening to the sound of their breathing.

At this point, participants have recourse only to their intuition. The exercise seems impossible. Yet when practiced regularly, a different type of listening develops, and magic takes place.[1]

When the group dynamic is good, there seems to be no particular order to the sequence of voices, yet a uniting factor sustains and facilitates an "orderly" process. Everyone becomes calm. Quietly, resolutely, the letters of the alphabet are enunciated one by one, from "A" to "Z." When a group hits a home run, all faces are happy.

To be able to work together as a group without explicit leadership, in the heat of the action and under the pressure of trying to reach a definite goal—this is when you know you have a real team.

The phenomenon that takes place during this exercise can be likened to the neural synchronization between human subjects that has been demonstrated in neuroscience experiments. George Burr Leonard, the author of numerous books on developing human potential, writes, "Meditation helps us become more sensitive to our own vibrations and inner rhythms ... [and] find ourselves in a great state of harmony with our environment and people around us."[2] Likewise neuroanatomist Jill Bolte Taylor describes how a severe stroke taught her that the more time she spent running on the deep circuitry of her brain's right hemisphere (traditionally seen as responsible for processing of visual and audio stimuli and artistic ability, among other things), the more likely she was to experience oneness with those around her.[3] This is what participants end up achieving in the ABC exercise. At some point, when a large majority of participants have finally accepted giving up mental control over the process of building the alphabet and are relying predominantly on their brain's right hemisphere, they enter a form of meditative state in which new brain capacities (such as higher levels of concentration and intuitive participation) can be attained.

This is comparable to what happens when people are so immersed physically and emotionally in a playful activity that they lose track of time—and, sometimes, even of space—and open up to new realms of their imagination.

This kind of playful exercise helps participants redefine their relationship to efficiency. It demonstrates how an underlying force in any group dynamic can be recruited to achieve more than one ever can through intense, willful, consciously directed effort. This idea remains a very foreign concept among business audiences. Yet this is the way our instinct ensures our survival. We breathe without any conscious effort, yet it happens without fail. And when we become more perceptive of our breathing, we can then do more with it—as, for instance, athletes do to improve their performance or singers do to reach a high note or sing a long musical phrase. But what's remarkable in this process of improvement is that neither athletes nor singers can access this higher level of performance by volition of the mind alone; they need to compose with their body and its physiology, and they need to be attentive and receptive to what their sensations and emotions indicate to them.

There is no way to explain the success or failure of the group by objectively analyzing the ABC exercise, step by step. It's no longer, properly speaking, about a conscious, linear, cognitive process among the group members. It's about a felt ability to listen, an intuitive perception. Herein resides the complexity. We don't develop intuition in the same way that we develop the rational part of the intellect. This is why play is instrumental in its ability to circumvent reason and allow us to reach parts of ourselves that live beyond the conscious mind.

The ultimate lesson of the ABC exercise is that when people give up the traditional agenda of willful linear efficiency, when they stop resisting confusion and chaos, they start being much more receptive to their environment. They connect with new parts of themselves. They start feeling their guts and become much more creative. Then they can far more easily adapt to change and consistently achieve high performance. Such is the power of play.

PLAY IS A CORE FACTOR OF INNOVATION

We often hear extremely productive people say that their vocation is also their avocation, that they love what they do, that they have fun at work. Too often we fail to realize what this tells us about the way they work; it is not solely linear reason and disciplined routine, it is fun. Many great achievers emphasize the importance of play and imagination in making breakthroughs. In an interview with Kary Mullis concerning how he arrived at his invention of the polymerase chain reaction, which won him the 1993 Nobel Prize in chemistry, he said, "I wasn't working, I was playing. I was letting things take shape before my eyes, and deep down I knew that I was about to find something that was going to be Nobel Prize winning.... And that's what happened!" What Kary Mullis demonstrates for us is that his Nobel Prize–winning breakthrough did not come from him following the linear path of logic and reason alone. In fact, breakthroughs *must* disrupt the logic of what we know; because they bring new knowledge, breakthroughs can come only from parts unknown to the conscious mind, and therefore unknown to reason. So breakthroughs—even the most intellectual and sophisticated ones—can manifest only at times when we disengage from what we know and from what we understand logically. Again, this is why play is so crucial: it disconnects us from reason and logic and opens us up to new and different thoughts we wouldn't otherwise have access to.

Too many of us handicap ourselves in life and at work by approaching problems analytically; we cut out play and imagination and consequently close ourselves off from a vast source of ideas. When it comes to innovation, common business wisdom tells us that reengineering structures and processes is the way to innovate. But a survey released by McKinsey in early 2008 suggests otherwise.[4] In this survey of 1,500 leading business executives from around the world, more than two-thirds of them said that innovation is really about people and culture, and that with the right culture, people will reengineer any structure or process that needs it, on the fly. The study went on to say that the executives were concerned about their ability to manage innovation

WEB

because they had been trained to deal with processes and structures but not with people and culture. Executives rarely see an opportunity in the fact that people have a natural inclination to play. The lesson here is to understand that if innovation is about people, then work must foster play in order to develop creativity and new thinking. Managers need to understand how to allow and foster play as part of a team's daily routine and integrate the fact that at times play will replace a more linear and rational approach to team management. With perseverance it will provide, in the long run, an interesting and effective creative culture, as it is play that leads to innovation, and innovation is the engine of growth for our corporations.

WHAT IS PLAY?

To understand how play works, it's important to understand what it is. It's also important to understand what it isn't. Play isn't some reprehensible at-risk behavior that threatens to make slackers of us all. Western culture, unfortunately, often sees it that way. Play is perceived to be, at best, a child's pastime, or an indulgence for the very wealthy, or, in the worst case, the hallmark of a slacker. Certainly play does not come across as something that serious people in serious businesses should be doing on a daily basis. In fact, play isn't even necessarily perceived to be beneficial for our children. It is often thought to be more of an at-risk behavior that prevents children from doing more important things.

Our traditional school systems, with their strict pedagogical protocols that separate learning time from playtime, reflect our culture's belief that the two activities are not related. Yet research proves otherwise. The results of a study published by *Scientific American Mind* in December 2010 showed that surgeons who play video games actually make "one third fewer errors in the operating room" than surgeons who don't—and that "video games can improve mental dexterity, while boosting hand eye coordination, depth perception and pattern recognition." It goes on to say that people who play video games a few hours a week have "better attention spans and information processing skills" than non-gamers, and "when non-gamers...spend a week playing video games...their visual perception skills improve." It also negates the idea "of gamers as outcasts," noting that "white-collar professionals who play video games are more confident and social."[5] Clearly play is a meaningful activity in business and an important factor to improve work productivity and work quality and to boost self-confidence and social skills.

Dr. Stuart Brown, head of the National Institute for Play, who has extensively researched the functions and purposes of play, believes that one way to overcome negative attitudes toward play is to offer skeptics a view of play that is closer to their comfort zone: the science of play. He says, "Our experiences indicate that executives require sufficient immersion in the science of play before they understand and value it. The intellectual and scientific basis of play can provide the understanding—and permission—to deploy new play-based practices in their organizations. But, they must also value the new practices; without a positive play ethic, the climate for innovation is spoken of as important, but is not acted upon."[6]

Should we be working or should we be playing? When we separate work from play, we create a false dichotomy, and, as is the case with so many prejudices, the target of our scorn is deeply misunderstood. We don't have to choose between work and play, because—as we will see in scientific research and real-life examples to follow—play done properly is the lifeblood of our work. It fuels human motivation and enables us to move beyond what we perceive as insurmountable limitations.

So what is play? Is it the same as fun? Sort of. The key ingredient in play is engagement: engagement within your own mind, with another person, or with an object. Play is always a dynamic experience. Play is really about immersing oneself in a pleasurable activity for the sake of it, with no other particular intent or specific goal. It can be about immersing oneself in reading a book, drawing, sculpting, or fixing a collector's item such as an antique piece of furniture for the love of restoring a beautiful object. Play can be experienced alone or in a group. In business, observing people play, I have seen the energy in the room immediately become both lighter and stronger. Play creates new ways of interaction, allows a different type of bonding, encourages trust among team members, lowers inhibition, and facilitates the production of original ideas because people dare to speak up and express themselves more.

According to theorist and professor Johan Huizinga, play is "a free activity standing quite consciously outside 'ordinary' life." He also described it as being "'not serious' but at the same time absorbing the player intensely and utterly."[7]

The National Institute for Play defines play as "a state of being that is intensely pleasurable. It energizes and enlivens us. It eases our burdens, renews a natural sense of optimism and opens us up to new possibilities." They go on to note, "Scientists — neuroscientists, developmental biologists, psychologists, scientists from every point on the scientific compass — have recently begun viewing play as a profound biological process."[8] In other words, play is a core aspect of human nature. As such, it needs to be an essential part of work in order to leverage all that people have to offer. When play becomes a key component of a healthy corporate culture, it fosters positive thinking and creative imagination.

If we choose to leave our childish things behind, we not only deny our essential humanity but also cut ourselves off from a tremendous reservoir of creativity with the potential to make us happier and make us more effective contributors at work, as in the case of the video-playing surgeons.

A few other findings confirm the essential role of play in our intellectual and creative abilities:

- Play is crucial for full neurological and personality development. People whose childhoods were play-deprived experience lasting deficits across a range of intellectual, emotional, and interpersonal measures.[9]
- Play unleashes and strengthens our problem-solving abilities as nothing else can. Brain imaging scans show that immersing in play maximizes the firing of right-brain neurons, which are involved in lateral thinking, innovation, and artistic and scientific creativity.

Play shifts us out of the linear processes that characterize our conscious analytical minds and carries us into the realm of both conscious and unconscious imagination.[10]

- Species of animals that are more playful, such as crows, dolphins, and chimpanzees, also show higher forms of cognitive intelligence and problem solving ability indicating a direct correlation.[11]

The very good news is that it's not too late for us. There is scientific evidence that human beings are hardwired for play and that we have a lifelong ability to grow our capacity for play. The most ancient part of our brain, the part that is responsible for our very survival, is where play is initiated.[12] And, unlike other mammals, humans retain their capacity for play throughout adulthood, into old age.

WEB

PLAY AND MOTIVATION

Play opens us up to the possibility that we don't need more of anything — time, money, knowledge, and so on — in order to produce more. It is a radical idea, especially in business, where we often hear the argument that budgets are limited and therefore the ability to innovate is limited. How can you get the same result with half of the resources? How is that possible? It's possible because human motivation is not linear; the way one person gets motivated is a complex function of many intertwined factors, which do not follow a linear continuum but which can be greatly influenced by play. When we tap into the part of people that responds to play and inspiration, we unleash possibilities and a huge potential for new sources of motivation that we could not have predicted or accessed otherwise. Thus when people are engaged in play, truly and deeply engaged, they lose track of time, they stop thinking about whether their paycheck is bigger today than it was yesterday, they form close and fruitful bonds with their playmates, they withstand discomfort and inconvenience, and more often than you might imagine, they create magic. Play moves people into an optimistic frame of mind, a place where they are more adaptable to change and more likely to improvise, and where they begin to dance in the groove of life. In that joyous groove, success and innovation become far more likely outcomes than they ever could be in an atmosphere of grinding unhappiness and perceived lack.

Take, for instance, a story of how dice games were invented, according to the ancient Greek historian Herodotus.[13] In pre-Roman times, 2,500 years ago, the kingdom of Libya was suffering a famine that left it only able to feed half of its citizens. The Libyan king invented a game—sheep knuckle dice—and established a policy that every other day every person in the kingdom would do nothing but play sheep knuckle dice. They would not work, they would not just hang out, and they would not run errands for their grandma. And they would not eat. Such was the level of immersion that sheep knuckle dice provided that the people managed to survive an eighteen-year famine.

What does this tale reveal to us? It shows that the impact of play reaches far beyond the realm of reason. It also tells us that the power of play is such that it can provide an effective distraction even from something as elemental as hunger. Play is a strong catalyst for changing behavior, helping people shift perspective and refocus their energy to overcome hardship or challenging situations without necessarily increasing material resources or the number of team members.

The power of play can change outcomes, too. In September 2009, when I began consulting with Unimedia, a publishing company that owns a number of world-renowned print and online publications, the company was hurting.[14] Sales were down, the competition was closing in, and neither executive management nor rank-and-file employees could see a way to regain lost ground. Morale was low. One year later, Unimedia was reporting higher year-over-year sales, and the bottom line was in the black. How did they do it? They used play to create a sense of possibility, help senior executives regain optimism, and fight against the erection of silos and hierarchical thinking. I offered the ABC game as a ritual in all of my seminars throughout the organization. I encouraged them to repeat this exercise at the beginning of their "village meetings," where all employees were invited to brainstorm new ideas on key business areas identified as strategic by Unimedia's executive committee. Soon an employee who had taken classes in theatrical improvisation offered another "silly" game, called Zip Zap Zop, to loosen people up, quickly create a bonding energy, and motivate people to take risks. At a moment when the company had very limited time and money to invest in innovation, these exercises, as simple as they may appear, significantly helped with the daunting task of reinventing the failing paper magazine business model and reimagining the media of the future. Because they were light, fun, and surprising, they increased the energy level during and after meetings, got people energized, fostered a climate of optimism, eased relationships, and built trust among employees—all necessary ingredients to take on the difficult task of designing disruptive solutions and implementing radical change in the way business was traditionally conducted. In a record period of time, the company came up with new digital solutions and creative marketing partnerships with major advertisers.

IBM consultant Peter Andrews' work on innovation at the IBM Executive Business Institute in Palisades, New York, confirms why play is a must-have in any company seeking high levels of innovation. In a 2006 essay, he identified five barriers to innovation: inadequate funding, risk avoidance, siloing, time commitments, and incorrect measures.[15] Research on gaming shows us how play can assist in dealing with at least three of these five barriers: risk avoidance, siloing, and time commitments.

In a speech at a TED conference in February 2010, Dr. Jane McGonigal, game designer and director at the Institute for the Future, discussed how gaming elicits the types of behavior and mindset that are greatly conducive to problem solving and innovation.[16] Dr. McGonigal specializes in pervasive gaming and alternate reality games. What she found in her research (which deserves more of our attention) is that gamers take to the virtual world with a fierce concentration and level of optimism that is too rarely seen in the real world. Why? Quite simply, because it feels good to them; they have fun playing. Dr. McGonigal is now leading the charge to find out how we can harness the energy she sees in gamers and put it to use to solve real-world problems like energy conservation, poverty, and war.

What about those of us who aren't game designers, but rather are managers facing constant pressure to innovate? In management it is widely recognized that adapting the task to the employee is far more effective than the other way around. If we decided to take that advice, how would we go about adapting the task of innovation to the employee? Maybe by creating a gaming-inspired atmosphere within our corporations. We will take a look at some ways to do this later in this chapter.

PLAY HELPS GET US PAST INERTIA

Once we start moving in a certain direction or doing something a certain way it is hard to stop or change. That is inertia. And while this is true for individuals, it is even stronger in a group dynamic. If you want to innovate, you need to change. And in order to effect change you need to overcome the natural tendency toward inertia.

Arie de Geus, an ex-Shell executive turned consultant, has researched why certain companies over one hundred years old have been so successful. The twenty-seven companies he studied were able to successfully get past inertia, sustain themselves, and grow over time. They managed to withstand economic changes while staying true to their mission, without resorting solely to the tactic of acquiring companies to stay afloat in their market. He found three characteristics common to these successful companies:

1. They practice fiscal conservancy.
2. They are open to new ideas from both inside and outside the organization.
3. They have established a strong community of values that resonates with their employees, making them feel they can take risks and not be fired if they don't succeed—the feeling of belonging to a community helps overcome the fear of failure and the anticipation of potential negative consequences at a personal level.

Although point one relates to classic best practices in business, points two and three tell us why play—something not in the typical business best-practices toolbox—is key in a work culture to ensure the longevity of an organization. Openness to new ideas and a fundamental level of trust are inherent in a playful atmosphere, and play, as we have discussed, is an essential ingredient in generating innovative ideas. But that's not the whole story.

It is relatively easy to see how play can generate fabulous new ideas, but what is less obvious is the critical role of play in giving those ideas a chance at life against some very serious odds. Innovation is change, and change sends many of us running for cover—for good reason. Change activates our survival instincts and is at least partly responsible for our tendency toward inertia, and inertia, again, is a serious barrier to innovation.

Experts agree that the critical stage of innovation is implementation. Implementation is where the rubber meets the road. It requires us to change our behavior, and changing behavior is not only an intellectual but also an emotional challenge. It also requires us to step into the unknown. But perhaps the greatest challenge is that it requires us to overcome inertia, and that is something that humans are hardwired to resist. That hardwiring is key to understanding how inertia works and what its function is.

The human brain wants to stay where it is, in the comfort zone. If we stay in our comfort zone, we don't have to struggle to survive. We minimize the risk to our survival by staying where we know we are safe. I often explain to my MBA students that the reason they take the same seat in class every week, and the reason we lay our towels in the same area of the beach every summer weekend, is that we are, at our core, instinctual animals. Once we have chosen a seat and made it through class safely without being attacked, the part of our brain responsible for our survival tells us that our best option is to repeat that behavior, because in a way it is the most economical use of our energy. As part of its strategy for survival, our brain wants to conserve energy, so once we sit in a particular spot and know that it's safe, we will subconsciously want to sit there every time and avoid having to reevaluate the safety of a new spot.

In a group, because relationships add complexity, the inertia grows exponentially more difficult to overcome. My inertia plus your inertia is more than $1 + 1 = 2$, and when we add a half-dozen colleagues, or try to take on a company with hundreds or thousands of employees, the task is truly formidable. Even if Kim decides she is ready to be brave and try a new way of organizing the Monday morning meeting, all of a sudden she confronts the realization that her change will affect her staff members. What if they don't like her new approach to meeting protocol? Will they refuse to cooperate? Stop having lunch with her? Go over her head, complain to her boss, and expose her to a negative performance review? Kim has a problem. How can she try something new without so unnerving her colleagues that they stonewall a potentially good idea before it ever gets off the ground?

So, in addition to the natural preference for staying with a mode of being that has proven itself to be safe, getting past inertia is also difficult because of the emotional reaction of others. You have to show people that change will be beneficial to them; you have to make it both nonthreatening and inspiring. Play is key to overcoming the emotional component of inertia.

You are probably familiar with the saying that you must fight fire with fire. Stuart Brown (introduced earlier in this chapter) concluded, after years of research, that "play is no less important than oxygen . . . it's a powerful force in nature that helps determine the likelihood of the very survival of the human race."[17] When we realize that the part of our brain that is responsible for our survival (the fight-or-flight response) is the same part of our brain that contains our capacity for play, it puts play in a new, more powerful, and clarifying light.

WEB

Play in fact lives eye-to-eye with inertia; both are rooted in our brainstem, where you also find the part of the brain responsible for our survival. Play and inertia are in the same weight class, peers in a very exclusive executive suite where core strategic decisions about our present and future are made. But they are having a little war. Inertia, the more conservative of the two, believes that the smart move is to not move at all, to stay with the plan that got us this far safely. Play, the wild child, wants to dream a little dream, take the afternoon off, find Atlantis and create a new society there, because sitting here is, quite frankly, killing its buzz.

Play—our wildly creative and childlike nature—opens the emotional door. It offers an arena in which people become naturally more flexible. For example, think about music. You go to a rock or jazz concert and when the music starts you may sit or stand quietly, taking it in, being polite, and behaving appropriately. But over the course of the evening the music takes you over and you become more comfortable, then relaxed; you may start tapping your foot or swaying in time with the beat, or even dancing spontaneously with the stranger next to you. You didn't go into the concert thinking about changing your behavior; your behavior just changed without any effort on your part. This is the magic of play. It creates the possibility for effortless change once you get started, provided that you have permission (internal or external) to submit to it. We are in fact playful by nature; we just have to get out of our own way, let our true nature shine through and take center stage for a while. We have to get comfortable with the idea that we can trust play. Knowing that play is rooted in the same brain area as our instinct for survival is a good enough reason to give it the benefit of the doubt.

Once you let the genie out of the bottle, once play is in full swing and inertia banished (at least at that particular moment), things can move fast. This is especially true with a large group, because just as it is harder to move a group out of its inertia, once the group does get moving, it can be a force to be reckoned with—in the best possible way. Then the challenge transforms into how to manage your newly creative, very energized team. How to channel their creativity into the winning innovations your company seeks without putting a damper on their enthusiasm. Playful energy will beget as many dead ends and failures as it will successes. You have to be able to tolerate this, and you have to create an atmosphere in which your team will be able to tolerate it—even better, embrace it.

NAVIGATING THE SHIFT TO PLAY

Because creativity is such an important factor of success in business today, play should be part of every CEO's mandate, and companies should be rated according to the level of playfulness of their culture in the same way as they are rated as a great place to work or as a socially responsible organization. A number of practical steps can be followed to navigate this cultural shift toward play, which then can become easier than it seems.

According to the 2010 IBM Global CEO Study series, the degree of difficulty CEOs anticipate, based on the swirl of complexity now engulfing the business world, has brought them to rate creativity as the most essential leadership quality in the next five years. For this study 1,541 CEOs, general managers, and senior public sector leaders who represent different sizes of organizations in sixty countries and thirty-three industries, were interviewed face to face. Asked to prioritize the three most important leadership qualities in the new economic environment, six out of ten cited "creativity as the most important leadership quality over the next five years, integrity came second, global thinking third."[18]

Senior executives recognize that leading creatively will require them to shed some long-held beliefs. Their approaches need to be original, rather than traditional. They must be distinct and, at times, radical in their conception and execution, not just marginally better than existing models or methods. Or, as one telecommunications CEO in India put it: "Creativity is everything."

Creativity is often defined as the ability to bring into existence something new or different, but the CEOs elaborated on this. Creativity is the basis for "disruptive innovation and continuous re-invention," a professional services CEO in the United States told IBM experts. And this requires bold, breakthrough thinking. Leaders, they said, must be ready to upset the status quo even if the status quo is successful. They must be comfortable with and committed to ongoing experimentation.

If innovation is key to corporate success, and if play is the door to innovation, then the next logical question (logic does have its place!) is how to create a corporate atmosphere that is conducive to play, how to turn workers into players.

Think about what play looks like. It is personal, engaging, and interactive. It is often exuberant and messy. It is filled with light, color, and sound. When you think about play, you may instinctively think about a children's playground or children's toys. Now, think about corporate offices, or, more specifically, corporate boardrooms. There are lots of straight lines in boardrooms (or perhaps, artistically, an elegantly curved accent wall); there is typically an imposing table made from fine polished wood or sleek metal. That table likely suggests a hierarchical seating arrangement that people intuitively understand: the boss will sit at the head of the table and the chief advisor will sit next to the boss or perhaps will anchor the other end. The rest of the employees will fill in the sides of the table. So, before the meeting even starts, everyone knows his or her relative importance. And everyone knows that polite behavior is expected: sit up straight, papers stacked neatly in front of you, a pen at the ready, BlackBerry close by in case of an emergency.

These rigid boardrooms are where major strategic decisions are being made about innovation and the future of our organizations. They represent a very logical environment geared toward conscious conversations that will unfold in a very linear and efficient way. They appeal to the 20 percent of our intelligence that lives in our conscious mind and seeks logic and rationality. Unfortunately, they don't appeal to the 80 percent of our intelligence geared toward our unconscious mind with its wealth of creative ideas, and the intelligence that we can reach through play.

Dr. Marian Cleeves Diamond, one of the world's foremost neuro-anatomists advocates the establishment of "playful environments."[19] I too believe that we need to create offices, boardrooms, and activities that engage our playful nature—a corporate sandbox or playground. We are playful by nature and efficient by necessity. So let's embrace our nature, and less effort will be needed for the same, or better, results. When we do this we can break through the mental barriers that are keeping us stuck. Certain corporations are already doing this. Some of the things that they do to create a play-friendly atmosphere include:

- Allocating significant time in which employees are explicitly encouraged to play
- Creating, or giving employees access to, physical spaces that are conducive to play
- Giving employees implicit and explicit permission to "fail" or be "unproductive" in their pursuit of innovation

Here are some specific examples of what these play-friendly corporations look like in action:

Google, known worldwide for both its analytical discipline and its offbeat corporate style, has exceptionally playful headquarters in Zurich, Switzerland. There employees can ride a slide into the company's gourmet restaurant, hold meetings in rooms shaped like igloos, or contemplate a vexing problem while sitting in a bathtub facing a flat-screen television with underwater images drifting past. In addition to interior design, Google has designed a strategy that attracts world-class talent and then incentivizes them to bring their best ideas forward for consideration. Engineers and developers within this giant internet company have the opportunity to spend 20 percent of their time on a personal research project, on the condition that the projects done during this time must be presented to their colleagues for peer evaluation. Because no one wants to be seen as less than competent or too dreamy, this has created an atmosphere of healthy competition and orients the research projects towards applications that can actually be created at Google. This strategy has many other positive side effects. It attracts people with extremely inventive minds, who wish to maintain their creative autonomy, and it promotes innovative creativity among teams (all team members want Google to accept one of their ideas and invest in it). The strategy also improves productivity (engineers must continue to maintain their regular workload with 20 percent less time) and creates a dynamic tie to the academic world because so many employees publish

WEB

articles about their research. One of Google's primary objectives is to avoid missing out on a brilliant idea — as the management at Hewlett Packard did with Steve Wozniak, the future creator of Apple, when he came to them with his idea of a portable computer!

Google's strategy has a predecessor at 3M, the highly diversified American industrial company most famous for the familiar green plaid–labeled scotch tape dispenser. The Minnesota-based company earns 25 percent of its annual revenue with the new products that it puts out on the market every year. Innovation is its official motto. It was by allowing their employees to spend 15 percent of their working hours doing what they wanted that the Post-It was created in 1980. Art Fry, an engineer at 3M and an amateur choral singer, was looking for a bookmark that wouldn't slide down his sheet of music while he was singing. He came up with the idea of a self-adhesive bookmark that used the weak glue invented years earlier by researchers in his division, and the Post-It was born. From the playful pursuit of a hobby sprang forth a need that motivated an idea that led to the international success that the company has today.

Even a company as inherently creative as Pixar, the animation film studio that produced such worldwide successes as the *Toy Story* series, *The Incredibles*, *Ratatouille*, and *Finding Nemo*, takes deliberate steps to create an atmosphere that will enhance their employees' capacity to innovate. When asked what makes people innovative, Pixar's Oscar-winning director Brad Bird said, "I would say that involved people make for better innovation . . . You want people to be involved and engaged."[20] To increase the potential for engagement across departments at the company's offices in Emeryville, California, Pixar cofounder Steve Jobs had a large central atrium designed where he "put the mailboxes, the meetings rooms, the cafeteria, and, most insidiously and brilliantly, the bathrooms. He realized that when people run into each other, when they make eye contact, things happen. So he made it impossible for you not to run into the rest of the company."[21]

Givaudan, one of the world's leading fragrance companies, hasn't actually created a specific space for play, but instead takes people outside of the office and puts them in an atmosphere more conducive to play. Givaudan turns employees loose in New York City to engage in trend-hunts. They walk around different neighborhoods and look at what people are wearing, what is in shop window displays, and how stores are presenting their merchandise. For the employees this exercise is both fun and informative. It is an opportunity to be with coworkers in a memorable atmosphere somewhere between fun and work.

A notable number of companies have artist-in-residence programs. American manufacturer Kohler Co., based in Wisconsin, is one of them. Since 1873 Kohler has been producing household equipment, including plumbing fixtures, furniture, tile and stone, and primary and backup power systems, as well as establishing award-winning hospitality and world-class golf destinations. Seen as a renowned leader in each of its four business groups, Kohler leads the way in design, craftsmanship, and innovation. One way they sustain a high level of innovation is through an ongoing collaboration between art and industry, at the John Michael Kohler Arts Center in Sheboygan, Wisconsin. Founded in 1974, it remains unique among all American artist residency programs. It has provided artists with an entrée to an industrial setting through two- to six-month stays in the pottery, foundry, and enamel shops at Kohler. Up to two dozen artists per year have the opportunity to learn new ways of thinking and working. Here they are able to produce entire bodies of work that would otherwise be impossible to execute in their own studios. Sophisticated technologies, unlimited access to technical expertise, materials, equipment, studio space, housing, and transportation, plus a weekly stipend, create an unusually supportive environment. Over time, hundreds of arts and industrial employees have built rapport as they work side by side and learn from each other's approaches to work. Through this arts program Kohler aims to give its employees the opportunity to learn from the proximity of artists at work. They can observe the artists' creative process, see how hard work has to become play to produce a creative outcome, and develop a better understanding of how to inspire creativity. They can deduce best practices about managing the creative process and see their value

WEB

in real life: the role of giving oneself permission to fail, the necessity of trial and error, and the importance of a space conducive to creativity.

Amdocs, a publicly traded provider of software and services to leading telecommunications companies in sixty countries worldwide, including AT&T, Sprint-Nextel, and Vodafone, places the pursuit of innovation at the core of their business strategy. In addition to their Open Innovation program, under which they explicitly invite start-ups and early and growth-stage companies to collaborate with them, Amdocs takes proactive steps to provoke and nurture the realization of new ideas from their employees.[22] To help achieve the latter, Amdocs hosts off-site "innovation camps." These are a perfect example of giving employees a different and more engaging physical environment to work in as well as the necessary mental space and free time to reflect creatively. For the June 2010 camp, which cost Amdocs $100,000 to host, hundreds of employees competed to win one of the seventy-five spots to participate in a week-long series of collaborative exercises that the company hoped would "identify entirely new business opportunities worth at least $100 million apiece in additional revenues."[23] After a day spent engaging in "a variety of wacky, mind-expanding activities, including learning skills such as origami, juggling, astronomy, and improvisational theatre,"[24] the participants brainstormed and came up with a list of hundreds of potential new business ideas. Those lists were honed down, refined, and thought through more carefully. The top fifteen ideas were presented to clients for feedback, and from there the top three were subjected to yet more refinement. The camp participants, now divided into three groups (one per final idea), spent a day developing presentations to be pitched to Amdocs' senior management. In this case two of the three ideas were green-lighted to receive funding for further development.

Companies like Shell, IBM, and DuPont use music to create an atmosphere that accelerates learning and optimizes memory. Music, as discussed earlier, is a powerful way to access a joyful, playful state of mind. It is also a powerful way to access a relaxed and meditative state of mind, which is another facet of being playful. We know today the impact of music on our emotional state, concentration, learning ability, and intellectual agility in new situations. Dr. Don Campbell has authored a few books on the subject; one of them is *The Mozart Effect*, which was greatly inspired by the work of late French ENT doctor Alfred Tomatis. Campbell writes that forty-three of the largest industrial companies in the world play music in their offices. Some of them have recorded productivity improvement through stress reduction; others have recorded up to 33-percent reduction in administrative errors. In times of intense mental concentration, our pulse and blood pressure increase, making it harder to concentrate. To counteract this, baroque music in particular is a very efficient way to induce feelings of relaxation because many compositions are performed at a tempo of sixty beats per minute, with long sections of music at the same tempo, mimicking a slow-paced human heartbeat and inducing a natural state of relaxation and improved learning ability. Recent research shows that music fires up certain parts of our brain responsible for memory, language, movement, and our sense of rhythm. Professor Anne Blood, a researcher in neuropsychology at McGill University in Montréal, proved that different types of music fire up different parts of the brain. It can be very useful to manage stress, anxiety, and attention deficit disorder on the work place.

In several of these examples you see how people are engaged physically. This is smart, because physical activities bring us closer to the unconscious part of our brain — creativity and imagination — where new ideas live. By eluding or disengaging from the rational mind, you open the door and allow what lies in the unconscious to rise to the surface.

WHAT HAVE WE LEARNED ABOUT PLAY, AND HOW CAN PLAY HELP YOU?

CEOs across a range of industries have begun to recognize that creativity is a key driver in the future growth of their companies. It is no longer seen as important only to businesses in the arts and entertainment. In addition, scientific research is giving us more and more insight into the role of play in our personal growth, creativity, and ability to perform better at our jobs. We have seen how play is essential to the survival of organizations in a complex and fast-changing market place. It enables us to elude the rational mind and opens us up to the part of the brain responsible for our survival: instinct. As much as we may be culturally prejudiced against instinct, because we associate it with animals and lower species, thanks to contemporary neuroscience we now know that our instinctual brain has a central role in human intelligence. Play enables us to influence this very powerful part of ourselves, helps us develop our cognitive abilities, and brings balance into our lives: playing fosters the agility and creativity that are key to our business success.

2

the power and purpose
of instinct and intuition

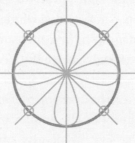

No, no! You're not thinking, you're just being logical . . .
—NIELS BOHR, Nobel Prize winner in physics

To date, our collective approach to human intelligence often relies on outdated concepts. The misplaced expectations we place on the ability of instinct and intuition to guide us in life often obliterates their original contributions. We expect intuition and instinct to give us black and white answers that logic can evaluate. It is simply not their function. Yet this misunderstanding of intuition and instinct, which is evident in questions like "Can I trust my intuition to make the right decision?" or "Can I rely on my guts to do this?" is often encountered in business. This in turn limits our ability to better understand the breadth and depth of a situation and make decisions with a broader perspective, which is exactly what instinct and intuition are meant to allow us to do.

It is necessary to better understand how our brain functions in order to better leverage its creative capacity for in-depth reflection, original thinking, and efficient and sustainable decision making. But with the exception of rare initiatives,[1] business schools and educational institutions in general seem quite resistant to change in this field of interest. Our economy is highly complex and unpredictable. This makes traditional decision making, which is predominantly guided by the laws of logic, inoperative or plain dangerous. Therefore we need to better understand our mental life—and its larger potential, which is hidden to the conscious mind yet accessible to the newly educated and insightful individual; this is where intuition and instinct come into play to help us identify in the midst of complex systems the decisive piece of information that would have otherwise eluded our rational mind.

Instinctual aptitudes can be instrumental in business. We will see, as the chapter unfolds, that people who employ instinct and intuition also have a more and more decisive competitive advantage when navigating in the new economy. But what exactly is instinct? Here are some simple definitions to keep in mind throughout this book:

- Instinct is our innate inclination toward a particular behavior (as opposed to a learned response).
- A *gut feeling*—or a hunch—is a sensation that appears quickly in consciousness (noticeable enough to be acted on if one chooses to) without us being fully aware of the underlying reasons for its occurrence.
- Intuition is a process that gives us the ability to know something directly without analytic reasoning, bridging the gap between the conscious and nonconscious parts of our mind, and also between instinct and reason.

In everyday language these three terms can at times be substituted for one another. Some people may also understand or define these words differently. But for the purposes of this book, these definitions reflect the specific meaning I attach to each.

CHIEF INSTINCTUAL OFFICER WANTED

April 15, 2008, Jouy-en Josas, France — Twenty minutes south of Paris, in the beautiful Bièvres River valley not far from the Chateau de Versailles, a sparkling slate grey Citroën C6 slows down at the entrance gate of HEC, Europe's leading business school. The luxury sedan moves through the open gate and parks in front of the conference hall. Jean René Fourtou gets out of the car and proceeds swiftly to the auditorium, where he is going to tell an unusual story to two hundred MBA students from fifty-five countries around the world.[2]

Six years earlier, Fourtou, then sixty-three, had retired after sixteen years as CEO of Rhône Poulenc, the global pharmaceutical company. His only plan in life was a Mediterranean sailing vacation with his family. But first he had dinner with two old friends: Valéry Giscard d'Estaing, former president of France, and Claude Bébéar, founder of insurance giant AXA, as of 2010 the ninth largest company in the world.[3]

To his surprise, Fourtou's friends started lobbying him to become head of the French-American conglomerate Vivendi Universal, a hodge-podge of operations including the Universal film studio and related companies. Fourtou was horrified; at the time, Vivendi Universal reported 35 billion euros in debt and an operating loss of 13.6 billion euros. He politely declined the offer and tried to change the subject, but his friends persisted. They knew him well and were confident he could not resist the challenge.

In July 2002, his vacation canceled, Fourtou was named CEO of Vivendi Universal. As he explained, "two weeks later the company stock was rated as junk," effectively locking it out of the capital markets and depriving it of new investment to fund a turnaround. A few days after that, "police entered the company headquarters in Paris to affix seals on file cabinets and corporate closets."

As the ordeal continued, Fourtou explained to the MBA students at HEC, he felt he would never survive it. Yet he kept going through corporate hell, trying to fix, in his own words, "the mess" he had inherited. Vivendi was on the verge of bankruptcy. There was no time for beating around the bush, and he did not trust the board members. After all, they had been there when everything went wrong.

So Fourtou began an amazing hunt for talent, expertise, and finances. The financial world thought his efforts were doomed and that Vivendi Universal was worthless. Indeed, the company's holdings were so complex that it took more than a year to establish its actual net worth.

During this year, against all odds and largely against the recommendations of his board, Fourtou staved off disaster. Against everyone else's advice and financial logic he refused to sell Canal+, a French premium pay television channel, which was the only asset he could trade for immediate cash in an attempt to avert financial disaster and stabilize Vivendi's economic situation. Within another year, he restructured the group and brought it back to financial health. As detailed in Fourtou's presentation at HEC, in 2004 the group's total revenue reached 17.9 billion euros, with a net profit of 3.87 billion euros, and since then it has continued to thrive. Even in the global downturn of 2008, Vivendi earned total revenue of close to 25.5 billion euros and net profit of more than 3.7 billion euros.

Maybe it's because Jean René Fourtou felt this experience was like survival in the jungle that he made all his decisions by pure instinct and against all strategic sense and logic at times. According to Fourtou himself, "the challenge was so huge, I thought I would die. So I did everything following my gut. I had no other choice. There was no time to gather all the data and make analytical decisions." The intonation of a voice on the phone, the first few minutes of meeting someone, sometimes even simply looking at a business card he had just been handed, would be enough for him to make up his mind and reach the most efficient decision. "Time was of the essence . . . every minute made a difference," said Fourtou.

From time to time, we've all felt our gut instincts and experienced how hunches can bring a moment of exceptional clarity. Fourtou puts it this way: "Management is not about organizing, it is about giving life!" In these moments of insight, we are closest to our creative nature and most able as executives to inspire teams, enliven organizations, and come up with innovative business solutions — in other words, we are at our best as leaders!

In the real world, life does not follow a linear path. Yet business is taught and too often practiced according to linear thinking. Fourtou's thinking, however, was not linear, and the merit of his approach revolves around two key elements:

- His incredibly rich professional experience and astute business mind
- His ability to trust his gut and remain composed in the chaotic and complex situation in which he found Vivendi when he joined the company

Fourtou, making business decisions against common financial wisdom, exemplifies how to use intuition to tap into one's gut instinct for swift and successful decision making. And as research shows, he is far from alone. In the 1960s, Dr. Douglas Dean, along with his colleague John Mihalsky, studied approximately five thousand executives. Eighty percent of them said they believed in extrasensory perception (ESP) and used it to anticipate and seize profitable business opportunities. ESP is casually referred to as a sixth sense, gut instinct, or hunch,[4] and for this reason ESP pertains to our subject matter: the importance and the role of instinct and intuition in decision making. This belief in ESP did not stem from the fact these highly successful businessmen had any theoretical knowledge of the subject, nor did it indicate that they would seek advice from a person with psychic abilities. It was simply the reflection of a direct experience with these abilities and their concrete applications to business. Dean and Mihalasky also studied a particular subgroup among the initial five thousand executives.[5] They focused on 165 presidents and CEOs of American companies who had doubled or more than doubled their company profits in a five-year period. They found that 80 percent of them had above-average predictive computer test scores; that is, they demonstrated precognitive abilities.[6] This piece of research on the use of everyday intuition for decision making in business led the authors to believe that precognitive ability was a reliable indicator of financial success. According to the authors, measuring potential aptitudes for ESP would be a much better indicator of professional success than other psychometric instruments.[7] Some of the highly successful global companies I have worked for, like Estée Lauder Companies and L'Oréal, do give great importance to intuition. Mrs. Estée Lauder herself would rely greatly on her intuition, and today Estée Lauder Companies CEO Fabrizio Freda insists on maintaining and supporting intuition — in conjunction with a strong analytical capacity — in the work of his teams as a fundamental aspect in the success of the company.[8] L'Oréal's former CEO, François Dalle, who built the beauty company into a world-renowned multinational, insisted on "intuiting what is arising" as a key competence the beauty company executives had to develop and work with.[9] This type of belief is not limited to the beauty industry. Konosuke Matsushita, Japanese industrialist and founder of Panasonic, once said, "No matter how deep a study you make, what you really have to rely on is your own intuition."[10]

Dean and Mihalasky's well-known research has been available since 1974, the year of its publication. It is not new knowledge. And since then, similar studies have produced similar results. Another study was conducted in the 1980s, using two thousand managers over a period of two years.[11] This study revealed that executives used intuition like "explorers" to "foresee" the correct path to follow, but they did so secretly.[12] A well-known 1994 study conducted at the Harvard Business School produced a global survey of more than 1,300 practicing managers in nine countries: the United States, the United Kingdom, Austria, Brazil, France, India, Japan, the Netherlands, and Sweden.[13] Of the 1,300 polled executives, 80 percent explained their success through decisions made intuitively, and 75 percent claimed they used intuition and logic equally. However, the study also shows that more than 50 percent of them would not publically admit to relying on intuition. These last two examples prove that gut feelings and intuition are widely resorted to in business, but that there is definite prejudice against this type of aptitude.

So how come organizations I know and organizations I hear about still evaluate executives on criteria such as team management, interpersonal communication, entrepreneurship, and, more recently, emotional intelligence, but they do not integrate in their evaluation templates the ability to manifest as well as encourage in others instinctual intelligence and intuition at work? How come classes about intuitive skills are still so rare in business schools? A first answer seems obvious: we are culturally uncomfortable with what's not exact and what cannot be demonstrated. Even if research shows that many successful business minds use intuition, it remains hard to conceptualize intuition and make it a tangible capacity that can be taught and measured. Besides, to share an intuitive opinion or to defend it in a fact-based environment such as a business presentation requires self-confidence and courage. All these issues are cause for leaving the challenging topic of intuition out of our modern society in which the scientific mind is clearly seen as a warrant for truth and reliability.

INSTINCT AND INTUITION CAN BE TRAINED

Aside from business executives, there are other professionals who use intuition and instinct, and in some cases it is about crude survival tactics. In war, life-and-death decisions must be made instantly, with little if any time for rational analysis. And what's more impressive is that the army has discovered that the ability to act effectively from gut feelings can be improved through training.[14]

Time after time, the army has learned that "the speed with which the brain reads and interprets sensations like the feelings in one's own body and emotions in the body language of others is central to avoiding imminent threats." The U.S. military has spent billions of dollars to protect against improvised explosive devices (IEDs), investing in hardware and technology to seek and destroy these homemade roadside bombs. But experts say it is the human brain that has proven to be the most perceptive detection system. Troops often credit their experience and perceptions—their gut feelings—for their ability to notice and foil IED attacks.[15]

U.S. troops are a central focus of a large effort to understand how it is that in a life-or-death situation some people's brains can sense danger and act on it well before others' can. As with Vivendi Universal CEO Jean René Fourtou, experience matters on the battleground. If you have seen something before, you are more likely to anticipate it the next time. Yet it is not just experience that matters. Research suggests that something else is at work too. "Small differences in how the brain processes images, how well it reads emotions and how it manages surges in stress hormones help explain why some people sense imminent danger before most others do."[16]

Unfortunately, for some time feelings have been perceived as having little to do with rational decision making. In fact, it has long been thought that they just get in the way of it. But according to Dr. Antonio Damasio, director of the Brain and Creativity Institute at the University of Southern California, "Now that position has reversed. We understand emotions as practical action programs that work to solve a problem, often before we're conscious of it. These processes are at work continually."[17] All scientific facts point to the evidence of an inner knowing preceding our rational mind.[18]

Before we discuss further how instinct and intuition actually work and what their actionable benefits are for us in business, it is important to first understand our cultural resistance toward instinct and intuition, to recognize our bias when we probe this aspect of human intelligence.

PREJUDICE AGAINST INSTINCT AND INTUITION

Gut feelings about potential threats or opportunities are not always correct, and neuroscientists debate the conditions under which the feelings precede the conscious awareness of the clues themselves. But our instinctual skills evolved to ensure our survival, and research findings suggest that in some people those skills are exquisitely sensitive. So although the many serious researchers who say that gut feelings are not always correct do have a point, they may be missing the most important point: gut feelings have other functions that transcend the logic of reason, and to leverage their role fully we should not evaluate gut feelings on a narrow basis of whether they are right or wrong.

When we engage in solving a problem using logical skills, we follow certain rules or protocols based on past experience with a similar problem. The rules and protocols we follow are generally well defined and measurable. If we succeed in solving our problem, we typically attribute it to the efficacy of the protocols we followed. If we fail at solving our problem, we can look back and analyze the steps we took to find where our approach failed.

Conversely, when we engage in solving a problem using our instincts, we follow a path that is highly specific to our problem and ourselves at a particular moment in time. If someone asks us how we solved the problem, we may be able to recount what we did, but even a detailed recounting of what we did will not necessarily apply to a similar problem. And that's fine, because instinctual problem solving isn't necessarily about replication; it's about dynamic adaptation to circumstances. The problem is that when we are successful, we (and others) may attribute our success simply to luck, even though calling on our instincts is a skill we can develop. So although we may never be able to measure the efficacy of instinct-based problem solving precisely, that doesn't mean it is a random phenomenon. The difference between logic-based problem solving and instinct-based problem solving isn't necessarily efficacy; the difference lies in our ability or inability to precisely identify cause and effect. And when we can't identify cause and effect, we feel out of control or inefficient.

As the studies mentioned earlier show, many of us—even when we experience success—are uncomfortable with the idea of using our instincts as a guidance tool. We are embarrassed to say that we follow hunches, we mistrust the sometimes-cryptic messages that our instincts send to us, and consequently we diminish our capacity to leverage the power of our own instincts when we need them most. Our discomfort with the idea of relying on our instincts is based on millennia of cultural prejudice.

Leaving all commentary on the value and importance of religion aside, we can still make the observation that most Judeo-Christian religions arrived, in one way or another, at the conclusion that our often crude instinct-driven impulses for food, pleasure, and aggression can stand in the way of spiritual growth and ascension. Think of the common phrase, "We are not like animals." It tells us that the assumed difference between humans and animals is humans' ability to reason with our instinctual impulses, and the unspoken message is that reason is a higher and better quality to possess. The thing is, not only are we *like* animals, we *are* animals. However, we are animals with the distinct advantage of having both instinct and reason at our disposal. So we don't actually have to reject either morality or instinct; rather, we have the capacity to honor and call upon both.

What's more, as much as we may associate "animal instinct" with predation or violent "dog-eat-dog" behavior, the truth is that animals also have an extraordinary capacity for collaboration and playfulness, even with partners who are their enemies (or their lunch) in the animal kingdom. Dr. Stuart Brown, whose important research into the value of play was discussed in chapter one, has observed animals at length.[19] His research shows an extraordinary series of photographs taken in Manitoba, Canada, by a photographer who captured a chance encounter between a 1,200-pound wild male polar bear and a pack of huskies, the beautiful domesticated dogs that are typically used to pull sleds. In the first frame, the polar bear is seen approaching the huskies with a distinctive predatory gaze. In the next, we see one husky come forward toward the polar bear in what Dr. Brown calls a "play bow," wagging her tail. In subsequent frames we see the polar bear's attitude toward the husky transform from predation into playfulness. He withdraws his claws and softens his gaze. They begin to play together and dance around. The polar bear allows the husky to playfully bite his jaw, and the husky allows the polar bear to playfully bite her bared neck. The sequence ends with the polar bear cuddling the husky under his neck.

WEB

Instinct can level an otherwise unlevel playing field, as it did with the polar bear and the husky. The husky's playful approach was the first step in shifting the polar bear's approach from predatory to conciliatory. With instinct, a quantifiable power advantage can be disabled, which is both a fantastic realization and simultaneously a daunting responsibility. What we can take away from this is that instinct is about relationships and instantaneous adaptation to circumstances, and it is about reproduction, territorial protection, and aggression alike. What matters is intention and choosing how we use instinct. As humans, it is our duty to channel our instinctual powers and put them to creative use. Repressing them or devaluing them in the name of logic, or assigning instinct roles it cannot fulfill (such as to be analytically predictive or rational) are not appropriate answers. As we saw in the previous chapter's story about famine in the ancient Libyan kingdom, play is an inventive way to leverage instinct; we will see later in this chapter how rituals can help in a powerful way to channel our instinct into a creative and productive force. This is where intuition and its ability to enter in communication with instinct become key. Yet the prejudice toward intuition is no less than that toward instinct.

Intuition is traditionally associated with femininity; it is an internal, hard-to-define capacity. It is not about having a sheer physical or scientific advantage, and its power can't be measured in the same way. So bringing instinct into the corporate world with the help of intuition threatens our well-established male, scientifically oriented culture at a fundamental level. It threatens not just men, but women too, simply because it calls into question old assumptions about the nature of power. Too often these old assumptions equate intuition with dominance and control, and they have only been strengthened by the advent of modern science and the industrial and technological revolutions.

But we don't have to reject scientific logic or the advantages of sheer physical power in order to benefit from instinct. We can honor and call upon all of these tools, and we can seek balance. And by seeking this balance we will finally bring all of the resources of our brain into action. Until about a hundred years ago science wasn't even aware of the role of our unconscious, but as we have seen, studies now show that only 20 percent of the brain's gray matter is dedicated to conscious thoughts, while 80 percent is dedicated to nonconscious thoughts.

As a point of clarification, I refer to "conscious" as the part of the mind we are aware of (our conscious thoughts and clear emotions), to "nonconscious" as the part of the mind that we cannot possibly be aware of (which governs most physiological actions of our organs), and to the "unconscious" as the part of the *mind* that is not conscious (the unknown motivation behind an action, for instance), but which we can become aware of through conscious effort. Culturally we have a highly developed relationship with the part of our brain that is conscious, but we lack the same relationship skills with our unconscious. Which brings us back to the observation that gut feelings aren't always correct. The question is, how does one come to that conclusion? A relationship — or dialogue — with the unconscious part of our mind is very different from one with the conscious.

Our conscious mind excels at answering clear questions with logical answers.

> *You:* What should I wear today?
> *Your Conscious:* Well, what is the weather like today?
> *You:* I checked the Weather Channel, and it says it's going to rain.
> *Your Conscious:* Wear a raincoat.
> *You:* Good idea, thank you.

Our conscious mind is less effective at answering questions for which there isn't a successful predictive model to follow.

> *You:* How do I come up with a new marketing campaign for my widget?
> *Your Conscious:* Use last year's campaign as your model.
> *You:* But things have changed since then.
> *Your Conscious:* So tweak it.

You: How?

Your Conscious: Do a study on changed consumer priorities.

You: What questions should I ask?

Your Conscious: Find a proven model and replicate it.

You: But there aren't any!

Your Conscious: There must be; look harder.

And the question-answer dialogue goes on, but it's all about a linear relationship with the past, present, and future. The conscious is an expert at logic and will use it relentlessly. Conversely, the unconscious mind searches through the past, present, and future and connects with hunches and feelings in a nonlinear way. Its process is cryptic to the logical mind, as it defies the conventional laws of time and space.

You: What should I wear today?

Your Unconscious: Red.

You: Red what?

Your Unconscious: I don't know, just something red.

You: Why?

Your Unconscious: Feels good.

You: But I have an interview today; isn't red too aggressive?

Your Unconscious: You're missing the point.

You: What's the point?

Your Unconscious: You like red. It makes you feel happy.

You: What has happiness got to do with this?

Your Unconscious: Everything.

You: How?

Your Unconscious: You'll see; just trust me on this.

So maybe you wear the raincoat and it rains, and you say, oh, logic is my protector. Or you wear the raincoat and it doesn't rain, and you say the Weather Channel was wrong but your logic was correct. Maybe you wear red and it turns out that the interviewer likes you because you were the only person brave enough to not wear black. Or maybe the interviewer doesn't notice, but just wearing red has put you in a good mood, and that good mood translates into your performing better in the interview. Who knows? The point is that when it comes to understanding the intelligence of our guts, analyzing the validity of what it is telling us solely through the tools of our logical mind is not the right approach. What's more, it is virtually impossible to engage in a dialogue with the unconscious and benefit from its wisdom if we insist on speaking to it in the language of logic.

Our instinctual intelligence and our logical intelligence do not fulfill the same purpose, nor are they two opposites on one continuum. The opposite of instinct, according to Nobel Prize winner in economics Friedrich A. Hayek, is not reason, it is death, "If we stopped doing everything for which we do not know the reason, or for which we cannot provide a justification . . . we would probably soon be dead."[20] Indeed, soldiers in the battlefield making split-second decisions to avoid being attacked do this without conscious forethought. Similarly, people driving on the highway are able to reflexively avoid dangerous objects or cars on the road at the last minute. Culturally we readily overrate and overextend the role of logic, and we tend to forget about and sometimes even deny the value of instinct. Of course, we also tend to repress instinct and get our way with logic, but are we really *getting our way*? The Intuitive Compass does not deny the value of reason and replace it with the exclusive or inappropriate use of gut feelings; rather, it establishes a balance between these two very distinct aspects of human intelligence so that they can enrich one another.

INSTINCT, INTUITION, AND THE BRAIN

For all that scientists have studied it, the brain remains probably the most mysterious human organ—and now it is the focus of billions of dollars worth of research aiming to penetrate its secrets. But for all its complexity there are still a number of deeply rooted cultural assumptions about the brain that we can challenge to better understand both the role of instinct and the process of intuition.

To understand instinct we need to understand the whole human brain of which it is a part. The late Dr. Paul D. MacLean, of the National Institutes of Health, devised a triune brain theory that offers a very useful model. Although his theory dates to the 1960s and is today challenged on many levels by current neuroscience, it remains overall a valid organizing theme for the purpose of this book. You will find in what follows a highly simplified representation of the human brain to help us understand why people do what they do and how they do it. It casts a very different light on human behaviors. Once we look at the human brain through this model, we cannot think of management and leadership in the same way, nor can we think of human organizations or business in the same way.

According to MacLean, the human brain is in reality three brains in one: the reptilian complex, the limbic system, and the neocortex.

The reptilian brain is the center for instinctive reflexes, primitive impulses, sexual drive, and aggression.[21] In common language, it is the seat of our guts. It is responsible for the survival and the reproduction of our species. It is inherited and not acquired. It follows the rules and necessities of human nature. Of the three brains, the reptilian brain is the first to be formed during prenatal life.

The limbic system is the center of our emotional life. Its development occurs from birth until around the age of five, and it is influenced by the child's relationship with his or her mother. This is why the emotional brain has a strong feminine side. Emotions are rarely simple. They sometimes are contradictory. They have lots of nuances that can be hard to identify at times. Our limbic brain is our second brain. It is the seat of our sensitivity and empathy. Emotions intersect with our feelings, which relate to our heart and its empathetic nature.

The neocortex, our third brain, grants us our ability to reason, engage in logic, master calculus, speak a language, and use abstraction. It functions in a binary way; it is dualistic: a proposition is either right or wrong, a business meeting can happen only before or after

Labor Day. It follows the rules of logic and reason. It sees the world in hierarchical terms and evaluates it by continuously establishing comparisons. It typically develops when children begin school, around the age of five or six.

The reptilian is our first brain not only because it is the first one present in us but also because, being responsible for our survival, it is programmed to get its way even when our emotions and our reason disagree. Our reptilian brain makes sure we breathe and that our heart beats. These are involuntary functions — they happen in spite of us and our will. Whether we feel sad or happy, depressed or energized, whether we decide to hold our breath or speed our heartbeat with substances, these functions at some point will have to come back to a normal state, unless there is a medical problem. Whatever we may think or feel, in the end our instinct will have its way, because we need to breathe and come back to a regular heartbeat, as much as we need to eat, drink, and sleep to survive and thrive. I call it *the law of survival*. For this reason, our reptilian brain is very adaptive (it will find every way it can to secure our survival, and it has done so for millennia), but it is also very stubborn. Its agenda has to come first. Just try to appease with gentle and sweet words a newborn who is screaming with hunger; chances are you will not have much success.

Another trait of the reptilian brain is that it will not spend more energy than needed to satisfy its main mission (ensuring our survival). As steward of our safety, the reptilian brain can be very limiting. This is the explanation behind human inertia. As we saw in Chapter One, we tend to do what's safer because from the standpoint of the reptilian brain it makes more sense. I call it *the law of human inertia*. This law is key in motivating teams to change or to be creative; because creativity is about stepping into the unknown, the law of inertia explains why being creative can be a difficult task. At the same time, our reptilian brain will get us to run faster than ever when fleeing from a threatening wild animal or will spur a mother to jump into flames or raging rapids to save her baby. It can help us mobilize talent, resources, and character beyond what we can imagine. I call it *the law of reaching beyond boundaries*.

These three laws, all based in the reptilian brain, are three fundamental forces we have to reckon with if we want to grow in life.

To further understand the human brain, though, we need to also remember that a decade ago Dr. Antonio Damasio, the neuroscientist from the University of Southern California mentioned earlier, developed the hypothesis that rational thinking cannot be separated from feelings. According to Damasio, we can no longer assume that our rational thoughts are generated by the neocortex independently from other parts of the brain or that instinct has no influence over our choices.[22] Actually, as we saw earlier, recent neuroscience research has proved the exact opposite: that all our cognition is somehow embodied; that is, our cognition and our body influence each other at all times. These studies suggest new ways of thinking about learning and leading. Learning should be approached as an interaction between the primitive structures of the brain and the more evolved part of the brain, our cortex.

This interaction between the primitive structure of the brain and our cortex as a factor of influence over learning and leading speaks to me because it synchs up with my experience as a business owner and leader. I believe one of the main reasons I was able to execute a fast turnaround in the publishing house I co-owned in Paris is that I led the company using my gut feelings and intuition as much as I was using my intellect and reason to make decisions and motivate others. However, I am not sure that at the time I would have been able to articulate clearly how this impacted the company's success. Leading is not simply a product of the most "intelligent" part of our brain, the neocortex, which is always seeking to analyze in order to understand what is occurring. No one part of the brain rules our life, nor are the parts interchangeable. Leading is an interaction among instinct, feeling, and reason. When we allow this, we adapt much faster and our motivation is much stronger.

Some people believe that logic rules our lives, but this is not true. Some would like our instinct to be rationally logical and exact, but this is neither its function nor its *modus operandi*. Logic and instinct truly are of different natures. This is where intuition becomes instrumental.

As we will see in the next section, intuition communicates and is equally at ease with both our logical mind and our instinct.

A CLOSER LOOK AT INTUITION

We may ask: what, exactly, is intuition? *Exactly* may not be the best word choice. Intuition has been referred to as an "inner voice" that is incredibly important to leadership when listened to and trusted.[23] It has also been described as "knowing for sure without knowing for certain."[24] Others will say it's the same as a hunch, a gut feeling, or an inner knowing, and in common language we may assign it the same characteristics as instinct and use the words interchangeably.

Perhaps virologist Dr. Jonas Salk offered both the simplest and the most appropriate definition when he said, "The intuitive mind tells the logical mind where to look next."[25] As I stated at the beginning of this chapter, I understand intuition as our ability to know something directly without an analytic process or reasoning. Intuition contributes to the decision-making process and is separate from the outcome (as I understand it for the purpose of this book, the outcome is the hunch). Intuition gives us the opportunity to access nonanalytic data and incorporate it into our decision making. Intuition is the means to bridge the gap between the conscious and nonconscious parts of our mind, between instinct and reason. It enhances analytic thinking and focuses on the present situation, providing insights as to timing, specific strategy, and creative ideas. It feeds our decision-making process, but it is not the whole process itself. It navigates the nonconscious and unconscious parts of the mind and does not logically evaluate the information it encounters. It operates in an associative, creative, and holistic way, which does not relate to logic. So to judge intuition as you would logic not only is inappropriate, but also misses out on and denies what intuition has to offer—an entrée into the irrational, paradoxical, and nonlinear aspect of life. If intuition does not deny logic (because intuition is not about denying or opposing; rather, it is about embracing, deepening, and revealing), it still reaches far beyond the confines of logic, so much so that it can help us be much more efficient than we could be with logic alone. It gives us light-speed access to flashes of insight and immediate knowledge that is otherwise hard to gain access to, and that's what makes it uniquely useful as we will see in the following story.

WHAT HAPPENS WHEN INSTINCT AND INTUITION ARE IGNORED?

Kevin, a twenty-one-month old boy, was brought to a leading American teaching hospital with one of the best pediatric departments in the nation.[26] Abandoned by his father and greatly neglected by his mother, Kevin was in very bad condition when he entered the hospital: pale, undernourished, significantly underweight, and refusing to eat. Noticing that needles and blood draws were aggravating Kevin's overall state and his refusal of food, the young doctor taking care of Kevin understood intuitively that the best approach for his young patient would be to minimize any invasive treatment and provide a caring environment. Kevin's health improved and he started to eat again. Soon enough the disapproving hospital specialists took the child away from the young doctor's supervision because they disagreed with his approach (they saw it as a lack of treatment) and started the diagnostic machinery, ordering multiple tests and examinations. For nine weeks Kevin was subjected to multiple tests, but they still couldn't find the cause of his problems. Unfortunately, during this period he stopped eating again and, despite blood infusions and intravenous feeding, Kevin died. After his death an autopsy was performed to determine the cause, but nothing conclusive was found. After all of this, one physician said, "He was spared no test to find out what was really going on. He died in spite of everything we did."

The reason I tell this tragic story is not to criticize doctors, who in many ways can be true miracle workers, but to expose what can happen when the power of logical reasoning is misguided. Even in one of the most altruistic and well-meaning contexts, like a reputable hospital, the outcome can be the exact opposite of the intention. We're quick to denounce the excesses of emotions and instinct, such as in a crime of passion or a decision based on irrational feelings, but we resist looking with a creative sense of responsibility at the faults of logical reasoning.

I have found that this same fault explains the lack of sustainability in business and economic development. When we base decisions on gut feelings and things go wrong, it's easy to blame intuition. However, when logic fails us, we explain it away with logical reasoning, not factoring in the fact that our approach to development is divorced from the organic way in which life unfolds, which is through a combination of laws identified by science and a series of unpredictable accidents present throughout the history of the universe.[27] In an effort to improve everyone's quality of life, our modern societies—driven by so-called scientific progress—have, in spite of or because of reason and logic, created pollution and depletion of resources, subjected animals to industrial feedlots and questionable slaughtering practices, and left our fellow human beings to suffer from increasing poverty and rampant viral diseases. Our approaches look very similar to the logic-based approach the doctors took to Kevin's treatment. They meant well, but in the end their efforts did not succeed at improving Kevin's quality of life. Yet we seem incapable of evolving our thoughts and ways of decision making beyond the one way of thinking that we know well, which is predominantly logical and analytical.

WEB

It seems that we often act without feeling or intuition. When faced with an unknown outcome, and the anguish that can come with it (like the anguish hospital specialists probably felt about their inability to heal Kevin), the overwhelming nature of our confusion leads us to seek logical answers as relief from our emotional discomfort. But it does not have to be this way. Logic alone is not always enough to ensure our survival in the short or long run and to provide appropriate creative answers. This is why we need to resort to other human capabilities, alternative approaches that are sustainable and are no more difficult to execute.

We can see the three laws of the reptilian brain in action in Kevin's story:

- The first is the *law of human inertia* that can take away common sense and creative autonomy. Medical science has its goals and therapeutic protocols well thought out and defined, but even in the face of obvious human suffering and the patent inefficiency of the system, the doctors were not able to critically and creatively reconsider their process.
- The second is the *law of reaching beyond boundaries* (that is, the perception of self-imposed emotional and intellectual boundaries). Too often we have too little faith in our (intangible) ability to grow and evolve without recourse to external material resources. Kevin started to heal when he was embraced emotionally. It took nothing more than caring attention and love for him to start to feel better; no material expense, no scientific knowledge, all intangible means, all free and available at all times.
- Finally, the third is the *law of survival*, which is powerful, adaptive, and cannot be fully understood by logic. To support, enhance, or tap into our instinct and capacity for survival, we need options other than those that logic can provide. Logic is too limited and blind to what lives outside of logic. Our limbic brain, which holds our capacity for empathy, is the only instrument we have that can fully comprehend the law of survival. This is the law the young doctor who first took care of Kevin was going by and the same law his colleagues denied. The intuitive doctor felt that the logic of systematic testing for best diagnosis was not right and conflicted with Kevin's self-healing capacity, which is sustained by the law of survival.

In business I see these three laws constantly underestimated and often dismissed. Yet thanks to the structure of the human brain and the deep mechanisms in place that ensure our survival and well-being, taking these three laws of the reptilian brain into consideration is the most powerful way to engage employees, communicate efficiently with audiences, and innovate and drive the growth of a company.

As we will see in what follows, some leaders understand well how to leverage these three laws, and science itself is now experimenting and researching how to mimic the laws of life and human nature to optimize human efficiency. Following the three laws of instinct necessarily leads to the path of least resistance and of the most economical use of energy to ensure the survival of our species.

RITUALS ARE GATEWAYS TO OUR INSTINCT

Ritual is powerful and can be used to engage people in ways that words alone cannot. As Dr. Antonio Damasio explains it, the mind is *embodied*—to clarify, the mind is inseparable from the body and the body influences the mind and vice versa.[28] Rituals are meant to affect the body through regular repetition and dramatic staging; as a consequence of that drama and repetition, they affect us at an instinctual level and influence the mind in ways much deeper than logic and reason. From sacred ceremonies including christenings, Passover Seders, and Ramadan to secular ones including school graduations and the public swearing in of elected officials, they mark the most significant moments of our lives, individually and collectively. On a more mundane level, they help us navigate through the average day—the morning cup of coffee, a hot shower. They send a signal to our brain that something of note is happening. In all cases they help us harness energy, stabilize our minds, and have faith in the future. In doing so they channel our thrust for survival in constructive ways. By conveying a sense of purpose to important aspects of our lives, they help us find meaning, go past inertia to move through the challenges of life, and creatively reach beyond the bounds of logic. Rituals powerfully harness the law of survival, the law of reaching beyond boundaries, and the law of inertia. This was demonstrated in an experiment related to the treatment of chronic disease conducted by two leading medical institutions.

In a study published in December 2010, researchers at the Harvard Medical School (HMS) Osher Research Center, and Beth Israel Deaconess Medical Center (BIDMC) found that placebos work even when the doctors giving them tell the patients very clearly that they are in fact placebos. Placebos are typically used in research as a control mechanism. A portion of the study subjects are given a drug that is expected to have some therapeutic value, and a portion of the study subjects are given a placebo, which has no known therapeutic value. None of the study subjects are told whether they are receiving the real medicine or the placebo. For many years researchers have been aware of the placebo effect—the phenomenon that a portion of the study subjects given the placebo will experience relief from some of their symptoms. Because research projects typically require the researchers to not disclose to the study subjects whether they are receiving a placebo or an actual drug, it has been posited that these study subjects were influenced by their own thought that the placebo might in fact be a real drug. In short, they believe that the drug is real, and that very belief heals them.

In the study by HBS and BIDMC, the subjects all suffered from irritable bowel syndrome (IBS), a chronic functional gastrointestinal disorder characterized by abdominal pain and discomfort associated with altered bowel habits. IBS is one of the top ten reasons why people seek medical care and is prevalent in 10 to 15 percent of the global population.[29] The study notes, "few therapies have been shown to be effective and safe in relieving the global symptoms of IBS," and "previous research has demonstrated that placebo responses in IBS are substantial and clinically significant."[30]

The researchers wanted to find out if the placebo effect would be neutralized or diminished if the IBS patients were aware that they were being given a placebo. In this study, half of the subjects were given nothing and half of them were given a sugar pill. What they found was startling: 59 percent of the patients who were treated with the placebo, and fully aware that they were taking a placebo, experienced relief from their symptoms. In contrast, only 35 percent of those who were given nothing experienced any relief. Further, the relief the 59 percent experienced was "to a degree roughly equivalent to the effects of the most powerful IBS medications." The study notes that while scientists aren't sure what to make of the findings, they suspect that the ritual of taking a pill is one of the factors that made the study subjects experience relief.[31] Dr. Ted Kaptchuk, an associate professor of medicine at Harvard Medical School, is a researcher on the placebo effect. He led the research on placebo and IBS. He describes the placebo effect as presumably about the appearance of things, the belief in things, the ritual of things. "There is something inherently unscientific about it. A ritual depends on belief, religion and imagination. The idea of ritual is what science detests."[32]

Rituals can also help in the business world. BETC, the most successful advertising agency in France, provides an example that can easily be adapted to many different businesses and industries. The founder and chairwoman of the agency, Mercedes Erra, insists that whenever a brief on a new client or project is brought in by an account executive, it is and should be treated as a pivotal moment in the life of the agency. The brief is the first step in the development of a new campaign. Its arrival becomes a celebratory moment. It is the trigger for a professional ritual in which importance and meaning are conveyed. Food and drinks are brought into a special room, and all of the people who will be working on the campaign gather together to talk about the future of the project. It is fun and play and serious work all at the same time. Key elements of the brief are clarified, including the strategic context of the project. There is discussion about the agency's or individual team members' relationships with the client, and any convictions or doubts about the client, their company, the brand, or the communications plan that they want to launch. But what happens could not be achieved through an exchange of emails or written notes because they would not have the same impact. Allowing time, staging the meeting in a different way, and having the chairwoman attend the briefing all have a special emotional impact and show the significance of the event. People can feel its significance, and feeling it is more important than understanding it intellectually when it comes to harnessing creativity and enthusiasm. Feelings make an impact on our bodies, which in turn influences our ability to solve problems and imagine new solutions. Such a meeting reaches into people's psyches, and the meeting's perceived significance has a long-lasting effect. Rituals are powerful, as they help us go beyond what's tangible and conscious. They reach deep into our unconscious, engage our instinct, and convey meaning.

Mercedes Erra knows that she's in a business where creative talent and strategic thinking are everything and she needs to mobilize and encourage both all the time. Advertising is a high-pressure, demanding business, and she is a hard-working executive and a demanding person, so these moments of celebration are also her way of reenergizing her teams and thus compensating for an unavoidably high-pressure work environment. Mercedes says that about once a year she reminds everyone at her agency about the crucial importance of brief rituals to their ability to succeed; without this constant attention to ritual, she knows that the pressure of deadlines and demands of clients simply push the more subtle—yet far more powerful—management of the invisible aspects of the advertising business to the side.

This type of leadership is needed all the more in times of deep transition like the one we live in today. When we need to make creative choices in a complex context, or entrepreneurial decisions in a fast-evolving environment, when we need to mobilize more of our employees' energy to reinvent a business model, or to stimulate creativity and agility to adapt to rising competition from emerging markets and cheaper labor, logic alone will not deliver what's needed to do the job well. The new economy we are doing business in asks for much more disruptive thinking, whether in people management, business strategy, or even financial planning. This is why rituals are more needed and more relevant today than ever before. Their ability to mobilize teams at an instinctual level, create longer-lasting engagement, connect people with the deeper part of their psyche and therefore their creativity, and help them reach beyond their assumed limits and overcome inertia, cannot be replaced by logical reasoning.

THE NEW ECONOMY CHALLENGES LOGICAL THINKING

One of the most important forces driving economic performance in the United States and other countries during the 1990s was the rise of information technology. New technology has had such a significant impact on the economy that "the new economy" emerged as a popular term in both the media and academia to refer to a technology-based economy. In addition, the rapid evolution of technology makes change much faster. It lowers barriers to entry and challenges business models and distribution logistics, as we have seen most publicly in the media and music industries with the emergence of new music or media distribution channels like iTunes and Netflix. It has also given consumers expanded power via social networks.

When advising clients, I ask them to carefully factor into their business strategy, in addition to the rapid evolution of technology, the following four key elements of the new economy:

- A complex global playing field
- New consumers
- Unpredictability
- Sustainability

Each of these four elements demands new ways of doing business. Each indicates the need for new thinking and new levels of agility and creativity within organizations. Let's take a closer look at these four key elements, all of which are crucial to success in the new economy.

A Complex Global Playing Field

The impact of technology, combined with the so-called emerging economies—such as the BRIC countries (Brazil, Russia, India, and China), among others[33]—has led to a new relationship in global commerce and industry. There has been a noticeable change in the world economic order, which makes the economic environment even more complex. The number of players has largely increased. The G7, a meeting of the finance ministers from a group of seven industrialized nations created in 1976, has been paralleled since 1999 by the G20, a group of finance ministers and central bank governors from nineteen countries plus the European Union. The former leading powers of the world (the United States and the European countries) now have to integrate their activities with new economic and political powers such as China and, to a lesser degree, India and Brazil. Africa, with its natural resources, is courted today by China as the Middle East was courted by Europe and the United States fifty years ago. Whereas twenty years ago high school students would study Spanish as a foreign language, many today study Mandarin. A couple of comparisons illustrate this radical shift.

The cumulative gross domestic profit (GDP) of the BRIC countries was twice that of Germany's GDP in 2006 and almost three times it in 2010; it is believed that it will be more than four and a half times Germany's GDP in 2020.[34] This change in the world economic order influences trade negotiations, currency values, and, of course, marketing strategies focusing on new consumers with different needs that are based on their sociocultural habits and level of economic development. By 2020, of the top fifty richest cities in the world, twenty are expected to be in emerging markets.[35] This is an economic trend that has already changed the face of the retail industry, in which, for instance, there are flagship stores in more countries than ever before, and corporate organizational structures with an expanded presence of centralized administrative services or distribution platforms on three or more continents.

Obviously, business leaders who want to succeed in an interdependent world economy can no longer simply focus on the United States and Europe. They need to address new markets and devise new strategies to respond to new competition. In addition, we are moving away from an East-West dominated focus and now must also look to new economic territories in the Southern Hemisphere, due to the accelerated growth of countries in Africa, South America, and Southeast Asia. As a result, the ever-increasing service economy in developed nations requires workers with more sophisticated skills and competencies, so the practices that organizations need to develop is very different from what it was even ten years ago. Research in the field of corporate innovation shows that "Demand for workers who understand complexity is increasing. Over 75 percent of the U.S. work force does information work, which requires workers to collaborate with other information workers to make judgments and solve complex issues."[36] In today's workforce, information workers, also called knowledge workers, are valued for their ability to process, exchange, and act on knowledge within a specific subject matter through focused analysis and deep understanding of the subject. They use research skills to define problems and to identify alternatives. They leverage their expertise and insight to help solve those problems in an effort to influence company decisions, priorities and strategies.[37] Knowledge workers can be found across a variety of information technology roles and also among professionals like teachers, librarians, lawyers, architects, physicians, nurses, engineers, and scientists. As businesses increase their dependence on information technology, the number of fields in which knowledge workers must operate has expanded dramatically. This calls for more creative added value and a whole new set of creative skills among employees.

New Consumers

From ancient village meetings overseen by the town elders, to parents associations and the Elks Lodge, human beings have always organized themselves in communities. People are more likely to buy from people within their community. The difference today is that the communities are broader in geographic scope, narrower and more varied in focus, and devastatingly fast in broadcasting abilities through new technology. Take, for example, what happened in Los Angeles in 2009 when gas prices spiked: consumers began "tweeting" (via the increasingly ubiquitous online social network called Twitter) the gas prices at locations across the city so that their fellow drivers could find the best deals in their area. On a much larger scale, the Foursquare[38] application gained attention for its use in marketing campaigns by major retailers in the United

States and Europe, including McDonald's, Starbucks, and Domino's. Even if social media measurement remains a challenge in marketing strategies, it is still a sign of the advent of a new digital age to notice that household names like McDonald's, Starbucks, and Domino's are in conversation and in pilot programs with Foursquare for their marketing campaigns. What this means is that today's consumers behave and shop differently from the way they did even ten years ago. Consumers are more and more active online; e-retail on average across categories grew in 2010 at a yearly rate above 20 percent, which is greater than the growth of physical retail space in Europe and in the United States.[39] As a consequence, retail brands cater to this new set of consumption habits and develop new ways to engage consumers in the digital space.

Consumers have a wealth of information at their fingertips, they organize themselves in social networks, and they use technology to gather and communicate. So the winning business strategy is to become a part of that community. Businesses can do this by first looking for a way to establish and enjoy a relationship with community members (and prospective consumers) that is value based, creates a sense of shared interests, and builds loyalty with an array of valuable free services and community initiatives. When you first provide value you then will naturally build a strong and lasting relationship under your brand name and eventually make money. This is the new order.

Unpredictability

Rapid changes in technology, shifts in the location of labor, the emergence of new markets, and the influence of new consumers all add up to one thing: unpredictability. Yes, there is some underlying order, but the predictive models that we have used in the past are insufficient tools for today's world. As we saw in the IBM study of CEOs, complexity in the marketplace is one reason that the CEOs see creativity as the most important leadership skill in coming years. If we can't predict via logical models, we need to be fully aware of what's happening in the moment—to be able to adapt and have creative responses to new circumstances. The attributes of the creative mindset—agility, flexibility, the ability to overcome inertia in oneself and others, and openness to new ideas — will best enable us to address unpredictability and complexity. The old model, in which executive minds could be trained to rely on purely logical models, is far less relevant in the new economy.

Sustainability

Sustainability wasn't much of a consideration in doing business in the old economy. But the creation of the new economy coincided with a greater awareness of and concern with our global consumption and environmental resources. The traditional profit-centric business model has had negative side effects, which have been publicly felt on a global scale. It has contributed to unacceptable levels of poverty, health epidemics, pollution, and the exhaustion of natural resources — so much so that the balance of our natural and socioeconomic ecosystems is threatened. Public regulations and corporate systems have been implemented to reduce those levels, but doing business in the new economy means we need to not only comply with those regulations, but also find ways to proactively do more.

This is why the concept of *triple bottom line* (TBL), also known as "people, planet, profit," emerged in the early 1980s. It articulates a spectrum of parameters and criteria for measuring organizational (and societal) success: economic, ecological, and social.[40] With the ratification in early 2007 of a TBL standard for urban and community accounting, jointly produced by the United Nations and the International Council for Local Environmental Initiatives (ICLEI, more commonly known as Local Governments for Sustainability), this became the dominant approach to public sector full cost accounting. In the private sector, a commitment to corporate social responsibility (CSR) implies a commitment to some form of TBL reporting.

Today, between industry regulations, media coverage by investigative journalists, and increasingly aware consumers who readily broadcast their opinions via blogs and social networks, there isn't any organization of significance that can escape the demand for CSR in some form or another.

Adam Werbach, chief sustainability officer of Saatchi and Saatchi, notes that business strategy has always been about making profits first, and this cannot change.[41] But what can change is how we go about making those profits. I would take this one step further and replace the priority given to profit with a holistic focus on sustainable value, which obviously includes profit and compensation of shareholders' risk. In my experience this shift in focus always brings a direct positive impact both on profit and the business strategy.

PATHWAYS BEYOND LOGIC

Logic and reason alone can no longer guide us toward innovation or success. They will not be enough to get us to the level of creativity and reinvention we need to address the challenges of the new economy. We need to deal with the deeper part of human nature: intuition and instinct. Science, evidence in the real world, and experience tell us that our intuition and our instincts, although sometimes difficult to completely understand, very often point us in the right direction. Sometimes they can even save our lives. To positively influence the deeper part of ourselves, we need to appeal to the heart and engage the guts. We need to honor the sometimes-cryptic clues sent up from our guts, and realize that, in doing so, we follow in the footsteps of a great many accomplished people in science, industry, and the military. As business leaders we can take steps to create a corporate atmosphere that speaks to the hearts and instincts as well as the minds of our employees. Doing so puts a great deal of agility and creative power to work for our companies. One powerful way we can harness the creative power of our teams is by introducing rituals at key moments in business ideation and development. Management and leadership—which increasingly require dealing with human motivation, behavioral change, and, now more than ever, sustainable innovation—are much more about the intangible part of business than about what's tangible, much more about the unconscious part of human interactions than about the conscious part.

Part Two

A Novel Model and Skill Set

3

the intuitive compass: a model for creativity and agility

The world is not to be put in order, the world is order incarnate.
It is up to us to put ourselves in unison with this order.
—HENRY MILLER

The business world has been turned upside down by the rapid adoption of technological innovations and the globalization of many industries. Today, the creativity of corporate executives is increasingly called for in all areas of business, and courageous behavior is needed as much as creative thinking. Increasingly complex market scenarios laden with erratic disruptors require executives to have the confidence to step into the unknown and make decisions even in the face of confusion. Although traditional business thinking typically focuses on three- to five-year strategies created with sophisticated analytical processes and logical reasoning, this approach is no longer ideal. Because the future is uncertain, expert systems software or scenario planning methodologies are at best limited tools. Today's fast-emerging, often unpredictable scenarios call for an agile imagination to seize emerging opportunities, and a new model that allows for such.

The Intuitive Compass was designed to help us develop new behaviors and new ways to make decisions. It is a tool to help us access our instinct and leverage play in order to innovate, develop disruptive ideas, imagine new sustainable business solutions, and reinvent the way we approach value creation. The Intuitive Compass was invented to help organizations thrive in the new economy while enhancing the sustainability of our practices.

We've already begun to look at the influence of play in our approaches to innovation, the role of instinct in leadership and value creation and the tensions that each faces: *play* lives in tension with our need for results, and *instinct* lives in tension with our cultural inclination toward reason and logic. Play and instinct are the roots of creative imagination, and they both influence our behaviors at their core. We are instinctual beings by nature and logical beings by culture. The Intuitive Compass simply shows that linear efficiency and logic do not necessarily have to dominate our approaches to life and work, and it provides alternative ways to conduct business. It indicates how to balance and integrate the best of what both logic and instinct have to offer.

THE INTUITIVE COMPASS

The Compass is organized around the usual four cardinal points one finds in a navigation compass: north, east, south, and west.

In the north you find *reason* (our capacity to conceive ideas and analyze data) and opposite, in the south, you find *instinct* (our capacity to survive and adapt). In the east you find *results*, representing the outcome of linear efficiency, and opposite, in the west, you find *play*, which represents an erratic process comparable to the creative process. This diagram shows play and instinct coming together in the southwest quadrant, where creativity can be unleashed. The Intuitive Compass is designed to help people better understand where creative ideas come from and how to access their own genius and uncover meaningful ideas.

FIGURE 3.1 The Intuitive Compass

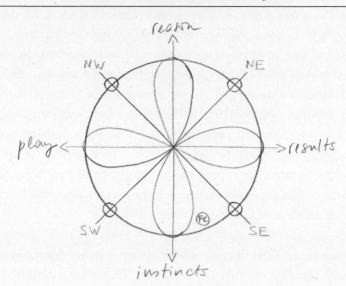

It makes the complexity of the creative process simple to see and it provides a clear roadmap to creative problem solving.

The North-South Axis

The vertical axis (north-south) shows reason facing instinct. In the north, you see reason: think of the brain resting atop your body. In the south you find instinct: think of the guts. Why these positions? In our modern societies we see reason as our highest form of intelligence. During our school years we train to develop our analytical intelligence, and we get praised mostly for our ability to reason. As adults, most of us rely on this skill to communicate our ideas to others, ideas that in turn often get evaluated for their logical value. Reason is at the basis of modern social interaction, decision making, and life evaluation. Analytical intelligence reigns in our world regardless of evidence showing that other forms of intelligence are equally as important if not more so.[1] As we saw in Chapter Two, parts of our instinctual brain are involved in our most sophisticated decision-making processes (as shown in 2005 neuroscience research at the Massachusetts Institute of Technology [MIT]). We now know that in our guts there is an undeniable capacity for helping us to make intelligent choices among complex data.

Because our instinct is responsible for our survival, it actually makes complete sense for it to be heavily involved in sophisticated decisions. It has been doing that job for thousands of years. So it follows that, in important matters that will affect our lives, our instinct should be the first and foremost judge of whether or not a decision is good. A study conducted by neuroscientists at Princeton University confirms this fact.[2] The aim of the study was to demonstrate how a gut feeling may arise before a person becomes conscious of what the brain has registered. In the study, students were

> *directed to pick out figures — people or cars — in a series of photos that flashed by on a computer screen. The pictures flashed by four at a time, and the participants were told to scan only two of them, either those above and below the center point, or those to the left and right. Eye tracking confirmed that they did just that. But brain scans showed that the students' brains registered the presence of people or cars even when the figures appeared in photos that they were not paying attention to.... The brain tallies cues, big and small, consciously and not, it may send out an alarm before a person fully understands why.[3]*

A gut feeling is often the result of some part of our brain taking in and processing information that we are not conscious of having taken in and processed. This study demonstrates how we sometimes are not consciously aware of all of the information that we in fact have already registered at some level — in this case, visually.

When a gut feeling arises before a person becomes conscious of it, it can enrich their ability to make a decision. Not only that, but sometimes logical problem solving is simply not the best option. Sometimes the best way to come up with an appropriate answer to a logical problem is to base it on a gut feeling. Dr. Gerd Gigerenzer, a psychologist who has studied the limits of rational thinking in decision making explains that, contrary to popular wisdom, sometimes there is no optimal strategy attainable to solve a problem.[4] He gives the example of a presidential candidate who has to plan a fifty-city tour. The candidate would like to start and end in the same city and obviously cover the shortest distance. There are so many possible itineraries that not even the fastest computer can optimize the candidate's choice in a lifetime, a century, or even a millennium.[5]

When optimization is out of reach we must rely on our gut feelings instead of logical deduction. And this applies to any situation in which rules are not completely explicit, uncertainty is prevalent, or rule breaking is an option. This obviously pertains to winning a negotiation, leading an organization, marketing a new product, investing in the stock market, or training executives. Of course, for every one of these endeavors good enough strategies exist, but for us to find and choose these valid strategies we need to resort to what Gigerenzer calls a "rule of thumb," which he defines as the product of a mental process that tries to identify the most important information and ignore the rest, taking advantage of an evolved capacity of the brain to do so. For Gigerenzer, expert of the intelligence of the unconscious, "it would be erroneous to assume that intelligence is necessarily conscious and deliberate." He adds, "We know more than we can tell."

Notwithstanding this information about the way our brains work, our school systems still rely predominantly on logic-based tests to select individuals. The underlying assumption in business education is that modern decision making still relies mostly on rational criteria and processes. But this very logical approach to life does not match the latest information offered by neuroscience. The way we make decisions is obviously more complex than linear, logical decision making would have it. Of course, the idea here is not to pit reason against instinct. On the contrary, the intent is to develop a dynamic synergy between the two. This is the explanation for the figure eight on the Intuitive Compass, which links reason in the north to instinct in the south. One cannot be without the other. Reason and instinct are intertwined and constantly cooperating.

The East-West Axis

The horizontal axis (east-west) shows *results* facing *play*. In the east we find *results*. Think of the east as the place where the sun rises and casts light, allowing us to see the results of our action. And in the west we see *play* as in creative play, an essential characteristic of the creative process. Think of the west as the place where the sun sets, leaving us in the dark, representing the unknown inherent to the creative process. In life we need to achieve a number of tasks to get things done and move projects to completion. It is essential. However, if we think about the Buddhist proverb, which says that in life it is not the destination but the journey that matters, then we're forced to think twice about the way we focus on results, the way we engage in an action. What the Buddhist proverb underlines is that nothing new can be encountered if we're only thinking about where we're going.

Imagine yourself driving to someone's house for a surprise birthday party. Every guest has been asked to arrive at a certain time to keep the surprise a surprise. You left home late. You're in a hurry. You're now focused on the road in order not to be late. You don't want to miss the face of your friend completely surprised, between tears and laughter. You're completely absorbed in one goal: to get there as soon as possible. You don't have "time" to notice the surroundings. You're all about the destination. There's no real journey, because you're not taking in what's around. And if someone asked you whether on your way over you saw a house under construction a mile away from your friend's house, chances are you'd say that you had not seen it because you were too focused on trying to be on time.

Now imagine yourself this time driving along the same road. The road goes through the Colorado Rockies. You're here on vacation. This is the first time you've ever been in Colorado. It's Sunday. You don't have to be anywhere at a particular time. No real plan for the day besides reaching your next destination at some point, whenever you get there. You set out early. You have plenty of time ahead of you. Chances are this time you will enjoy the spectacular scenery, very aware of what's around you; you'll notice the particular light on that day, the colors of the mountains, the vegetation, and many other minute details.

Same road, same person, two totally different attitudes; one is about the destination (result); the other is about the journey (play). So if we accept that creativity is essential in life in order to adapt to change and to keep evolving (whether as individuals or organizations), then we need to allow for and cater to the journey, the playfulness that defines the creative process. Being obsessed with results leaves out the playful, imaginative dimension of life. Our tendency is to focus too much on results, because our rational mind tells us that focusing on results is the best way to make good decisions. This focus also feels more comfortable and gives us a sense of control over the situation we're in. This is why we tend to approach efficiency in a linear way. Yet as we saw in Chapter One with the ABC exercise, in a highly complex environment—such as the circumstances of the theatrical exercise—linear efficiency is not the answer.

Again, it's really not about results and play being in opposition. It's about understanding the need for a collaborative synergy between play and results in order to reach a creative outcome. Obviously we need to get things done. But without a balance between the two, we run the risk of either never getting anywhere or getting someplace but not being aware of the changes in our environment. This is why it is important that in our approach to life, or a project, we keep a dynamic relationship between linear efficiency and the random nature of creativity; hence the figure eight linking results and play.

Before we learn how to leverage and balance all of the skills and talents that are represented within the four quadrants of the Intuitive Compass (the action that is represented by the figure eight in the diagram), let's take a closer look at all the quadrants to understand their unique qualities.

CHARACTERISTICS OF THE FOUR QUADRANTS

Each of the four quadrants of the Intuitive Compass is representative of a personality or approach to life or business. Once you get to know what the quadrants represent, you might say that some people have a very *northeast* approach to life, that a particular company is dominated by *southeast* behaviors, that a team operates by *southwest* principles, or that certain initiatives are based on a *northwest* tactic. Of course, the approaches that people, teams, and companies have toward decision making or just plain living are always a mix of all four quadrants, but by understanding predominant characteristics we can begin the work of balancing and integrating to improve performance.

The Northeast

The northeast quadrant is all about reason and results. It is the quadrant of linear efficiency, the zone of administering and organizing things to optimize outcomes and deliver predictable results within well-defined constraints. This is where you will find a traditional accounting firm, a school administrator, or a government agency. When we look at government agencies, such as those that manage education or health care, we see the difficulty they encounter when they try to evolve or innovate. Even when great ideas are presented it will often be very difficult for these ideas to be implemented because of a lack of agility and flexibility, due to the agencies' natural focus on institutional processes and structures. Also, since a typical northeast entity's performance is measured by the ability to follow rules, they lack the competitive and gutsy spirit characteristic of the southeast quadrant (where there is always the incentive to break the record, sell more widgets, and increase commissions) and the playful, instinctual qualities of the southwest quadrant (where hidden opportunities are revealed).

The Southeast

The southeast quadrant is also focused on results, but it achieves results more through instinct than through reason. High-achieving salespeople and athletes tend to have a southeast disposition. If you push the salesperson out the door, she will come back in through the window; when the champion athlete's usual tactics aren't working and time is running out, the athlete will mobilize his instinct to devise and execute a unique game-winning play. There is a great deal of efficiency and charisma in the southeast quadrant, but it has its shadow side. When the southeast dominates at the expense of the controls of the northeast, the longer-range view of the northwest, or the respect for the natural flow characteristic of the southwest, the ultimate outcome can be highly destructive. A case in point is what happened when a rogue trader at Société Generale, Jerome Kerviel, blatantly ignored banking regulations; ultimately his actions — which had been delivering spectacular financial results for some time — imperiled not only his employer, but indeed the entire global financial system.[6]

Mr. Kerviel is a French trader who was convicted in the January 2008 Société Generale trading loss incident for breach of trust, forgery, and unauthorized use of the bank's computers, which resulted in losses valued at €4.9 billion, a figure far higher than the bank's total market capitalization.[7] Société Generale claims Kerviel worked these trades alone, without its authorization — assertions that have been met with skepticism from expert commentators and analysts alike. Kerviel told investigators such practices are widespread and that turning a profit causes the hierarchy to turn a blind eye. Kerviel published a book, *L'engrenage: Mémoires d'un Trader* (Gears: Memoirs of a Trader) in May 2010; in it, he alleges that his superiors knew of his trading activities and that the practice was very common.

Whatever Kerviel's motive (he is not thought to have profited personally from the suspicious trades), this incident illustrates how instinct, when left completely unchecked by the rule of law and reason, can create unprecedented damage. Excesses of unchecked instinct in the financial world, unfortunately, have abounded in recent years.

The Inside Job is a documentary released in 2010 in which a number of high-level bankers, economists, financial regulators, and elected officials are interviewed about the 2008 global financial crisis. It gives us a close look at how the drive to build personal fortunes or personal power bases compels some people to make decisions that offer short-term gain but are ultimately highly destructive. What's most riveting about the movie is the palpable discomfort that some of the interviewees display when being asked if they knew, or even strongly suspected, that the actions they took (or failed to take) during that time were contributing to the creation of a crisis that would ultimately cost $20 trillion dollars and hundreds of thousands of jobs worldwide. The visceral reaction of viewers to this movie is most commonly anger: "look at what they did to so many people and what they got away with!" However, another reaction might well be the realization that this is a cautionary tale that can inform us about the dangers of unsustainable business models. When underlying value is not in place, it is as if some invisible compensatory force eventually works to restore order and balance. In the end the victories of this period were not only destructive, in many cases, to the very people who initially benefitted, but also unsustainable. Southeast behavior is about a single-minded dedication to the achievement of results. However, when left unbalanced by influences from the other three quadrants, it can lead to the excesses and destruction that are illustrated in *The Inside Job*.

The Northwest

In the northwest quadrant is reason—the analytical mind—applied to the creative process of play. This is where you will find strategic planners, management consultants, psychologists, marketers, graphic designers, and architects—the people and firms that develop ideas and visions about the future that are creative and backed up by logic and analysis. They are creative problem solvers and, very often, the "gurus" we look to when we want to take a leap forward but we also want assurances about potential outcomes. The positives in this quadrant seem obvious: creativity plus logic! The potential drawback is that if we rely on the northwest alone (creative thinking and great plans) without the pragmatic measures of the southeast (where performance and actual results occur), or the administrative expertise of the northeast (organizing things to optimize outcomes), then what you are left with is wishful thinking. You have the exhaustively researched, extensively discussed, and beautifully printed Strategic Plan that sits on the shelf.

Take, for example, the EZ Pass system. In New York and New Jersey the roadways are heavily trafficked, and for years—decades—toll bridges and tunnels routinely become clogged with cars and trucks inching their way forward to stop and pay the toll to a toll taker in a booth. The Port Authority of New York and New Jersey (PANYNJ) came up with a great plan: give travelers the option to buy an electronic device (an EZ Pass) to put in their windshield that could be read by another electronic device in the tollbooth. No need to stop, pay, and wait for your change and receipt; just slow down a little and move through the tollbooth. But what if they had stopped there? What if every tollbooth still would accept either cash or the EZ Pass? Congestion would not have been remarkably reduced, and people would not have been highly motivated to buy the EZ Pass and use it. Instead, PANYNJ tactically set aside a large percentage of the tollbooths to exclusively serve EZ Pass holders: this very northeast tactic, combined with a southeast focus — manifesting the potential of a great idea through the implementation of a well-thought-out and detailed plan with a determined focus on results, no matter the frustration of drivers who have not yet adopted EZ pass and now need to wait in longer lines because of the newly limited number of cash-only booths — transformed a great idea into a productive, innovative outcome.

The Southwest

The southwest quadrant is where we find instinct applied to the creative process of play — a heady combination of nature's most powerful and least predictable forces. This is where great artists, scientists, and adventurers thrive, oblivious to the lure of comfort and stability. This is where the germ of an idea for an innovative product possesses us to mortgage our house when more rational minds refuse to lend us money to build the prototype. Here you will find a person who has the instinct of the champion athlete or top-performing salesperson, but you won't find the same focus on results. Instead, the person who operates from a southwest perspective enjoys activity for the sake of the activity, play for the pleasure of it, and exploration without necessarily having a clear destination in mind. But — and this is a critical point — the southwest quadrant is also the invisible hand behind a great many leaps forward in science, business, politics, the arts, and culture as a whole. So why wouldn't we want to live in a world dominated solely by the southwest? Because it would be too much intensity and uncertainty for most of us to bear. However, we wouldn't want to live in a world bereft of the influence of the southwest quadrant either. And, as we will see later in case studies about Maytag, Hewlett Packard, and Blockbuster, when companies cut themselves off from the richness and strength of a southwest approach, they limp along at best, and fail miserably at worst.

UNDERSTANDING THE SYNERGY AMONG THE FOUR QUADRANTS

Three of the quadrants—northeast, southeast, and northwest—are relatively straightforward and easy to understand. Metaphorically speaking, as it pertains to sustaining ourselves, in the northwest quadrant we plan ahead and make sure that we have enough food for tomorrow in the fridge, in the northeast quadrant we do quality control and confirm that what's in the fridge is still fresh enough to eat, and in the southeast quadrant we produce what we need to eat—meaning we either make money or grow food. These three functions are adaptations to life. They're part of living, but they are not life itself. Life itself is really about unconscious processes that allow for play, and the southwest quadrant is where the life force lives and thrives. The danger if you live too much in these three quadrants—the northwest, the northeast, and the southeast—is that you are managing your life well, and making it highly efficient, but you are not embracing life fully; you're leaving out the underlying force that sustains it and that is at all times available to you.

The southwest quadrant, which is the hardest to harness because it's all about instinct and random play, is essentially part of an unconscious experience of life. The combination of play, which by its nature cannot be organized or planned, with instinct, which is not fully intentional or rational, is where long-term value is generated both personally and in the business world. No great scientific breakthrough, innovative idea, or artistic achievement can be born except in the southwest quadrant. So the more you are able to integrate the southwest quadrant, the more you are actually leveraging that life force, and the more you're being carried through life's ups and downs. You will be carried by something that doesn't feel very clear to you, because it's an invisible force and it may follow an order that seems random to you. But it will have a real substance that will carry you further and deeper than volition alone could.

On a personal level, if you obsess too much on the first three quadrants, you end up focusing too much on managing your life and keeping things in control. If you do this, your life will not be supported by the vital force encountered in the southwest quadrant, and you will, in fact, be drifting away from it. The more you drift away from that life force, the less sustainable your life will be, and the harder you will have to work to sustain yourself. You may ultimately end up being depressed. The same dynamics are true for business enterprises.

As discussed in Chapter One, research conducted to analyze companies over one hundred years old, to determine what accounted for their long-term success, showed that they have three characteristics in common: fiscal conservancy, openness to new ideas, and a sense of belonging and shared values that enabled employees to take risks.[8] Although fiscal conservancy lives somewhere between the northeast and southeast quadrants, the second and third characteristics are classically northwest and southwest.

The Intuitive Compass is not meant to result in four teams or approaches to business excluding or opposing each other or fighting for supremacy. As we can see from the preceding descriptions of each quadrant, no single quadrant offers a complete solution to the complexity of life and business situations that confront us today. No matter where you, your company, or your industry fall on the compass, you can and should create and optimize dynamic relationships with all four quadrants. Sales teams should also focus on innovation and great ideas. Just because you are a lawyer doesn't mean you can't be creative. Diplomats can also be poets; artists can be champion athletes. Reason and instinct aren't oil and water, destined for a life apart; they can and should function together. There's no such thing as pure southwest living, no such thing as pure northeast being. The quadrants allow us to understand the impact of different competencies, but it's not about which is best; we need to respect and include all of them.

The Intuitive Compass gives us a way to look at each quadrant constructively and then, in times when we need sustainable innovations, to point our attention to the most critical one in terms of creativity and agility: the southwest quadrant. The southwest quadrant, integrated intelligently, gives us the raw materials and inspired ideas that help us to lead in a very uncertain and complex environment.

As noted earlier, in IBM's 2010 Global CEO study, the level of complexity and pace of change in the business world have prompted six out of ten CEOs to identify creativity as the most important leadership quality over the next five years. What these CEOs have intuited is that we are no longer on a playing field where logic and efficiency will deliver the results they need in order to remain competitive. They know that in order to achieve breakout innovations they must develop new skills and an entirely different relationship to strategic thinking. By way of analogy, let's look at two different board games.

One of the most highly regarded board games of all time in the western world is chess. Great chess players are revered for their ability to plan and execute winning strategies within a set of specific rules and defined protagonists. Your ability to win is determined by your ability at the start of every move to compute as many turns ahead as possible. The IBM chess-playing computer Deep Blue is said to devise strategies that compute up to fourteen moves ahead. For centuries chess has mirrored the kind of strategic thinking that has resulted in successful military campaigns, political superpowers, and strong businesses. Not anymore, or at least not exclusively. In today's environment, rational, logical, predictive systems based on the past are no longer in operation or dominant enough to secure our success in the future. As technology catapults us forward at a breakneck speed, creating new markets and new consumers, we might instead look to a Chinese board game called Go for inspiration. In Go, two players place tokens on a grid, each trying to circumvent the space of the other and dominate spatially by surrounding and neutralizing the tokens of the other in a bit-by-bit move into the opponent's space. You move, I move; you cannot think ahead, you can only respond contextually. It's like martial arts; you work with the energy of your opponent in response to his moves. This is similar to the interaction between instinct and play in the southwest quadrant. Play is forever evolving with circumstances and imagination, and instinct is adapting to its environment to ensure survival. It's an interaction that doesn't follow a set, predictive causal model.

Now let's take a closer look at how to tap into the creative force of the southwest quadrant.

MANAGING IN THE SOUTHWEST

Often, after I give a seminar on the management of innovation, executives will pull me aside and confess that they don't feel that they themselves are very creative and they are uncertain of their ability to manage creative minds. I always tell them that whether or not they are creative, if they seek creativity in their teams, their own behaviors can make a huge difference. Research conducted by the Center for Leadership Studies at SUNY Binghamton in New York explicitly shows that although the creative process does not really follow rules, there are still key aspects to the management of creativity. Risk taking, openness to new ideas, tolerance for confusion, and passion are all part of what's needed to manage creativity positively. The following are some necessary and practical steps that some very successful companies have taken to protect and better encourage creativity and a southwest culture.

Give Away Time

It is important to encourage employees to follow their own instincts when it comes to innovation. One of the easiest ways to do this is to give them a valuable resource: time. The luxury of time, and the unspoken message that it sends — that you trust and value your employees — help to stimulate new ideas and foster creative impulses.

I started my career in a small business, a publishing house that had thirty-five employees when I joined the company. The owner and president worked very hard, including Saturdays, and almost never took a vacation. As a result, employees would work long hours, often come to the office on Saturdays, and rarely take vacations themselves. We were in a highly creative business in which most employees had to come up with new and original ideas every day—for a new book, a new layout, new ways to motivate the sales force or optimize logistics, and so on. So in my ongoing pursuit to boost creativity I, as the managing director and co-owner of the company, decided two years after I started to work there to go away on vacation for a few weeks to send a strong signal that it was acceptable to take real breaks and restore oneself. Changes in behaviors followed. Employees bit by bit started to take longer vacations, and consequences were soon felt. I observed that people were more relaxed, more available to communicate with one another, more productive and efficient, and more creative—and sales jumped up. This wasn't exactly a radical or particularly innovative form of giving away time, but even in this most basic form, it gave people a chance to refresh and return to work with the energy and attitude that would allow them to be more creative, more engaged, and also more efficient.

We've also seen this already in Chapter One with Google, 3M and Amdocs. As you may recall, 3M has a long-standing policy that allows employees to spend 15 percent of their time pursuing projects outside of the scope of their assigned work;[9] Google allows employees to spend 20 percent of their time on such projects, provided that they present their projects to their peers for critique.[10] Similarly, Amdocs, the global telecommunications giant, has invested significant time and money to take some of their most creative employees to an innovation camp where, for an entire week, in an atmosphere completely separate from the daily requirements of the normal work routine, all they do is brainstorm and refine potential new product ideas.[11] In all three cases the message is that new ideas are worthy of investment, and employees are trusted partners in the pursuit of innovation.

Give Away Toys

When you think about the tools and supplies that your employees need in order to be productive, you should think beyond desktop computers, multifunction printers, and pens and pencils; give them tools to spark the imagination and playfulness that give rise to innovative ideas and an innovative culture. IDEO — the Palo Alto industrial design company behind many of the most recognizable consumer products of the last few decades, including the original Apple mouse and the first successful handheld, the Palm Pilot — is an actual playground. Art supplies abound, toys are commonly seen in meeting rooms and lobbies, and employees are given the tools and encouragement to develop rough prototypes of products in the course of the meetings themselves.[12] Perfection is not the goal; idea generation is the goal.

In my seminars I often pass around Play-Doh, colored pencils, and origami paper to help people access creative ideas about their vision of their own company or industry. I ask them to make collages that represent trends of the future: children's education, future transportation, beauty consumption habits, or whatever might be relevant to the success of their organization. This helps participants get out of their heads, shift into play mode, and let their imaginations come out so they can express themselves more freely and come to innovative solutions more easily.

Give Away Space

Space affects moods. A beautiful space can make people happy; a small cramped office can make them feel depressed. But more important, space also affect behaviors and communication. Open space offices allow an easier flow of communication among team members and can convey a strong feeling of belonging, but they also can make it harder to focus. Separate offices allow for more privacy and concentration but can easily create silos that separate people and teams. Depending on what you're trying to achieve, you need to be ready to manage space not only from a budgetary stand point but also from the perspective of what it is your creative teams actually need in order to be creative and in a position to deliver the level of innovation your company needs. To achieve this, some companies will have to literally give away space—that is, to sacrifice space for its positive impact on the environment, the company culture, and ultimately the creative output.

Office space is an expensive commodity, especially in the world's most competitive markets, and historically offices have been designed and furnished to maximize administrative efficiency and minimize facility costs (private offices only for senior executives, "cube farms" for lower-ranking personnel). But today companies are looking at efficiency differently, and consequently they are looking at space differently. They are looking for ways to maximize the creative output of their employees, and from that viewpoint the most efficient use of space is one that supports creative interactions. For example, as discussed earlier, Pixar's California headquarters—where bathrooms, mailboxes, and meeting rooms are clustered at the center of the building—are designed to ensure that employees from different divisions of the company are certain to run into each other throughout the day. This facilitates informal and random conversations among diverse team members and allows creative ideas and collaborations to be born. I once had a client who wanted to close off an open space in their New York City offices; I struggled hard to convince them otherwise. The company needed more private meeting rooms. Moving out of their existing facility was not an option, nor was renting another floor, so the president of the company wanted to build elegant glass walls to enclose what in his opinion was wasted space.

My observation was quite different. This open space, which offered an inviting round table nestled by a large staircase, was the only place in the office where different members of the product development team would spontaneously sit to discuss their projects. Account managers would stop there after coming back from client meetings to share the latest developments about those clients and their projects. In other words, it was the perfect spot for an informal communication and feedback loops. In the end, this precious open space was saved in spite of financial pressures.

Give Away Ideas

Ideas are the lifeblood of great companies, and as any creative person will tell you, the inspiration behind great ideas can come from the most unlikely sources. Maybe, as described earlier, it's the spontaneous conversation with a colleague that happens in a well-placed sitting area after an internal presentation, or maybe it's exposure to a new piece of information available on the company intranet at just the right time. It does not always have to be strictly relevant to the life of the corporation to spur interesting and useful thoughts for the business. To set the stage for the generation of great ideas, Louis Vuitton hosts regular seminars and presentations in its Paris headquarters on a variety of topics that, at first glance, appear not to have a direct link to their line of business and range of products, which includes luxury luggage, clothing, and accessories. Employees are offered lectures on ancient civilizations, sociological studies, and artistic movements as a source of inspiration and rejuvenation.[13] The important element here is to open the walls of the company to new and different ideas to spur employees' imaginations.

Give Up Perfection

From the mailroom all the way up to the C-suite, employees have developed an exceptional capacity for reading between the lines. The boss or the shareholders may say they want innovation, but the unspoken message may be, "but only if it's risk-free." If we want innovation, we have to tolerate risk, and we have to make it safe for our employees to take those risks. When corporate leaders make it clear in their words and actions that employees aren't expected to be perfect—that "mistakes" are not only acceptable, but are indeed just part of the process of getting to winning ideas and products—then employees can relax in a way that supports their own creativity. And when employees get creative, innovations can happen.

Cirque du Soleil, which reinvented the traditional slow-growth genre of the circus and in doing so became a multinational company with four thousand employees, twenty simultaneous shows running worldwide, and one hundred million spectators in less than twenty-five years, embraces risk taking and sees occasional failures as simply part of the creative process. In an interview, Lyn Heward, president of their Creative Content Division, explained that at Cirque du Soleil "employees are offered the protection and support that they need to take risks on the company's behalf."[14] Successes and failures are seen as the result of a team effort, and this reduces the fear or shame that is associated with personal failure. As a result, individuals feel encouraged to take risks and even protected from adverse consequences.

Making failure an acceptable part of the creative process is also a core value at Mango, a men's and women's fashion company. Founded in 1984, Mango now has the biggest design center in Europe in a highly competitive industry, and is present in ninety-one countries, with 1,220 stores and 7,800 employees. Mango explicitly promotes "the practice of a culture of mistakes" in their written policies. As their 2009 annual report puts it, "Our organization encourages a climate of trust and communication, working in teams, and learning from our mistakes."[15] They acknowledge that the final design for a dress does not always manifest in the designer's first draft. And they go as far as to recognize that not every single final design of the eighty millions articles shipped out throughout the globe will necessarily become a success. Mango executives know it is essential to acknowledge this important part of their business, because not accepting it and denying the possibility of human error can become very stifling to the creative process of fashion designers.[16]

Give Clear Constraints

Fostering an atmosphere of creativity and innovation doesn't require business leaders to concede all control or throw all rules out of the window. In fact, the judicious and clear application of constraints frames the challenges that employees are asked to address. By setting a goal and laying out the constraints, business leaders can create excitement. Most people like the experience of overcoming some obstacles; constraints are the obstacles that make the finding of the solution exhilarating.

"It is common knowledge that Cirque designers don't like budgets, deadlines, and limited resources," says Lyn Heward, but she adds, "Privately however, even they will admit that these 'constraints' force us to become more resourceful and more creative! They require us to come up with solutions we'd never thought of before...and they actually become motivators for getting the job done. In fact, some of our most inspired ideas arise from moderately Spartan situations."[17] Cirque du Soleil enforces very strict budgets, and creative teams have to abide with nonnegotiable deadlines.

This is just one of the many paradoxes of operating in the southwest quadrant. As leaders and managers we need to both establish constraints and free our employees from self-imposed boundaries. In short, we need to find balance. Along with budgets, time is of course one of the most obvious constraints. Deadlines, as daunting as they may seem to creative people, are also their best ally and help them move through the fear of the white page and the unknown. However, time pressure needs to be handled with a serious sense of balance. A study by two Harvard Business School professors shows that to develop the creativity of team members it is better in the long run to be careful with excessive time pressure as it easily leads to high levels of stress and potential burnout.[18] In my experience with creativity, efforts to save time by accelerating the process can sometimes end up costing time. Creativity often requires patience, because it follows its own rhythm and entails moments of what I call "active inactivity"—moments when creative teams need to lie fallow. Creativity is quite often about problem solving, and problems by definition have some established factors. Once the confining factors are clarified, the goal is identified, and balance can be more easily achieved, creative minds are more able to find inspiration to overcome challenges. A paradox of time management applies: time constraint is productive, but too much of it, repeatedly, leads to the risk of burnout. This paradox cannot be resolved by following a fixed rule. Managing the time of creative teams requires the ability to manage paradox and feel one's way through it, depending on how your team members react individually and collectively, which talent(s) you are most heavily depending on, and how much leeway with constraints you have in any given situation.

Give Up on Uniformity

Giving up on uniformity is really about acknowledging in tangible ways the fact that different people require different conditions in order to perform at their best. So rather than requiring everyone to follow the same rules within the workplace, you make allowances that enable all concerned to pursue their responsibilities in the way that best suits them. Creative people have a tremendous capacity for teamwork, but they can also have a tremendous need to follow their own rhythms or work style. It is very likely shortsighted to force creative talents to follow rules that inhibit their creativity without adding anything to your company's goal of generating innovations. For example, it may be important for all team members to show up to a weekly progress meeting, but is it really important for everyone to show up at 9 A.M. and stay until 5 P.M.? They may be more productive working at different hours or not coming in at all on some days. When you manage by exception you honor people's individual requirements for freedom, and when you manage for inclusion you make sure that everyone feels a responsibility for the collective success (or failure) of the project. When I was a publisher, my experience in working with authors was that each author was very different and required adaptation and careful attention to approach their creative talent in a unique way. Over the many years I have worked in the fragrance industry, I have observed the same thing with perfumers. Creative talent is rarely separable from the individual's personality, because it has a lot to do with imagination, sensitivity, and feelings. This is why seeking uniformity in management is rarely the way to go. Management by exception will bring much more efficiency.

Create Rituals and Symbols

As we've seen, rituals are significant and powerful. Symbols can have a great impact, as they communicate beyond words and convey meanings without explicit explanations. Rituals and symbols play an important role in the success of managing the southwest quadrant because they speak to our subconscious, comfort our unspoken fears, enable us to tap into solutions that cannot be found in a linear fashion, and connect us emotionally to our friends and colleagues.

Ritual is a powerful way to harness the life force that lives deep down in every one of us. The way rituals impact us is through rhythm (rituals occur at well-defined moments: Sunday mass, birthdays, the end of puberty, end of year graduation) regular repetition (Thanksgiving every year, morning ablutions, Sunday family lunch) and dramatic staging (Christmas tree, sculpted pumpkins, candles for a Valentine's Day dinner).

Rituals imply a certain level of ceremony and require time, but they are profoundly efficient in both the short and the long term. For example, think about how football players huddle before they go onto the field at the beginning of a big game. It is a moment that may include a prayer or words of encouragement from their coach, but most important it is time that they set aside to reach beyond self-doubt and turn fear into audacity by connecting to their guts. In Rugby Six Nations Tournaments, national anthems are played at the beginning of the game to invoke a sense of pride and responsibility for the success of the team.

Rituals are transformative because they help us deal constructively with the intangible dynamics within us and within groups. They productively channel instinctual forces into creative powers. Ritual is what allows us to gather the energy needed to achieve great things, often beyond what we could imagine ourselves capable of. When managing the creative process, celebrating wins and awards is one effective way to reassure creative teams, whose members often question their own talent. And one thing is certain: not celebrating wins can cause a lot of damage to the spirit and motivation of your creative team.

Navigating the southwest quadrant is rarely easy; it often entails a lot of unknowns and a lot of erratic moments. No matter how seasoned and brave you are, self-doubt and fear are simply unavoidable in the process of creation. Rituals address fear of the unknown, self-sabotage, and procrastination, which can all happen during any creative process—hence the importance of rituals in southwest management.

There are many ways to spark creativity and establish an atmosphere that resonates with creative teams. These are effective ways to improve creative output that you can apply to your business. Consider how many of them you've thought about before and how many of them you actually implement in your management. Leaving these out is not a valid option. The following are a few cautionary tales.

The Consequences of Imbalance

Corporations are living organisms, and when one area is overtaxed or another area is neglected, those respective areas cease to operate well and the entire organism suffers. Likewise, when strategy neglects one quadrant entirely or is based on another exclusively, things fall apart. Here are three real-life examples of what happens when business strategies become overly reliant on a single quadrant of the Compass at the expense of the others.

Hewlett Packard: Prioritizing the Northeast at the Expense of the Southwest

In the first half of 2009, a number of articles in the business media took stock of Mark Hurd's then three-year tenure as CEO of Hewlett-Packard (HP). It was noted that Hurd focused on rationalizing operations and cutting budgets and expenses to improve profitability, and it was suggested that there was little more advantage to be wrung out of these command-and-control measures. His cost reductions included a 5-percent pay cut for most employees in 2009, lower spending on research, and plans to eliminate at least forty-eight thousand jobs. Costs including research and development, marketing, and general and administrative expenses were actively cut from 17.6 percent of sales in 2005, when Hurd started, to 13.5 percent of sales by the end of 2010.[19] At the same time, rumblings within HP made it clear that the focus on optimizing administration, an approach that resides in the northeast quadrant of the Intuitive Compass, was putting pressure on people in the research and development department, an area that resides in the southwest quadrant.

This dichotomy is represented in Figure 3.2, showing Mark Hurd's approach in the northeast quadrant. He applied rational thinking to achieve better financial results. This is an approach that is valid, yet can exclude or marginalize the southwest quadrant, and in this case that is exactly what happened. Hurd's approach didn't allow for the means and space R&D needed to thrive. Indeed, as the graph below shows, the creative process inherent to the work in research and development requires being open to improvisation, the randomness of play and the highly adaptive quality of your instinct.

Hewlett-Packard's R&D staff felt that their jobs had lost value and become less respected because they had to spend more time on reporting, budgeting, planning, and rationalizing the organization.[20] Accordingly, they had less time, money, drive, and focus to dedicate to actual research when competition was becoming stronger.[21] In fact,

FIGURE 3.2 HP Research and Development

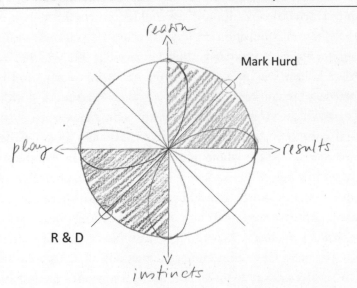

between 2008 and 2009, R&D spending was reduced by 20 percent while net revenues decreased by only 3.2 percent.[22]

Hewlett-Packard's R&D people take justifiable pride in the company's history of scientific breakthroughs and technological innovations. They see R&D as the pumping heart of the company and its long-term success. Indeed, as per Hewlett-Packard's mission statement, its raison d'être is more about technological breakthroughs and innovations than it is about accounting or rationalizing its management processes.[23]

It's not that Mark Hurd necessarily followed a bad road. It's just that he focused on one goal to the exclusion of all others. There needs to be a solid balance between the implementation of cost-containment actions and the investment of time and money to support R&D activities, because R&D relies heavily on its engineers to be creative and its teams to be entrepreneurial. Top management must establish some sort of a dynamic, conscious relationship between the northeast quadrant and the southwest quadrant, in order to sustain the company's ability to innovate, invent new patents, and build long-term asset and profitable value for the company.

HP's acquisition in July 2010 of Palm Inc., the smartphone manufacturer, certainly brought HP a substantial library of valuable patents. Hurd boosted sales and shareholder returns through more than $24.3 billion in acquisitions.[24] Indeed, when HP announced financial results for its fiscal quarter ending January 31, 2011, its net revenue of $32.3 billion was up 4 percent from the prior-year period both as reported and in constant currency.[25] Yet this represents a slowdown in HP's growth over the two previous years, with an average of 7-percent annual growth.[26] According to analysts, HP will grow at the same 4-percent rate for the whole of 2011 and 2012. Leo Apotheker, who became HP's new CEO in November 2010, asserts that "HP has lost its soul" and has short-changed innovation, in part because of Hurd's emphasis on cost-cutting at the expense of research and development and product quality.[27] According to Apotheker, HP has cut enough costs. The new CEO communicated publicly that his new strategy, which revolves around cloud computing, a new set of acquisitions to beef up HP's software capability, would accelerate speed to market and place an emphasis on quality.

According to financial analysts, winning investors over will be tied to Apotheker's efforts to ramp up HP's innovation power and reenergize its staff. Clearly the HP leadership team will have to respect and cater to the requirements of the southwest quadrant in its management culture for its own best short- and long-term interest. You cannot mandate innovation. People need empowerment to go the extra mile innovation requires.

Maytag: Misplaced Reliance on the Northeast and Southeast

After enjoying extraordinary brand equity and customer loyalty for most of the twentieth century, home appliance giant Maytag changed its approach to business and lost both in less than a decade. Founded in Newton, Iowa, in 1893 by Frederick Maytag, the firm manufactured the Pastime, its first washing machine, in 1907. Its innovations in creating a better-functioning automatic washing machine, including the aluminum tub and the vane agitator, put the company in a leading market position and enabled it to survive the Great Depression. Its reputation for outstanding quality and customer service was exemplified in their advertising campaign by a lonely Maytag repairman, endlessly waiting for the phone to ring, because no customers are calling for repair service. Maytag was also known for having the highest level of profitability of its industry.[28]

An interesting anecdote illustrates Maytag's reputation for outstanding quality. In 2009, a Mrs. Thomson of Sand Springs, Oklahoma, called Maytag's customer service to inquire whether the door latch could be fixed on her Maytag dryer, which she had purchased in 1957 along with a Maytag washer. Her fifty-two-year-old appliances were otherwise still working well. Customer service found it so unique that they offered to replace her antique appliances with brand new ones from their new Centennial line if she would allow them to place her vintage pink washer and dryer in the Maytag Museum in Benton Harbor, Michigan.

Mrs. Thompson agreed, but wisely told Maytag that if the new washer and dryer didn't work as well as her old set she wanted her old set back because she knew "they just don't make 'em like they used to."

Mrs. Thompson was right to be cautious. Since the early 2000s Maytag's corporate management had dramatically cut investments in new product development and made an expensive acquisition of a competitor, and the company was experiencing increasing customer dissatisfaction that led to expensive legal problems.[29]

Maytag built its original product line of washers, dryers, and dish-washers with a niche market of consumers in mind: those who were willing to pay a premium. By the 1980s this niche began to diminish, as those targeted consumers began to lose their ability to differentiate between premium-priced and lower-priced appliances. While May-tag implemented operational efficiencies to reduce costs, new foreign players entered the U.S. market, and competition for share of wallet continued to be an issue.

To address these market conditions, Maytag took advantage of its cash reserves and embarked on several acquisitions, through which it diversified into product segments beyond the company's original scope in which it had proven competencies. It also expanded its distribution, reaching into new markets worldwide. Between 2001 and 2004 Maytag's revenue was relatively stable, but its return on sales diminished. It also expanded its geographic reach to newer markets worldwide. Maytag changed its traditional high-quality, high-priced positioning but failed to maintain its profitability.[30]

In 2004 Maytag was still producing 88 percent of its products in US based factories, but it had begun offshoring production to lower-cost plants, as other appliance manufacturers had done. The brand once known for producing premium products and being an industry leader also cut investments in new product development by 50 percent. In addition, it adopted a marketing strategy that encouraged its customers to buy new appliances before their existing ones needed to be replaced for functional reasons. Nonetheless, that same year it announced a loss of $9 million.

In the battle for market share, Maytag acquired competitor Amana, which increased its debt load.[31] More internal cost cutting in materials, manufacturing, and distribution followed. In another marketing strategy, Maytag launched Performa by Maytag and the Legacy Series. The latter was simply a rebranded Amana machine that was built in Amana's former plant in Herrin, Illinois. The Legacy Series, called "Amanatags" by unhappy customers, was deemed substandard and generated complaints about significant mechanical and durability issues. Customers were also dissatisfied with Maytag's slow response to complaints about its Neptune washers and dryers (which earned the nickname "Stinkomatic"). The Neptune line would ultimately be the subject of a nationwide safety recall by the Consumer Product Safety Commission due to fire danger. The company's reputation, so long stellar, was damaged, and it had to set aside $33.5 million to settle class-action lawsuits.[32] The Internet, where customers created the negative nicknames, only made exposure of the company's difficulties more widespread.

By 2005, Maytag was near the bottom of customer rankings in terms of satisfaction, the company's market share was at an all-time low, and sales were flat. In 2006 it was acquired by a major competitor, Whirlpool.

Such a decline stemmed from the combination of a number of factors — lack of vision (northwest), lack of competitive analysis (northwest), lack of margin control (northeast), and lack of trust in product innovation (southwest) — which led to less investment in product development, hence lower product quality and customer satisfaction, and reduced market share.

Again, the response of Maytag corporate management to the company's difficulties was to cut investments in new product development in half — a classic northeast quadrant approach in which reason and linear efficiency prevail — and amp up sales and marketing efforts — a southeast approach in which one tends to do whatever it takes to achieve sales results. Conversely, the southwest quadrant, which focuses on instinct and play and where R&D's innovative initiatives can thrive and newly patented inventions can eventually help the company beat the competition, recruit new consumers, and generate huge profits, was neglected and deprived of resources when new product investment was cut in half. A shortsighted move out of the southwest quadrant turned into a long-term failure.

The Fragrance Industry: Attempting to Innovate from the Northeast

The Intuitive Compass is applicable not only to the analysis of individual companies, but also to entire industries. In this case we will see how one industry, fine fragrance, has been approaching the development of marketing campaigns and product development with classic northeast tactics and, in the process, missing out on opportunities that might be revealed if they were to take a more northwest and southwest approach.

A study commissioned by fragrance industry leader Firmenich showed that in the United States between 2000 and 2009 prestige fragrance retail prices increased by more than 40 percent, and the number of launches doubled, yet industry revenue shrank from $3 billion USD to $2.5 billion USD, and two million users left the fragrance category altogether.[33] Fragrances are traditionally a high-margin, high-visibility business. Many brands have used fine fragrance to optimize their margins. Designers like Vera Wang and Tom Ford, and celebrities including Celine Dion, Sarah Jessica Parker, and Antonio Banderas, to name a few, have sought to extend their fame and make money with the launch of fragrances carrying their names. This trend has flooded the market with new products—some successful, others less so. Companies pursued this strategy because they were attempting to offer something different to consumers who already have so many options.

But within this trend we see marketers applying their analytical minds to the task of finding new fragrance concepts in order to secure maximum market share. They are highly focused on results, so they operate from the reason and results quadrant—the northeast—when by virtue of their function they should be operating from the northwest and the southwest. Why? Because the consumer has an instinctual relationship to fragrance. The sense of smell is processed by the reptilian brain; odors bypass our cortical brain and our rational screening. They immediately take us to places and times without any rational intervention. Fragrance consumers not only have an instinctual relationship to the product, they also have a very playful relationship to it. When you buy a fragrance, it's all about expanding your personality, putting on masks, putting on disguises, and really playing. Marketers have gone for easy results—leveraging the existing popularity of certain celebrities—rather than reimagining fragrance from the depths of the relationship that consumers entertain with it.

The relationship a consumer has with fragrance lives in the instinctual and playful southwest quadrant, but marketers' approach to fragrance typically revolves predominantly around the reason-and-results-driven northeast quadrant. As you can see in Figure 3.3, there's not much of an overlap between the marketing strategy (driven mostly by results—namely, winning new market share, and designed according to reason—namely, financial logic) and the consumers' experience, which lives opposite to the northeast quadrant, in the

FIGURE 3.3 Polar Opposites: Consumers and Brand Strategy

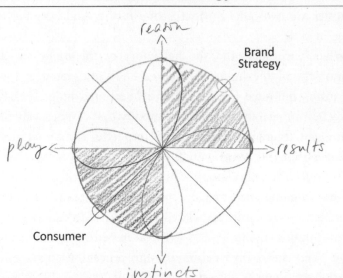

southwest quadrant between play and instinct. And as you can imagine, it's very hard for a marketer to get to the consumer in any effective way if their approach to fragrance stays in the northeast quadrant.

Again, it's not about giving up a rational analysis of market opportunities. And it's not about giving up your analytical brain to identify what would be a viable concept for a new fragrance. It's about taking that and running it by the consumers' playful and instinctual relationship to fragrance, or observing what the consumer desires (in consumer focus groups, creative brainstorming, or retail stores) and using that information to feed their analytical thinking rather than devising a solution that makes sense to the analytical mind and then trying to sell the resulting product to the consumer.

The same study has shown that heavy fragrance users (those who wear fragrance four or more days a week) represent 33 percent of the market, whereas non-heavy users (those who wear fragrance less than three days a week but have worn it sometime in the past six months) amount to 45 percent and the bulk of the market. The lapsed users (those who have worn fragrance in the past, but who haven't worn any fragrance in the past six months) represent 13 percent of the customer base. But understanding the market statistics and understanding the consumer are two quite distinct propositions. And here the findings are remarkable.

When we understand the behaviors of the users, we discover the problem of the industry. Studies have uncovered a downward slide from emotional involvement to functional usage. Fragrance is rapidly becoming a throwaway commodity that can be easily replaced, because new fragrances convey a less impactful emotional message to consumers. This is a tough situation, because consumers rarely return to a product they have stopped using. In the past, a woman had a signature fragrance, one that she consistently wore throughout her life or one that was instantly associated with her. Who can forget Marilyn Monroe's famous quote: "What do I wear in bed? Why, Chanel No. 5, of course." This isn't to say we should simply repeat the language and style of marketing campaigns from the 1950s and 1960s. What it does mean is that we should rekindle the creativity and mystery of the product by offering unique experiences and by inspiring passion, reverie, and sensuality that speak to the fantasies of today's consumers. This would help beauty industry executives to balance out market strategies that seem to narrowly focus on market share as if fragrance had merely become a commodity like nuts and bolts.

Probably because of fragrance's huge success up to 2000, this study indicates that the industry has always focused on the heavy users (33 percent) and has never paid attention to the others, although they are in fact the vast majority (45 percent non-heavy users + 13 percent lapsed users + 9 percent never users). We see that a focus on the northeast quadrant and managing what exists as usual—leaving nonusers and lapsed users out of marketing campaigns—in a linear way leads to a lack of creative thinking and misses out on enormous financial opportunities. Experts' calculations in this same study show that non-heavy users represent a $3 billion missed opportunity.[34]

In-depth behavioral research has shown that the fundamental reason consumers cease to use or never begin using fragrance is a lack of meaning. Fragrances today have lost their relevance because they are represented and staged in ways anchored in the past. Advertising for fragrances still represents women as highly seductive femme fatales or super-achieving wonder women. The same study shows that in order to grow and thrive, fragrances will have to reconnect with relevance and meaning in a modern way that expresses twenty-first-century social values: authenticity, collaboration, and balance. This is why fragrance has lost its emotional value and personal meaning.

We see here that the success the fragrance category has been riding for decades has led to a lack of creativity both in marketing (northwest) and product development (southwest). Abandoning a focus on the instinctual connections consumers have with fragrances for an easy sales-driven business approach that maximizes volume has led brands to miss out on a huge business opportunity (lapsed users and nonusers) and has also led to lower profitability per item sold, little product creativity, and, more gravely, a weaker relationship with the consumer and a loss of consumers in the category. In other words, not approaching fragrance buyers through the southwest quadrant of instinct and play where consumers intrinsically feel its value has kept an entire industry from remaining relevant and thriving.

NAVIGATING THE CREATIVE PATH

Creativity is not linear. To get to what is new and revelatory, we have to tap into the wisdom of our subconscious, be present, pay attention to clues, and then react. The Intuitive Compass provides us with a tool that can enable companies and individuals to make innovative decisions and get results that are based on instinct, reason, and playfulness. It enables us to understand, through the symbolism of the four quadrants, our talents and limitations, what drives our actions, and how different people or groups with different competencies operate. The compass shows us the synergies that exist, between north and south (reason and instinct) and east and west (results and play). It shows us how to access the genius of the southwest, without which the other three quadrants would simply enable us to function from day to day without achieving creative breakthroughs or deep transformation.

4

intuitive intelligence: rethinking the way we think

I ntuitive Intelligence is a set of skills that will help us integrate the southwest quadrant into business thinking and get the most out of the Intuitive Compass. We are used to thinking in linear, logical, obvious ways about problems and possible solutions, but Intuitive Intelligence shows us that there are other ways to think, other ways to understand, and by embracing them we enhance our capacity to arrive at innovative solutions. The Intuitive Compass provides a new way of looking at human performance and human creativity and understanding our various approaches to business and life. As we have discussed, every quadrant of the Intuitive Compass contains both advantages and limitations, but the key to success in achieving our business and personal goals is orchestrating a productive synergy among all four quadrants. In addition, the opportunities and advantages that reside in the southwest quadrant are the raw materials for the disruptive innovations we all seek today, and they require a type of management that many of us are unfamiliar with.

Intuitive Intelligence enables us to create synergies across all four quadrants of the Intuitive Compass and therefore can help shape a novel approach to business that focuses on innovation to drive sustainable growth and overcome the specific challenges of the new economy. There are four tenets of Intuitive Intelligence: thinking holistically, thinking paradoxically, noticing the unusual, and leading by influence. By engaging in each, we can enrich our experience and understanding of personal and business issues that arise, and when we use all four, our capacity for innovation can grow tremendously. But before we explore each of the four tenets of Intuitive Intelligence in detail, let's take a look at what it is about the current state of the business world that has so many of us searching for new and better ways to move our companies forward.

TAKING STOCK OF TODAY'S BUSINESS WORLD

The best business leaders want to innovate, embrace change, and create new business approaches because they recognize the need to evolve. And yet in business too many leaders still do things by the book and stick to the logic of reason and results (the northeast quadrant) to the exclusion of other ways of thinking. Too many of us think and operate primarily in the northeast quadrant, especially during difficult times. The uncomfortable reality is that disruptive ideas come from the southwest quadrant, so we're pretty much thinking backward when it comes to engaging innovation. We're rearranging our companies rather than exploring the many ways we could create a completely different kind of company. Organization (a northeast activity) has the potential to add the most value when it follows creative imagination possibilities (a southwest activity), not when it precedes it.

Popular thought says that by applying more analysis, focusing more on results, and working harder to get those results, we will get to the new and different. But that is not the case. This is a forceful approach to change, but it's not actually a smart approach to change. It's certainly not a very creative approach to change. Given this way of thinking, however, it's no wonder that we've developed business models that are hard to sustain. The fragrance industry, the car industry, and the media industry have all been predominantly operating in the same way for many years, still trying to innovate from the northeast quadrant, and still hoping that if they use the same business models and the same management models they will be able to capture the market, keep sales afloat, and maintain margins. But that is not in the cards. In fact, the odds have been against it all along.

On an even larger scale, it's no wonder that we've developed economic models that are not sustainable and that contribute to dwindling resources, climate change, and pollution. The way we've been thinking about development has been through the linear, rational management systems represented by the northeast quadrant. But life unfolds according to the principles of the southwest quadrant. Most likely, if we haven't integrated the fundamentals of the southwest quadrant into our development models, it's because we haven't conceived of them in the first place. Yet they present a huge opportunity.

It's clear that we have evolved, progressed, grown, and prospered through a model that largely excludes the fundamentals of our ecosystem. But we've reached a place where the disconnect is so big that we have no choice but to think differently—really differently—and innovate radically. Intuitive Intelligence shows us how to do just that. It shows how we can think in a way that includes the fundamentals of life, the randomness of play, and the power and adaptive nature of our instinct for survival while responsibly harnessing our propensity for aggression and leveraging our valuable scientific heritage and its instrumental tool called logic. And if we're able to do that, then we'll be able to innovate and change more easily. We'll also be able to prosper in a way that is more balanced between cooperation and competition, without compromising our ecosystems, our survival, and our legacy for future generations.

THE FOUR TENETS OF INTUITIVE INTELLIGENCE

Intuitive Intelligence is a different way to organize and use what we already know and what we are already capable of doing. It helps us understand how to make use of our inherent abilities and aptitudes in the task of creative problem solving and optimum decision making. Intuitive Intelligence activates the profound, yet often intangible, interaction between instinct and play. Again, the four tenets of Intuitive Intelligence are thinking holistically, thinking paradoxically, noticing the unusual, and leading by influence. Each tenet helps us to complement the dualistic and limited nature of the logical mind with the other parts of our mind, which are much more cryptic, much less articulate, but extremely powerful.

1. Thinking Holistically

Holistic means that the totality of a system is more important than the sum of its parts. It is always interesting to think and focus on a holistic approach because we can gain new perspectives and learn new things from it. This tenet is obviously important to getting all four quadrants of the Intuitive Compass to work in synergy and to stay in balance.

2. Thinking Paradoxically

We know many theories, we have had many experiences; they all contribute to our personal belief system and collective knowledge. Although there is definitely more of what we *don't* know than there is of what we know, culturally we tend to evaluate everything through what we already know. Embracing new situations and new ideas with an attitude that is as open as it is critical, as candid as it is discriminating, is the only way to enter uncharted territories and conceptualize new ideas. The unconscious does not follow the logic of analytical reason, yet new ideas stem from our unconscious. So we need to open our minds to the paradoxical logic of the unconscious to reach beyond common ideas and beliefs, which is exactly the meaning of the word *paradox*.[1] To do this it simply requires giving up our need for immediate logical understanding of a situation and trusting our other form of intelligence — at work, for instance when we get insights from our dreams or myths.

3. Noticing the Unusual

The third tenet is the ability to look beyond what's usual, to notice the odd and unfamiliar, and to embrace the paradoxical and mysterious nature of life, beyond what we know or what we're used to perceiving. To notice is to pay attention, and for this we use our senses. We can pay attention outwardly by seeing what's around us, or we can pay attention inwardly by feeling what's inside of us. When we notice things we can receive information in two ways; one is paying attention to what makes logical sense, the other is paying attention beyond the logical sense of what we contemplate. In the second case we have to open up to our feelings, our emotions, our sensations, and our intuition. We get closer to our instinctual nature, and our creative imagination gets triggered. We connect with our unconscious; we gain access to, and nourish, our imagination and creativity.

4. Leading by Influence

As explained in the introduction of this book, there is at the heart of any living system a self-organizing principle. The less we try to control it, the more we can reap its power and creatively engage with it. As we saw in the Poe story "The Descent into the Maelstrom," the worst way to deal with it is to try to control it; on the contrary, the best way to deal with its energy is to influence it. The same is true for the creative process. Any creative process is experimental and chaotic due to its unpredictability. Successfully leading disruptive innovation calls for someone who can lead by influence and leverage the self-organizing principle present at the heart of the chaotic process of creativity to facilitate transformation and guide the process towards effective change.

This following simple anecdote illustrates the practical application of the four tenets of intuitive intelligence. A student I met while teaching at the graduate program of Ecole des Hautes Etudes Commerciales (HEC) drove every day to the business school campus, which is in the countryside close to Versailles, approximately twelve miles away from where he lived. Because he is from Chile, he had been relying on his car's GPS to find his way each day. But one day, after a seminar on Intuitive Intelligence, he decided not to switch on his GPS and to instead rely on his gut instincts to find his way. He had a big smile on his face when he told the entire class that driving to the campus without the help of his GPS device actually worked perfectly and more easily!

So, this is how intuitive intelligence was manifested for my student:

- *Thinking Holistically:* Finding his way to the campus was transformed into a richer experience, one colored with emotional, intellectual, instinctual, and almost spiritual aspects; it was ultimately both a task and a game. It was about a journey of self-discovery and adventure as much as it was about achieving a goal.
- *Thinking Paradoxically:* He managed to get to campus more easily while taking a paradoxical problem-solving approach: relying on less factual information.
- *Noticing the Unusual:* To make choices at any given crossroads, he had to pay attention and be receptive to his inner perceptions, even if they were unusual (not reading instructions on a screen or taking visual cues on an digital map).
- *Leading by Influence:* He accepted giving up logical control over the situation and letting other seemingly random possibilities emerge to help him find his way as he kept focused on his goal: getting to the campus on time.

Now let's take a more in-depth look into each of these tenets.

Thinking Holistically

Our experience of life is holistic. What this means is that, to some degree, we all draw from each quadrant of the Intuitive Compass in order to live our lives. It is difficult to be content about one's existence if you don't have any insight about your future (northwest quadrant), or if you can't perform and acquire what you need to live a decent life (southeast quadrant), or if you can't keep things in a certain order (northeast quadrant). And even if you have the capacity to do all of these things, it still won't be enough if you don't feel the pulse of life and its deeper meaning (southwest quadrant).

This deeper meaning comes from the actualization of our values in our daily lives. That actualization can come in many forms. It may mean we raise children because we value legacy, or we contribute our talent for the benefit of others because we value self-expression, or we generally make it a point to help people because we value compassion, but in some way all people need meaning and values.

So what does this have to do with business? There is one simple truth about business that seems to be forgotten: business is both facilitated by people and meant to serve people, and people are holistic. What always strikes me in business is how often we hear "We're doing business here" or "It's about business" as a way to justify decisions that essentially boil down to choosing what will help make money. To limit business decision making to an evaluation of the financial outcome simply does not cohere with the true nature of the people who run business and whom business is for. At best it's aligned with an isolated financial logic. But financial logic does not live in a vacuum. Business unfolds as a whole in the same way that we experience life as a whole. It's hard to be content in life if you're very rich but suffer poor health or if you're very successful professionally but experience irreconcilable difficulties with your children or spouse. Human satisfaction is holistic. Our experience of life as a whole is more important than the sum of its parts.

Unfortunately, when it comes to business, too often we expect profitability to be the driver of satisfaction, and therefore of motivation. But this isn't actually how it works. When we want people to be creative, or to change, adapt, and innovate, profitability alone won't motivate them to do that. These activities require a deep commitment, and if any part of us is not engaged, we won't make that commitment.

This is why the first tenet of Intuitive Intelligence is the ability to think holistically; in other words, the ability to focus on value that goes beyond dollars and cents to include things like integrity, honor, and meaning. The legendary retailer Hermès Paris is a case in point. Hermès is a luxury goods house specializing in leather, ready-to-wear apparel, lifestyle accessories, perfumery, and fashion. Its undisputed reputation as one of the most prestigious luxury companies in the world comes from a tradition of impeccable craftsmanship and a holistic approach to business. Established in 1837 by Thierry Hermès as a saddle shop in Paris, Hermès today has fourteen product divisions, employs seven thousand people, and owns stores all around the world. Hermès reports a total billing of approximately two billion euros and a net profit margin of roughly 10 percent. This is a spectacular success. But what's even more remarkable is that Jean-Louis Dumas, who was CEO of Hermès for twenty-eight years until 2006, always looked at Hermès in a holistic way. His vision for Hermès was inseparable from the three core pillars that define the brand.[2]

First, using skills associated with the northwest quadrant, he strategically envisioned Hermès as always ahead of consumers and market trends. Second, he called on Hermès' creative skills associated with the southwest quadrant to invent luxury goods of exceptional value that exceeded users' expectations. Third, using skills associated with the northeast quadrant, he always stressed the fact that it was equally important to make sure that all Hermès products could feasibly be manufactured according to consistently outstanding quality standards. And fourth, reaching into skills found in the southeast quadrant, he determined that all goods produced had to be marketable, because Hermès is not about objects of art for museums and galleries; it sells consumer goods for the enjoyment of customers. This holistic approach, shown in Figure 4.1, which was first articulated by Dumas for Hermès, has been enforced ever since because it has consistently ensured the integrity of the Hermès reputation.

Although Hermès has Dumas' way of thinking to thank for its success, most companies don't approach business so holistically. One

FIGURE 4.1 Hermès Paris: The Four Pillars of Success

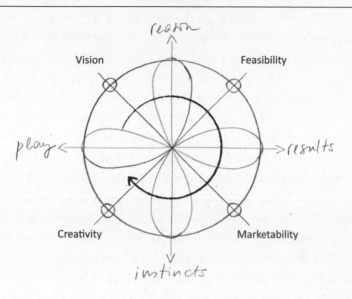

example of what happens when business is not grounded in the four quadrants of the intuitive compass can be seen in the story of the Concorde.

The Concorde was a supersonic airliner built by a consortium between Sud Aviation (known today as L'Aérospatiale) and British Aircraft Corporation. As a supersonic aircraft, Concorde moved faster than sound travels through the air. It was breaking all speed records set by other airliners. Because of the speed of the aircraft and the difference in time zones, you could leave Paris at 11:00 A.M. and arrive in New York at 9:10 A.M.—actually earlier in your new time zone than it was when you left the old one. Its exceptional performance and the level of technological innovation that went into creating the Concorde caused it to be seen as an aviation icon. Obviously this revolutionary aircraft was born in the southwest and the northwest quadrants of the intuitive compass but the business strategy, unfortunately, did not address the southeast quadrant and sales were approached traditionally.

The fate of the Concorde was challenged from the very start. In 1972, during the second public showing of the aircraft in the Middle East, sixteen airline companies placed seventy-four orders or first options to purchase. However, in 1973 a combination of factors led to the cancellation of almost all orders: the first oil crisis of the early '70s, financial difficulties of airline companies at the time due to the skyrocketing price of oil, competition from other countries' manufacturers like Boeing, and the fatal accident of the Concorde's Russian equivalent, the Tupolev, at an international air show. There were also environmental concerns due to the sharp crack of the sonic boom when the Concorde moved into supersonic speed and broke the sound barrier. These concerns limited the Concorde's routes, so it flew only from Paris or London to Rio de Janeiro, Washington, and Tokyo. In the end, only British Airways and Air France bought the supersonic plane. With only twenty aircraft built, their development represented a substantial economic loss, in spite of subsidies received by Air France and British Airways from their respective governments to buy the unique but expensive plane. And after twenty-seven years in service, on April 10, 2003, both British Airways and Air France simultaneously announced that Concorde flights would end in the following year. The reason they cited was lower sales due to the unfortunate crash on July 25, 2000, even though that crash was probably due more to negligence of the airport and of another airline than issues with the Concorde itself.[3]

But the commercial failure of the aircraft was also due to a lack of understanding regarding how to market and sell Concorde to passengers; they demonstrated a poor southeast approach (reason applied to get results: a good business rationale to support commercial results) to the marketing of an otherwise ingenious product. The experience of flying Concorde was not designed with the needs of modern business executives in mind. Yes, it was exciting to feel the thrust of the plane in your back as it moved beyond the speed of sound. And it was truly exhilarating to see the purple line delineating the frontier between atmosphere and stratosphere in the sky, something only Concorde passengers could see, because the supersonic aircraft was flying at an altitude well above any other top airliner (sixty thousand feet instead of forty thousand feet,) but the experience as a whole, which includes not just the physicality of the airplane, but also the scheduling and pre-, post-, and on-board services, was anchored in worn-out conceptions about luxury from the seventies when the aircraft was first offered to the public. After getting up early to get to the airport in Paris in time for your flight and landing in New York City's JFK airport, you had a whole day ahead of you. It was a long day indeed. You would finish working at 6:00 or 7:00 P.M. local time, which was midnight or later Paris time, and then go on to dinner. In spite of the predictably harsh schedule that Concorde travelers faced, Air France would offer heavy meals and plenty of drinks onboard to celebrate this great traveling moment, though most business travelers would likely have preferred something that would have mitigated the effects of their elongated day. A preboarding massage at the Paris airport, silence or relaxing music, room to work on board, and energy foods and beverages would have been much more beneficial (and probably much more welcome) than champagne and foie gras to the travelers who used the Concorde to do fast-turnaround meetings. Checking in was easy, thanks to dedicated desks and staff, but no helicopter transfer into Manhattan was made available at arrival, nor was there a special limousine service to pick you up at home or your hotel as Japan Airlines did at the time for its first class passengers. So even if Air France and British Airways made a very innovative plane available to their customers, the two companies did not bring the creativity of the southwest quadrant and strategic planning skills characteristic of the northwest quadrant to their approach to making it a profitable business. Sales promotions were plentiful but traditional and all about price rather than service. They scored poorly in the southeast quadrant (reason applied to results).

In both of these examples we see the power of holistic approach. Whereas Hermès CEO Jean Louis Dumas embraced the holistic approach and made the marketability of the brand and its products one of the pillars of the business, with the Concorde we see the opposite.

The approach that Air France and British Airways took to their business with Concorde was not holistic and lacked the necessary sharp approach to sales and marketing represented in the southeast quadrant. Every quadrant of the compass contributes to the success of a company and is actually necessary to facilitate long-term results. In addition, all aspects of business are connected and interdependent: to administer a business is important to the success of innovation, strategic planning helps with sales, sales help generate the level of profit necessary to invest in R&D, and so on. Taking a holistic approach is demanding but helps drive sustainable growth in the long run.

Thinking Paradoxically

Thinking paradoxically is an exercise in setting linear and logical patterns aside for a while and opening ourselves up to the possibility that solutions, answers, and new ideas can come from places that challenge common sense. To wit, Einstein once said: "Not everything that can be counted counts and not everything that counts can be counted." The question that follows, then, is this: what happens if a company departs from the traditional business approach of the northeast quadrant, where executives focus on reason and results and where everything that counts can and must be counted? Could this company still be successful with a business approach that reaches beyond conventional logic?

The best example is a company that designed the most playful and instinctual work environment we've probably ever known. This company is Google.

WEB

Google's European headquarters in Zurich, Switzerland, as we discussed earlier, offers a slide to take employees to a gourmet company restaurant, swing chairs hanging from the ceiling in study rooms, bathtubs to lie in and relax in front of lit fish tanks in rooms with low light, massage tables and masseurs available for employees' breaks, and igloo-shaped meeting rooms with penguins and snow as background. It looks like a kindergarten playground, not like the offices of a serious company. Yet it probably has one of the most analytical and efficient work cultures if judged by the number of patents it registers every year and its exceptionally high level of profitability. This is because Google fully embraces paradoxical business thinking.

First, let's remember that research shows human productivity does not follow a linear continuum with time. Specifically, according to Pareto's principle,[4] people produce 80 percent of what really matters in approximately 20 percent of the time they spend at work. So when I hear clients complain about summer hours, coffee breaks, or employees' short days, I always remind them of the results of this study. Timesheets for employees are a relic from the past. They made sense in the industrial era when the scientific management of labor was implemented to organize work in assembly lines. But in today's global economy more and more companies rely on their employees' creativity for their success. Because creativity does not follow a linear relationship with time, time management for creative employees shouldn't either. For instance, great advertising copy can take weeks or even months to be worked and reworked to final edit, whereas, conversely, a brilliant slogan may come to mind in just a few seconds. Time spent on copywriting is not a guarantee of success. So when Google provides employees with space and resources for a break, relaxation, or a massage they actually are managing the 80/20 rule of human productivity very well. They know that at some point in the day it inevitably becomes useless to require employees to sit at their desk. On the contrary, it's much better to help them relax and rejuvenate, encourage them to leave their workspace and get some fresh air to reignite their creativity and productivity. Google embraces the paradox of creative time management. In my work I regularly hear executives in creative firms stating along the lines of conventional wisdom that summer Fridays off are unnecessary and counterproductive and that employees sitting at their desk all day long is their ideal representation of productivity. They do not recognize the paradoxical nature of creativity management and have a hard time thinking paradoxically when it comes to managing employees' time.

And what about the slide to get to the restaurant? What does it do to people? What would it do to you? Do you remember the last time you went down a slide? It's a physical experience; for many of us, it's fun, but, for others, it may feel risky. In all cases, it involves our body and therefore engages us in our guts and puts us in play mode. Simply put, it sends people into the southwest quadrant of the Intuitive Compass where they can best access their genius.

Similarly, the swing chairs get us literally off of our feet and off of the ground, and take us away from verticality. Language first developed in human beings when we moved from a horizontal position (resting on our hands and knees) to a vertical position (standing on our two feet). So when we're sitting back in a swing chair we're away from the axis of language, which is the instrument of logic. Therefore sitting in a swing chair takes us away from our rational mind and opens us to our imagination. Here's the paradox: Google is extremely analytical and specific in the steps they take to engage their employees' creativity and commitment in a playful and instinctive way. Google is probably the greatest financial success in the history of capitalism. It's worth reflecting on the fact that Google handles the paradox of relying on hard-core brainpower and intellect very well, while simultaneously offering headquarters that look more like a school playground than a studious and orderly library. Google is not stuck in a northeast work culture. It obviously understands something that would very likely benefit many other companies seeking higher levels of innovation. If you wish to have creative and agile employees you need to embrace paradoxical thinking, because creativity does not follow any predictable rule, but rather demands specific ingredients: flexible time management, proper play, physical engagement, and some element of random collaborations, among other things. In the same fashion, if you wish to tap into more personal creativity you need to embrace paradoxical thinking, because new ideas will not come from common assumptions.

Noticing the Unusual

Creativity and innovative thinking are great, but the ability to notice the one pivotal piece of information in a creative brainstorming session is key to transforming an organization or making a project truly innovative. This is why we need to carefully pay attention and notice, with our senses open to the unusual or the irrational, but at the same time analyze and evaluate that information. Just because something does not make sense from the point of view of logic does not mean that it lacks value. A simple example: when Isaac Newton saw an apple fall from a tree, he did not simply see a usual phenomenon of nature. He was inspired to start thinking about a particular type of motion—gravity—which then revolutionized our perception of the universe. If he had not been open to his inner feeling of puzzlement, he would have simply seen an apple falling from a tree, and he would not have developed his novel understanding of the workings of the universe through mathematics.

This is why I advise clients to stop thinking and start feeling. If all we did was to think and only think, we would not allow the sensorial perceptions and emotions that come along with thoughts to feed our creative imagination. When we are anchored in our conscious mind, we know only what it knows. New ideas—ideas we don't yet know about—cannot be found in our conscious mind, because we already necessarily know everything that is conscious to us! So the ability to move beyond our conscious thinking and access our unconscious is key to creativity.

An excellent example of the business value of the skill of noticing the unusual can be found in the commercial airline industry. Many of us have probably wondered how air travel ever became so unpleasant. What began three generations ago as one of the most luxurious of consumer experiences, an event that people dressed up for and looked forward to, has degenerated to the point that the average consumer approaches it as if preparing for battle. Today it is an experience marked by bad food (or no food), a smelly environment, narrow seats, poor service, delayed flights, stern-faced flight attendants, shabby cabins, and outdated design. For frequent business travelers on tight schedules it's often challenging in both economy and business class alike. However, one company has been able to provide its clientele with quite a different experience: Virgin America.

Virgin America, a company that first put its planes in service in 2007, didn't become an award-winning airline in an industry-wide financial crisis by slashing costs or slashing ticket prices; they did it by raising the bar on design, service, and customer experience. Beautiful design, uplifting colors, clean cabins, warm and personable service, short waiting time to check in, and easy upgrades are among the many ways Virgin America has attempted to make passengers' experiences easier and more enjoyable. But more important Virgin understands our unconscious needs. The planes have a mood-enhancing lighting system on board that is reassuring because it relaxes the body and, by doing so, appeases our discomfort or fear of flying. Virgin America also gives all passengers on board the opportunity to order their own food from their seats through a personal digital screen, allowing them to eat on their own schedule. This last detail is genius because control of one's own eating schedule is key on an instinctual level. Whether we're conscious of it or not, managing our hunger at our own will is reassuring.

Both relaxing lights and food on your own time touch the passengers at an instinctual level. Many will say that they choose an airline based on cost or, for people who can afford it, comfort, and they'll most likely be sincere. What they don't realize, though, is that when they get on board, their reptilian brain is unavoidably evaluating whether they're safe or not. And when an airline caters to this basic need, passengers at some level eventually feel it and this positively influences their relationship to the airlines.[5]

So how did Virgin America come to think of these great ideas for the comfort of their passengers? They put themselves in the shoes of a passenger and truly tried to see and understand the way passengers feel rather than focusing first and foremost on the profitability generated by every ticket sold. They opened themselves up to their creative imagination by paying attention to two unusual aspects of traveling: lighting and food service. Two things that were never contemplated before. Virgin America has been voted the best North American airline three years in a row by readers of *Condé Nast Traveler*, a luxury travel magazine, showing that the ability to notice the unusual is a powerful aptitude, one that can put a company ahead of its competition. It can also have an impact on the industry as a whole: the European Aeronautic Defence and Space Company (EADS) has incorporated a mood-enhancing lighting system into its most recent luxury aircraft, the Airbus A380, the largest airliner ever put in service.

The study conducted by Arie de Geus that we discussed earlier in the context of play is also relevant to noticing the unusual.[6] The three key common factors of companies that display long-term success, according to the study, are fiscal conservancy, a solid community of values that conveys a strong sense of belonging among employees, and openness to new ideas for evolution and change. Clearly the last two factors are related to the third tenet of Intuitive Intelligence. Taking risks and being open to new ideas both require the ability to notice the unusual.

The ability to notice the unusual also explains how a company like Blockbuster missed the opportunity that Netflix seized and used to build a multimillion-dollar business. It took a curious and imaginative mind to see how the Internet could reshape the video rental industry. Netflix built a recommendation system that learns what you like and tailors film suggestions to your tastes. It beat out the competition by bringing simplified home delivery to the movie watcher. But the ardent fan base developed because Netflix facilitated a two-way dialogue where the user was at the center and could easily make personal referrals. And interestingly enough, statistics show that through this approach Netflix stimulated an interest in classics, training people to watch more than what was new.[7] Netflix viewers are offered home delivery with no late fees and the ability to browse the company's extensive library. Viewers' movie knowledge grows, as they can easily find great movies they otherwise might never have heard of. It's simple, fun, and hassle free.

Netflix executives changed the game by paying attention, noticing unusual solutions to doing business, and listening closely to their inner experience and feelings about ordering movies online. By doing this they were able to design a completely new system that appeals to a new kind of consumer. What kept Blockbuster from doing this? Probably many reasons, but one is certain: their inability to see new and unusual ways of doing business.

Blockbuster Inc. from Dallas Texas is one of the world's largest providers of in-home movie and game entertainment, with reported worldwide revenues of more than $5.5 billion in 2007 and $4 billion in 2009. As of 2007 it had been dominating the home video rental business for more than a decade with approximately 40 percent of the US domestic rental market.[8] However, in September 2010 Blockbuster filed for Chapter 11 bankruptcy protection because it was struggling under the weight of $1 billion in debt and facing growing competition from Redbox and Netflix.[9] This was a move that surprised no one. Actually, it might have been a surprise to one person: Blockbuster CEO Jim Keyes.

Back in August 2008, Keyes was quoted as saying, "I've been frankly confused by this fascination that everybody has with Netflix."[10] Mr. Keyes's apparent lack of understanding of the competition and customers' expectations seems unusual for a former president and CEO of 7-Eleven Inc. and someone who had twenty-one years of experience with the world's largest chain of convenience stores.[11] Equally bewildering to him was the emphasis on catalog size. "Why would anyone want to watch anything other than new releases?" he wondered. "I don't care how many movies are available to me ... as a customer, I want to watch the new stuff so whether we have 10,000 movies or 200 movies doesn't matter." Clearly, Keyes didn't understand the extent of a cinephile's many wishes and aspirations.

Blockbuster is perhaps the perfect example of a large, complacent company that is unable or unwilling to adapt to changes in technology or notice different, unusual, or new customer preferences. It took the company years to develop an online business component that mimicked the advantages of Netflix, and even then it was inferior in both execution and value to consumers. Ironically, one of the primary goals of the bankruptcy process was to escape from costly leases for some of its worst-performing stores. Though Blockbuster hadn't decided exactly how many locations it would seek to shutter as part of its bankruptcy, executives told the major studios it was looking at between five hundred and eight hundred. Blockbuster had already closed nearly a thousand stores in the previous year alone, a reflection of consumers' rapidly declining interest in renting DVDs from retail locations now that they could receive them in the mail or rent them from ubiquitous kiosks at grocery stores or via the Internet. Blockbuster shares, which in August 2010 was delisted by the New York Stock Exchange because of its ongoing low price and moved to the over-the-counter market, closed at the end of September 2010 at 11 cents, for a total market value of $24 million. In 1994, former owner Viacom Inc. had acquired it for $8.4 billion.[12]

In a fast-evolving market and shifting economy, the ability to notice what's unusual is crucial to anticipating consumers' deeper needs and to creating business solutions to meet the demands of the marketplace. Some, like Netflix's leaders, excel at this ability and succeed. Those who don't, like Blockbuster's CEO, rapidly see the impact of not being able to notice what's unusual and promising.

Leading by Influence

The fourth tenet of Intuitive Intelligence, leading by influence, is probably its most essential aspect. Leading by influence is about relinquishing control and allowing the natural creative process of evolution. This may seem paradoxical, but in other cultures it is not. In Zen Buddhism the master leads his disciples in their apprenticeship through questions (Kohan), not commands. When the chiefs of Native American villages were asked what decision to make (going to war, leaving the village in case of an attack, and so on), the chief would answer with a question, not an order. Exerting power and control is not necessarily the best form of leadership, especially not when you wish to develop autonomy and creativity among your team members. Although conventional wisdom regarding leadership is about aligning objectives, strategies, and people, leadership by influence recognizes that dissonance and tension, ambiguity and complexity, chaos and the unknown are equally important and necessary aspects of business. This is why this type of leadership cannot seek control: chaos cannot be controlled, and complexity makes it hard to determine the outcome of one's strategy, so influence is more effective than control. To lead by influence means to guide without control over the outcome. In a complex global economy in which creativity is rated the top business skill, a keen understanding of this new way of leadership is mandatory to innovate, reinvent, motivate, change, and make an organization successful.

Barack Obama's 2008 presidential election campaign offers a tangible example of leading by influence and why it is so powerful. Leaving politics aside, leading political strategists of all ideologies agreed on one thing: Obama's campaign was effective.

At the start of his candidacy Barack Obama had no executive experience, a short legislative history, no substantial financial backers, no real supporter base, and, in the context of United States history, the biggest challenge of all: he is an American of African descent with a familial tie to present-day Africa. He was a classic underdog. And what do you have to do if you're the underdog? You have to reinvent the rules of the game. So here is what Obama did.

Instead of focusing on the traditional swing states like North Carolina, Ohio, and Florida, where fierce competition would not have easily allowed him to differentiate himself from his well-established opponents, he strategically decided to deploy 50 parallel local initiatives and platforms.[13] The Obama campaign was based on the assumption that voters in New York care more about the relationship between Israel and the United States than do voters from other states; voters in Arizona care more about tax rates; voters in New Mexico care more about the border with Mexico; voters in California care more about clean air; and so on. State-specific campaigns were developed with customized themes to address local concerns and needs, at a time when Obama knew he could leverage local voters' participation as never before, thanks to social media. Whereas both Hillary Clinton and John McCain followed a traditional northeast quadrant approach (see Figure 4.2) by "doing business as usual" and managing for results in a linear way, the Obama team's fifty-state strategy challenged the status quo, displaying

FIGURE 4.2 Opponents: A Conventional Focus on the Swing States

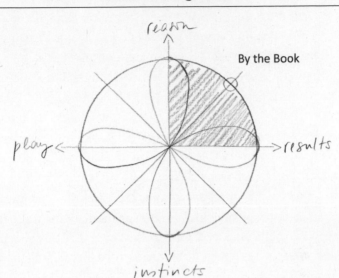

the creative thinking associated with a northwest approach, as shown in Figure 4.3.

But the fifty-state strategy probably would not have been enough if Obama had not delivered an even more radical message. At a Labor Day rally in Manchester, New Hampshire, on September 3, 2007, he said, "I am asking you to believe, not just in my ability to bring about real change in Washington . . . I'm asking you to believe in yours."[14] Going back to Figures I.1 and I.2, the pyramid represents a hierarchical view of the world and the yarn ball represents the interdependent and interconnected nature of life as we experience it, especially with the advent of modern technology. What Obama did with this message was embrace the net of interdependence even as he was clearly aware of his future responsibilities within a very defined pyramid hierarchy. The subtext of the message was this: *I am aiming for the top of the pyramid. I wish to become the president of this country to bring meaningful change. But I will not be able to do it without you; we're all in this together. I depend on you to get there and be enrolled as your master public servant.*

FIGURE 4.3 The Obama Campaign: A Visionary
Political Strategy

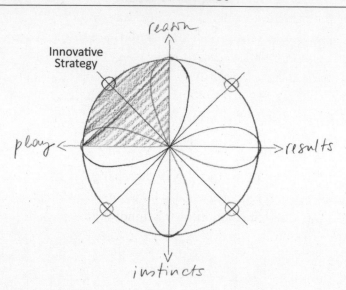

This is your chance! It was a rare call to action. And he was able to make it a reality with the help of the Internet; powerful, fast-growing social networks; and real-time communication.

The Obama campaign enrolled younger voters online and generated broad participation by recruiting creative talent for campaign images, music, and the like. Looking at his campaign through the lens of the Intuitive Compass, he took a creative northwest approach, grounded in the instinct and play of a bold southwest take on leadership by saying that it was not only about his ability to bring about change. He was ready to lead by influence because of his conviction about and understanding of where the world was heading and also because originally he did not have the means to impose or try to control the outcome. By stating publicly that the success of his campaign was not only his responsibility but the responsibility of all voters, he relinquished control from the perspective of a traditional type of leadership. On the one hand he chose to engage and influence fifty states rather than seeking control over the outcome of a conventional electoral fight focused on the swing states. On the other, he also stated principles such as oneness and interdependence to make people realize their responsibility in the outcome of the presidential election. He was shifting from a pyramid perspective that sees the presidential candidate sitting at the top and in control of the electoral process to a new image of leadership where both the pyramid and the yarn ball views of leadership mesh together. He clearly owned the fact that he was the presidential candidate (pyramid) and at the same time was one among all of us (yarn ball). He admitted a truism: he couldn't do it alone, but depended on voters; change was everyone's responsibility as much as it was his, and everybody depended on each other to bring about change. Because leading by influence gives everyone space to display autonomy, his teams managed the northeast implementation of this innovative fifty-state campaign quite remarkably. No detail was neglected, especially when technology could be leveraged. For example, people who signed up to receive text messages from the Obama campaign would be signaled when contacts in their address book were former Democratic voters. They were invited to call these contacts to remind them to vote and to invite them to cast their ballot for Obama. That level of detail in execution had never been reached before in American political history.

From the perspective of the Intuitive Compass, this is the equation behind Obama's success (see Figure 4.4):

northwest creative thinking + southwest reinvention
   + northeast execution = record-breaking results in the southeast

- Northwest: challenging the status quo of the swing state approach
- Southwest: embracing the deepest level of meaning: "We Are All One" to ground his leadership by influence
- Northeast: delivering an exceptional level of execution
- Southeast: achieving exceptional results[15]

Clearly, for the Obama campaign, influence worked better than control. In the debates with John McCain, Obama was not confrontational, because he was not after control of the outcome; yet he was

FIGURE 4.4 The Obama Campaign:
A Record-Breaking Approach

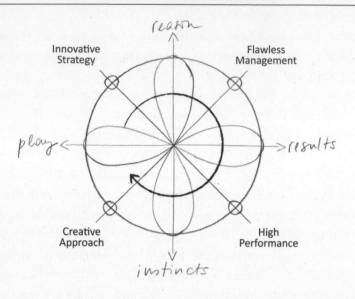

determined to influence viewers to rally around his campaign themes (such as changing politics in Washington, provision of health care to every American, and withdrawal of troops from Iraq). Whenever you cannot control a situation (and this is obviously the case when you're an underdog), influence works better. The more you want people to be receptive, autonomous, agile, proactive, and creative in their approach, the more you should try and influence them rather than trying to control them. It should be obvious, yet in a hierarchical worldview this is not common practice. Hillary Clinton and John McCain overlooked this fundamental principle and paid a very high price for it. Interestingly enough, in their concession speeches both Hilary Clinton and John McCain were particularly eloquent, engaging, and convincing. Indeed, these speeches were about influence, as they had been forced to relinquish control over the outcome of the election.

As much as innovation and agility may be part of the corporate strategic mandate in organizations, I still see many more attempts to control organizations than to influence them. This is the exact reason why many CEOs are disappointed with the level and speed of change they see in their organizations.

BUILDING YOUR INTUITIVE INTELLIGENCE TOOLBOX

Leading an organization today requires us to approach business in a radically different way and to rethink the way we think. Popular thought has always told us that if we work harder and more logically, we will get to the results that we need, but that's not the case. We need to think differently. We need to think and act in ways that unleash the power of the southwest quadrant, where innovative ideas and winning concepts are born. The Intuitive Compass and Intuitive Intelligence provide an actionable model and skill set to do just that. The four tenets of Intuitive Intelligence—thinking holistically, thinking paradoxically, listening for the unusual, and leading by influence—activate the profound and yet often intangible interaction between instinct and play that resides in the southwest quadrant. They enable us to overcome inertia and evolve more quickly, adapt with agility rather than respond from fear, and imagine sustainable solutions that serve our businesses and our customers. Importantly, the four tenets of Intuitive Intelligence enable us to create synergies across the four quadrants of the compass. These synergies are the fuel that drives the new and better business innovations our companies need to remain competitive in today's dynamic marketplace.

Part Three

From Theory to Practice

5

a practical approach to driving innovation for sustainable growth

In the previous chapters, we looked deeply into the importance of playfulness and instinct, the tensions that exist between them, and our desire to achieve results via reason. We have also looked at using the Intuitive Compass to create new and different approaches to getting results in business, and we have seen the impact that Intuitive Intelligence, or the lack thereof, has had on a number of high-profile companies. Now we move from theory to practice and take a look at how the Intuitive Compass and Intuitive Intelligence can be applied to address concrete business situations and deliver satisfactory solutions to succeed in the new economy. As we saw earlier, in this new economic environment companies cannot continue to approach their markets as they have in the past. Companies need to react quickly and creatively. Therefore innovation is a must to reach sustainable growth, and motivation to change must be harnessed at all levels of organizations. Developing record-breaking products and getting the most out of your colleagues' and employees' creativity and agility may require major shifts in the way you do business, or you may be able to achieve these goals with novel approaches and tactics that are in fact very easy to implement once you are aware of them. In this chapter we will look in greater detail at how four different companies have adopted management strategies that exemplify Intuitive Intelligence in action in order to achieve growth.

UNIMEDIA PUBLISHING: RETHINKING HIERARCHY AND LEADERSHIP

Unimedia Publishing, one of the world's largest and most glamorous publishing companies, has historically been an industry leader much admired by the most talented professionals in the field. But, like its competitors, in 2009 it faced the impact of fundamental shifts in the industry, and, for the first time in its history, it fell behind. The print magazine business used to rely heavily on advertising revenues, but as advertisers began to increasingly invest in digital media, they proportionally decreased their investments in print media placement. Also, since the beginning of the same decade, magazine readership had been progressively dropping with the advent of websites with so much free access to information and images online.[1] Given the digital competition, print media could not raise advertising prices or charge readers more for their magazines in order to compensate for the loss in revenues.

In 2010 the company's revenues had been declining dramatically compared to 2007, before the September 2008 financial crisis.[2] CEO Michael Baum and his team had done everything they could think of to get back on the road to success, but none of their efforts had made a significant dent. They had retained leading strategic management firms and implemented their suggestions, but this produced only incremental improvement. Michael Baum was looking for disruptive innovation, but he didn't know how to go about it. He was at a loss.

In September 2009, Michael revealed to me the deep quandary he was in about how to save his company. A highly accomplished businessman with a sound ability for strategic thinking, he had actually been doing everything right. Throughout his tenure as CEO, he had implemented changes to his internal organization and business management that were quickly recognized as strategic and valuable by his competitors, who copied them without delay. Michael would get a step ahead and then find his competitors right at his heels once again. He was concerned about morale at the company. Though we met only two weeks after a holiday weekend, he could see that his team was already exhausted. This told me that he understood Intuitive Intelligence at a fundamental level, though he didn't seem to realize the significance of what he was saying: people need to be energized in order to be creative, let alone disruptive. I asked him, "What about you? Do you feel energized and engaged? Playful and happy?" He looked at me with disbelief, like I was off my rails, and said with a wry grin, "The idea of fun at work is something I left behind thirty years ago." My answer was: "This is a problem."

Michael's employees were living in a tense atmosphere, and he was too. Their approach to innovation and to getting better financial results was mostly logical. But continuing with that logical, linear approach, expecting to somehow *northeast* their way out of this situation, would be futile. The critical question at this point was how he personally wanted to move forward, because the CEO sets the tone for the whole organization. If he didn't fully embrace everything that needed to be done and lead the reinvention, then at some point the team would hit a wall, and the process would come to a halt. As we saw in McKinsey's 2008 study, innovation is a matter of people and culture more than process and structure. Management has to leverage play and engage instinct in order to innovate disruptive ideas and motivate people to change their behavior and implement those ideas. So I told Michael that he was going to have to relearn how to approach his job, have fun at work, and experience genuine excitement.

This statement got a big smile from Michael, because even though, in his very logical mind, fun had no place at work, he knew he needed to change something about his leadership style and that his employees needed him to change. So we began our nine-month journey to turn things at Unimedia around.

We began with an in-depth conversation about his style of leadership, including his professional and personal values and belief systems and his managerial behaviors and attitudes. I shared with him my convictions about business and innovation. I explained how the Intuitive Compass works and why Intuitive Intelligence is key. We worked for a few weeks, and although he enjoyed the process, he was still confused. He couldn't connect the dots between the work he was doing on himself and the need for change in his company.

One day he told me: "I really don't know where it's all going!"

"Neither do I" was my answer.

"But we need to know where we're going for all of this work to lead to something!"

"Actually, I'm not sure I agree with you!" I explained that lots of inventors, scientific researchers, and great adventurers who discovered uncharted territories did not have a clear vision of where they were heading. After a long debate—in which Michael tried to convince me that no company can be successful without a clear vision and that as the CEO of Unimedia he should have a vision—I asked him, "Who in this industry can claim today that they know where the media business is going?"

He admitted he knew no one. This is when I told him, "The one thing we both know, though, is that Unimedia cannot stay where it is. The company has to evolve and move forward. So for now I suggest Unimedia's vision is its reinvention."

Michael looked at me, surprised, and after reflecting for a couple of minutes said, "OK, I like it. It makes sense."

"Good! So our next step is to pass on the message to the rest of the company."

Next, we organized a two-day seminar, which all members of the executive team and Michael attended. As the heads of different publishing units, the executive team members were more accustomed to thinking about the piece of business under their direct management than about the strategy of the publishing house as a whole. This was the first barrier that needed to be surmounted. During the seminar Michael was extremely tense because he was not used to bearing that level of ambiguity, especially in front of his executive team. As the facilitator, I was committed to allowing a new team dynamic and a consensus to potentially emerge around the new vision: reinvention. To impose this obviously would not have made any sense. Yet Michael wanted me to exert more control on the team process. I told him that his choice was to either go back to his old mode of leadership—the one that never produced the disruptive thinking he needed—or to let go. To let go means to give the team a chance to go beyond its silos and develop new convictions, or—which was equally possible—the opportunity to reject the whole experience.

The seminar went according to plan, following a three-step process:

1. We first worked on clarifying the CEO's mandate of reinvention: clarifying its intention, discussing the need for it with the hope of reaching a team agreement. It was the most delicate moment of the seminar, as I had to get the group to face the reality of the need for radical change, even though they hardly knew me at this early stage.
2. Next, we had to articulate a new pathway to success with a new business approach, through the concept of Intuitive Intelligence and the model of the Intuitive Compass.
3. Finally, we used the Intuitive Compass to brainstorm original solutions to help reinvent the business model while reimagining the consumer value proposition of Unimedia.

Although the experience caused Michael to be stressed and on edge, and few tangible results came out of that initial session, I knew that the company and its leading team were already moving miles ahead of the competition and the industry. A chief innovation officer (CIO) was appointed in the afternoon of day two, and we began to create an organization chart that would run parallel to the company's official organization chart. This new organization chart allowed for much more unpredictable flows of information, creative energy, and creative ideas than were possible in the traditional hierarchy. The new organization chart liberated people from thinking about their job description in such a restrictive way. It enabled them to see their job as doing whatever it takes, in a collaborative and entrepreneurial way, to help the entire company achieve its collective goals. They could take more initiative. The new organization chart—or, more specifically, the impact that it had on the mindset of the employees—would eventually foster a totally different work culture, one that revolves around play, fun, optimism, autonomy, proactive thinking, trial and error, and entrepreneurship; one in which you don't ask for permission, but rather ask for forgiveness after the fact

Members of the executive committee were inspired by the courage and commitment Michael showed, and everyone felt a new sense of possibility. So much so that new ideas were created and implemented almost immediately. The group decided to create a company social media network that would allow for direct communication among team members, contribution of new ideas from every employee, a loosening of the prevalent hierarchical mindset, regular informal communication from Michael to the entire company staff, and an easy way to communicate with Michael directly. The ability to communicate across all levels so quickly and easily supported the intention behind the creation of the new organizational chart: to remove all possible barriers to the flow of ideas, energy, and information. It also empowered people to feel a greater sense of responsibility for the success of the company. In parallel, to further emphasize the need for change, internal communication messages were designed around Unimedia strengths and commitments to the future.

To jumpstart the reinvention strategy and give clear evidence of senior management's support of it, the new CIO, Karen Hilton, launched a series of "village meetings" and personally led valuable brainstorming sessions on key strategic subjects. These village meetings were meant to acknowledge and draw out every employee's creative contribution and build team spirit. Along with the vice president of communication, Karen started holding regular breakfasts during which the CEO could meet the rank and file of the company. Many of them had never even seen their CEO in person before. Both Karen and Michael took the opportunity that these breakfasts presented to disseminate keys messages about the reinvention and its rollout in the company. It engaged rank-and-file employees so much so that some of them resuscitated innovative media solutions that had been developed years before but lain dormant since; they presented them to the CEO and the executive committee so that those ideas finally received the attention they deserved. This not only was very motivating for these employees but also helped the company start developing breakthrough products for its clients. A steering committee made of heads of functional departments (digital, marketing, social media, technology, and so on) was formed to cut through the expected inertia of the traditional corporate decision-making processes and swiftly turn innovative ideas into concrete business solutions, avoiding undue and toxic delays. Also, the CIO, COO, and CEO decided to meet regularly throughout the week to evaluate the progress of the company reinvention all around.

We created an incubator, called the LAB, to boost and accelerate the process of developing cutting-edge solutions for advertisers. LAB was the name for a subset of the people who were taking part in the reinvention strategy; it included seven people. Entrepreneurial ideas were brought to the LAB for analysis and discussion. The LAB was empowered with an incentive program, typical of a start-up, to catalyze and support the rapid development of the best ideas. It enabled the company to further overcome inertia and historic barriers within the company. In the LAB the CEO was no longer the CEO; he was just another team member with weight equal to all other team members. To help the members of the LAB team adjust to this new power arrangement, and get into a playful state of mind, we began, of course, by playing a game. Although I had planned to begin with the ABC game, on the first day one of the team members suggested a game called Zip Zap Zop that she had learned in a theater improvisation class, so that's what we did.

Zip Zap Zop is both simple and very efficient. Everyone stands in a circle and one person begins by looking another person in the eye and saying, "Zip." The person who receives the "Zip" then looks at another person and says, "Zap." The person who receives the "Zap" then chooses another person to look in the eye and says, "Zop." And it goes on. There is no order to the people chosen; the only real rules are the order of the play words—Zip, Zap, Zop—and that you look people in the eye when speaking or being spoken to. This game helps people loosen up emotionally and connect at a human level because it is silly; it helps defy and alleviate the weight of hierarchy and the inertia it creates. It requires agility and responsiveness—just what one needs in a time of business crisis.

After the game was over, LAB members sat in a circle to symbolize equality and solidarity and to help create a free flow of information, an open communication, and a sense that every contribution matters. Participants weren't allowed to wear shoes during their LAB sessions. This is not as trivial as it may appear: like suits and ties, shoes are elements of formality that keep us separated from the spontaneity of our instinct and playful nature. It's one part of our persona that is stripped away when all participants attend a meeting without shoes. Hence it allows for more direct and creative confrontation of ideas, even if some may be a little discomfited at first.

Although the seminars, the LAB, and the reinvention initiative as a whole got most people excited and engaged, it was not all smooth sailing. For starters, one member of the executive committee—the head of Unimedia's most successful and renowned publication, which had just recently outperformed its historical competitor by selling more advertising pages—was skeptical of and irritated by the initiative of companywide reinvention. He didn't feel it was a good use of his time. He even began not so subtly entertaining the job offers that had been coming to him from competitors for some time.

Because his publication was a very bright spot in Unimedia's weakened portfolio, these veiled threats to leave the company created anxiety in the CEO. His anxiety brought him to focus on the very real fact that, although Unimedia's vision was its reinvention, the road ahead was still unclear at best. There were no magical answers, only a process that we hoped would lead to unforeseen solutions. Michael descended back into pessimism and told his shareholders that he didn't see a way to rescue his sinking ship.

The executive committee member's reaction to the reinvention process and Michael's subsequent reaction to him are not at all unusual. Implementing these kinds of changes can make people uncomfortable, especially if, like the executive committee member, they have personally been doing well within the previously existing set of rules. Intuitive Intelligence offers great value, but putting it into action requires a willingness to change. And change, as discussed earlier, frightens people.

Notwithstanding these difficulties, progress was made at Unimedia. I brought in an associate of mine to work with the executive committee on the fundamentals of becoming a high-performance team. They developed a new process to focus on strategic decisions. Whereas before they had generally reported up about the state of their business, we got them to value the importance of working cooperatively and collaboratively. They increasingly began speaking and acting together to find and implement solutions for the greater good and the reinvention of the company business model as a whole, versus the interests of a particular business unit.

The LAB team continued to meet and brainstorm new ideas. Michael was increasingly impressed by the positive outcomes from the LAB group. He began to see the tangible evidence of the innovative power of a group of people who are committed to a common goal. Michael was proud to have participated in creating the new dynamic in the LAB and his executive team, and he started taking action to nurture and protect it. He continued to participate in the LAB meetings, thus providing the high-level validation that his employees were looking for. Six months later, a highly innovative iPhone application was developed to help users create videos. Without any particular promotion or marketing effort, the new app reached number 6 of all apps in Apple's iTune store. Michael also fired one executive committee member because of his rigidity and difficulty tolerating the confusion of the reinvention process. This member's inability to contribute to the long-term success of Unimedia had become an obvious drag on the other employees' efforts.

The unhappy director of the very profitable magazine finally accepted a high-profile position with a competitor. In the short term this caused great trauma, not just for Michael but also for the company as a whole. The feeling was, *We lost our star!* But within a few months something happened that was seen as a miracle. Through his network of contacts, the COO identified someone who had an even better profile and exceptional credentials in both the print world and the increasingly critical digital world. This new hire made a huge statement to the company's employees and to the industry at large, showing that the company was able to attract a powerhouse name. This also turned out to be a big professional victory for Michael, whose accomplishment in landing the new director was recognized throughout the company's leadership internationally.

At the same time, the LAB was working on the reinvention of the business model; it was actually still in its beginning phase. The core of the conversation about the business model revolved, of course, around the consumer value proposition. The paper magazines had lost some of their appeal to consumers because of the many alternative online destinations on the Internet, which were building audiences by the millions. No one could really figure out how to formalize this new consumer value proposition. It took a while for them to accept and work with my initial recommendation: to remember the fundamentals of the new economy. I explained, "You're no longer dealing with consumers in the traditional sense of the word (one who uses up goods and articles); you're dealing with community members who have the potential to influence an entire brand and make, with more and more discernment, value-driven choices. You need to move from a consumer value proposition to a community member value proposition." I explained to them that a merchant at a farmers' market selling produce to a customer does not behave the same way as a parent in a conversation with another parent at the meeting of their children's school parents' association. The goal of being part of a parents' community is not to sell anything. The goal is to have meaningful conversations and productive actions to foster the mission, purpose, values, and improvement of the community. However, if you've been a member of this parents' association for a while and need a lawyer to help you with your home purchase, you may think of hiring another parent whom you have come to know well who is a real estate lawyer. Being part of a community is not about business, but it does not exclude business; quite the contrary. Community membership can actually facilitate great business opportunities.

A couple of months after the creation of the Unimedia LAB, I attended a meeting with the COO, CIO, and CEO to review the reinvention process. I synthesized my recommendation and led them to focus on four strategic priorities for the reinvention of the business model:

- *Place technology at the heart of the new media.* Traditional business model reinvention would have consumer value proposition at its heart and technology as a side factor. But in the case of media, technology is inseparable from the value proposition. Unfortunately for Unimedia, although executives in the digital and technology departments were the most knowledgeable about the Internet and the new economy, they were not represented on the executive committee because they were seen as technical experts with no strategic perspective on the business. To rectify this, both the LAB and the steering committee were expanded to include executives from both the digital and technology departments, immediately bringing in a wealth of new ideas.
- *Collect and resell consumer insight.* Consumer insight is a rare and costly commodity for advertisers, yet Unimedia did not have a system in place to collect this information, let alone sell it to advertisers. It was missing out on large potential revenues. Once identified, this was also changed rapidly. Systems and processes

were put in place to collect consumer insight in a formal manner, and publishers were given selling guidelines to leverage the value of this data with advertisers.

- *Create new marketing alliances.* It was important for Unimedia to build strategic partnerships with advertisers. Many brands were seeking new ways to engage more and more discriminating consumers beyond traditional one-way-street advertising. An initiative was put in place to meet with chief marketing officers (CMOs) at advertisers' companies to present them with new opportunities to take advantage of Unimedia audiences in original joint ventures. New multimedia consumer engagement platforms were designed and offered to advertisers to enable new conversations and exchange of information in the fast-developing digital marketplace, where consumers were increasingly found. These new platforms enabled Unimedia's clients to gain a larger share of wallet from their customers.

- *Present content in a new way.* In an age when so many Internet users share useful information derived from real-life experience, I thought it was important to blend professional content with public content. For instance, not too long ago someone looking to buy a Ford Mustang could turn to only Ford or magazines like *Car and Driver* or *Automobile* to find information on the car (price, options, gas mileage, cost of maintenance, and so on). Today thousands of Mustang owners continuously share information online about the experience of owning a Mustang and what's available to improve the experience of driving a Mustang, but it can take some digging for a buyer to find exactly the information they want. A respectable magazine can then use today's search engine technology to organize and optimize all this valuable community-generated information and present it to car buyers in a more user-friendly way. And what's true for the car industry goes for most industries: food, hospitality, interior design, gardening, fashion, and more. So it was important for Unimedia to go beyond traditional editorial material and develop a strategy and process to publish Content 2.0 — that is, content generated by staff writers and independent expert bloggers as well as content derived from *curated* consumer-generated information.

These four directions gave a strategic focus to the LAB in their efforts to effectively reinvent the Unimedia business model. And after nine months, the company was back in the black. Great strategic thinking combined with an entrepreneurial attitude had led to new opportunities and partnerships far outside of the company's core business. The main reason for returning into the black, though, was not putting in place new deals outside of their traditional business, but the sense of possibility that the CEO had been able to infuse throughout the organization and the immediate impact it had on the sales teams and editorial staff.

Figure 5.1, on the following page, shows the change in thinking at Unimedia. The Intuitive Compass on the top shows Unimedia's work culture before the reinvention initiative. It was a culture focused on sales (southeast), where planning and reporting (northeast) stifled any entrepreneurial spirit (southwest), and where there were tentative trials to spur creative thinking (northwest). This is characteristic of a sterile administrative agency. The Intuitive Compass on the bottom shows Unimedia's work culture after the reinvention initiative. It had become a culture open to entrepreneurial initiatives (southwest), where planning and reporting (northeast) were in the service of strategic planning (northwest) and had a direct favorable impact on sales (southeast). This is characteristic of a limber organization capable of innovation — and consequently efficient at delivering financial results.

It takes tremendous courage to bear the fear of the unknown, and Michael Baum bore it. He knew that he couldn't stay where he was, and he committed to change even when it felt dangerous and uncertain and the destination was unclear. His commitment to the reinvention and his focus on empowering people (including himself) in lots of different ways created a culture of entrepreneurship, creativity, agility, and boldness. Even better than the solutions that have already been

FIGURE 5.1 Unimedia Work Culture: Before and After

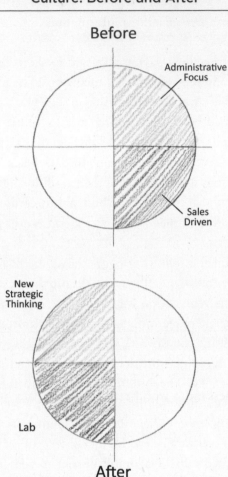

generated, he now has a culture capable of, and interested in, generating innovations over and over again.

SEMCO: TRUSTING A NEW ORDER

A big part of the difficulty that Michael faced is that Unimedia Publishing is a massive international company with well-established rules, lots of quarterly reporting procedures, and a very traditional hierarchical approach to internal relationships. Over the years, Michael had become adept at steering his company cautiously, with lots of safety procedures and checks and balances. However, to succeed in the new economy he ultimately had to throw a bit of that caution to the wind and learn to drive creativity. The question is, is it possible for a very large organization to be managed with the agility that is more commonly seen in small, entrepreneurial companies?

There is a company that always comes to mind when this question of balancing the needs of a large company with the dynamics of today's economy arises: SEMCO.

SEMCO is often called one of the most interesting companies in the world, and it lives up to this description. This Brazilian manufacturing company, whose total billing went from US$4 million in 1982 to US$35 million in 1994, and since then has reached hundreds of millions of dollars annually, is organized unlike any other company I know.[3] It operates without job titles, written policies, a human resources department, a headquarters, or even a permanent CEO. It is the brainchild of Ricardo Semler, the son of SEMCO founder Antonio Semler. When Ricardo told his father he had to leave the family company because it was too hierarchical and regimented, to keep him from leaving, his father resigned as CEO and put Ricardo in charge. Ricardo then catalyzed this small local business into a world-renowned company and an important player in South America's manufacturing industry.

The new work culture Ricardo Semler designed for his company allows for constant innovation, reaps the rewards of leadership by influence, and takes full advantage of the southwest quadrant's creativity. Rejecting "legacies of military hierarchies" in favor of letting employees follow their own intuition, Semler says that his job description is to be a "catalyst . . . broaching weird ideas and asking dumb questions. . . ."[4]

At SEMCO, senior executives pass on the title of CEO every six months, and the rest of the more than three thousand employees are all associates. The employees set their own salaries and working hours. Everybody shares in the profits. Everyone in the company knows what everyone else earns. Every employee receives the company's financial statements and can take classes on how to read them. Subordinates choose their managers by vote and publicly post their evaluations of them. All meetings are voluntary, and two seats on the board are open to the first employees who turn up. All of this creates a remarkable level of employee loyalty, with a low 1 percent to 2 percent turnover in the course of more than two decades.

SEMCO was created in the 1950s as a company manufacturing centrifuges for the vegetable oils industry. Over the years, the company has modernized by expanding its range and investing in other businesses, moving heavily into the services area, always in association and partnership with world leaders. After successfully developing several businesses in the environmental consultancy area, facilities management, real estate consultancy, inventory services, and mobile maintenance services, SEMCO Group is currently market leader in the industrial equipment area and solutions for postal and document management in Brazil. How does such a large company that offers such a broad range of complex products and services manage to be so successful with such a seeming lack of structure? Ricardo Semler offers this explanation: "I let the system work for itself."[5] He has fully embraced the principles of the southwest quadrant as a leader, and he has empowered his employees to bring a southwest approach to their work. He has created a culture of profound trust, saying "We want employees who are ready and willing to work. If that means they only come twice a week, that's okay. It's about results."[6] The work process he has allowed is about play, and SEMCO has reached this great dynamic balance between east (result) and west (play) on the Intuitive Compass.

I have found, in my own businesses and consulting, that hierarchy is a hindrance rather than a necessity, and when it can be partially removed or tempered, companies can succeed beyond expectations. What's more, by removing the hierarchical structure — by moving from the pyramid view of the world to the intertwined yarn ball view of the world, or by adding an open organizational chart in parallel to traditional hierarchies, as was done at Unimedia — we create a refreshing opening whereby energy is naturally generated. Whereas hierarchy and the traditional corporate structure are really about control, open power structures foster a culture in which people's autonomy is encouraged and supported. When employees are offered more autonomy, they naturally function at a much higher level with less supervision. This is really the future, because it creates an atmosphere in which people are more likely to take risks and come up with solutions—an atmosphere suited to creativity.

Not every company work culture can or should be like SEMCO's. But every company has the potential to evolve within what I call a degree of "cultural elasticity." So although the changes that Michael implemented at Unimedia Publishing felt radical to him and to many of his employees, in comparison to SEMCO they are not so radical; if Michael and his employees had been working at SEMCO for a few years or even a few months, then what I was asking them to do would have felt much more normal. It's all about habit, belief systems, attitudes, and mindset—all things that can be changed and learned.

RALPH LAUREN FRAGRANCES: REIMAGINING VALUE FOR YOUR CONSUMER

In the first half of 2009, prestige fragrances posted a decline of 10 percent in U.S. dollars compared with the first half of 2008,[7] and Ralph Lauren Fragrances was no different from the rest of the industry. When I began working with Ralph Lauren Fragrances in January 2009, I was told that they also faced some difficulty in confronting the new economy. Like Unimedia, Ralph Lauren Fragrances was asking itself deep questions about its future, due to this difficult phase in the U.S. economy following the financial crash of 2008. However, in the case of the fragrance company, it was more of a traditional marketing and branding problem than a business model reinvention. Because of their concerns related to lack of sustainability in the fragrance industry Ralph Lauren Fragrances needed to figure out how to make one of the world's most traditional products—fragrance—appealing to increasingly skeptical young consumers.

Ralph Lauren's brand has always been defined by high-quality, elegant, "classically modern" America. Although Ralph Lauren has offered fragrance since 1978, it is known primarily as a fashion brand and has not always had a leading image in the fragrance category. In fact, it had had two big fragrance launch challenges in 2007 and 2008 and was experiencing a steady decline in fragrance sales. In addition, in spite of its historical success in the men's fragrance category, Polo Ralph Lauren's male client base in fragrances was aging. To stay current and build their brand for the future, Ralph Lauren Fragrances needed to attract a younger audience to their fragrances. For this they had to offer a new approach in men's fragrances and move beyond their three traditional yet successful Polo fragrances: Classic, Blue, and Black.

As we saw in Chapter Three, the fragrance industry had been steadily declining and losing up to 1 percent of its American customer base per year since 2007.[8] For the most part, the fragrance industry hasn't adapted its marketing to address changing consumer desires and values. Young Americans are less interested in fragrance for two very specific reasons. First, because it is chemically based, they believe it is not good for their skin or their bodies. Second, they believe it is not environmentally friendly, which conflicts with their growing concern for the environment and desire to respect the earth. Bottom line: fragrance doesn't inspire American youth as much as it used to. And because fragrance is not perceived as a necessity, inspiration is absolutely critical. So if Ralph Lauren Fragrances wanted to capture the interest of young potential consumers—those who have the least personal history with fragrance and therefore the least loyalty to it—they were going to have to think far outside of the traditional box of fragrance marketing.

When I began working with Guillaume de Lesquen, in January 2009, he had recently been appointed president of Ralph Lauren Fragrances. He asked me to assist in the launch of a new collection of fragrances, so we engaged in extensive research related to this project. The launch was critical, in light of recent difficulties.[9] The idea for the launch of the new collection was proposed by Mr. Ralph Lauren himself, and it would carry a name—the Big Pony Collection of Fragrances —based on the brand's very successful Polo shirts line, The Big Pony Collection. This line had gathered a tremendous following worldwide across generations, ethnicities, and countries. It offers a fresh take on Ralph Lauren's classic elegance—aristocratic yet inclusive, energetic, and youthful. In spite of a great vision, we faced some challenges: the saturation of the fragrance market and the fact that to market a fragrance collection meant we had to convince distribution to take on four fragrances, which historically has never really worked. We had to do a lot of research to find an appropriate angle to deliver value to the American male consumer.

In addition to using a 2007 study by the NPD Group, Inc., a leading North American consumer market research firm, on the fragrance category in the United States, we commissioned our own worldwide study on the likes, dislikes, habits, and aspirations of Generation Y.[10] As part of this study we conducted focus groups to test the concept and execution of bottle and packaging design, explored the best ways to engage young people via an internet presence, and hosted multiple internal brainstorming sessions.

This study confirmed Mr. Ralph Lauren's creative direction, which was to create a collection of fragrances and launch them simultaneously. It was a disruptive departure from the traditional launch, in which only a single unique fragrance is launched on its own. But the younger generation today seeks variety, praises diversity, and wants many options to choose from. It is all part of what keeps them engaged.

On the one hand, based on all the findings, I was convinced that launching an additional collection of new fragrances into a saturated market would not be successful—yet I was equally convinced that we could successfully sell the Big Pony Collection of Fragrances, even in an already saturated market, to a generation whose interest in fragrance was low and waning. This is a perfect example of paradoxical thinking.

My insight, based in intuitive intelligence, was this: Generation Y's lack of loyalty to and lack of interest in fragrance meant that we needed to engage in a deeper conversation about value, rather than focus on a classic fragrance marketing strategy to conquer market share. If we were to do this—specifically, if we made the effort to notice the unusual (one of the four tenets of intuitive intelligence) — then I believed that we could successfully launch a collection of fragrances, provided that its purpose and the value it would deliver reached beyond simply offering another fragrance to consumers. The question the Ralph Lauren Fragrances team needed to answer was, what value are we bringing with our fragrance to a new consumer who likes fragrance less than has been the case for older consumers? When we began discussing value in numerous meetings, conference calls, and via a constant exchange of emails, it opened up lots of possibilities and interesting paths for new approaches, generated by a volley of ideas among Guillaume, his counterparts at Ralph Lauren Fashion, and myself.

Once we started to think from the perspective of our target audience, we began to really think about what it is like now to be a twenty-something young man. We then addressed the questions of what they have on their minds and what they aspire to. In brainstorming sessions, based partly on our own memories of being young and based partly on information from our research, we came up with some ideas. These young people want to succeed, have a girlfriend, be stylish and relevant to society, prove themselves, have a sense of adventure in their life, and do all of this in spite of the normal doubts and insecurities linked to their age and the early stage of their life journey. What became obvious to me is that they would welcome empowerment. If the Big Pony Collection of Fragrances could convey empowerment, then it would be delivering something valuable. It also became obvious that this was something we could legitimately offer to them. Why? For two reasons. First, because Mr. Ralph Lauren is probably the designer in the best position to offer this. As a self-made entrepreneur he is a heroic figure, and as creator and designer of a huge fashion brand he is a mythological figure. It is easy to see why young men would trust the brand bearing his name for its capacity to empower them. Second, fragrance itself is often a means to feel better, to feel empowered. What do we do when we have to go to an important meeting in the morning after we've been out late and not gotten enough sleep? We take a hot shower and, often, we spray fragrance on ourselves to shore up our energy level. Fragrance is, for many, a part of that "morning after a late night" ritual. So there was an actual congruence between the empowerment this younger generation of men wanted and what a Ralph Lauren fragrance naturally delivers.

We determined that in order to attract the highly-sought-after eighteen-to-thirty-year-old market, Ralph Lauren Fragrances would have to:

- Move beyond its product category by offering more than fragrance and presenting these new fragrances as means of empowerment
- Develop energizing scents with an exceptional fragrance manufacturer that could deliver the high level of quality expected from the Ralph Lauren brand[11]
- Design and develop inspiring modern points of contact that resonated with its brand DNA; for example, an original in-store and internet presence that would rejuvenate its image and inspire customer engagement
- Help our young audience gain easier access to Ralph Lauren products with interesting and generous promotions that made purchasing the Big Pony Collection of Fragrances even more valuable

To get the attention of Generation Y, we needed to speak to them in their language and make the Big Pony Collection of Fragrances the obvious first step into the enticing, legendary lifestyle associated with Ralph Lauren. To make the lifestyle accessible and tangible, Ralph Lauren Fragrances and the Ralph Lauren advertising agency created an elaborate and interactive online presence. For example, Bruce Weber, the internationally renowned photographer who has shot Ralph Lauren's fashion collections and fragrances for years, created a film for TV and the Big Pony Collection of Fragrances website. The film portrayed four young men, seen as the players on the team, empowered by each fragrance, and featured music by the popular group OneRepublic. It also resonated with the Big Pony DNA and embraced the aspirations of its young audience by showing the Ralph Lauren style on beautiful young models, as music that is popular with this audience plays in the background. On the website visitors were invited to create their own short films by freely editing a large number of clips drawn from the making of the film, giving them another opportunity to learn about each fragrance in the collection. Helping consumers understand what the collection was about in such an emotional way was an important aspect of the communication campaign.

Again, we also had to address the challenge of launching a collection of fragrances. I went to different department stores to better understand why this has historically proven so difficult. Observing my own reactions and listening carefully to what beauty assistants and store attendants had to tell me, I gathered important information on my shopping expedition. First, it clearly confirmed purchasing a fragrance is very subjective. Subjectivity leads naturally to a certain amount of self-doubt, because there is no right or wrong answer to what we feel. When presented with the multiple choices that a collection of fragrances gives us, we can easily become overwhelmed. Second, it stressed the fact that after you smell a couple of fragrances, it becomes difficult to differentiate them or choose a favorite, and that leads to frustration. Moreover, fragrance is an intimate accessory, which makes the choice even harder. For this reason the experience felt disheartening; it left me unsatisfied. Finally, buying three fragrances felt too expensive, and buying one or even two fragrances from the collection and leaving one or two behind felt incomplete.

I came to the conclusion that if the ultimate goal is to get young men to eventually purchase the entire collection of fragrances, then each fragrance had to be part of a strong, unifying, and irresistible whole. This simplifies the process of choice. It is no longer a matter of choosing which one to buy over the others; it is a matter of deciding which one to buy first, second, third, and fourth. This is why, with the team, we made sure that the Big Pony Collection of Fragrances offered a clearly unifying and compelling holistic thread. In this case, the concept that formed the holistic thread was "A Team of Fragrances." The team consisted of four distinct scents, each one expressing one of four archetypal aspirations or dimensions of success for a young man at the beginning stage of his adult life and the four fragrances correlated to the four men in the film.

Each fragrance was shown to clearly relate to each of these archetypes with the promise of bringing about clear results. Blue was associated with *sporty*, Red with *seductive*, Green with *adventurous*, and Orange with *stylish*. This invited young men to buy all four and feel fully empowered to achieve their goals across all aspects of their lives.

In the summer of 2010, the Big Pony Collection of Fragrances broke all historical sales records in the men's fragrance category at Macy's and Bloomingdale's in the United States as well as in Europe and Asia. Just a few weeks after its launch in August 2010, Big Pony Fragrances reached an unprecedented 6 percent U.S. market share without the support of any television advertising, which didn't start until December. For the first time in decades, a collection of fragrances was successful, and the four fragrances sold evenly. In early January 2011, the Big Pony Collection of Fragrances won the Duty Free News International Product award 2010 for the best new men's fragrance. Equally important, the success of the Big Pony Collection of Fragrances actually boosted the worldwide sales of Ralph Lauren's "World of Polo" Fragrances. This last fact not only was good for sales volumes but also meant that Ralph Lauren Fragrances had achieved the acquisition of the new and young audience it had aimed for.

Examining the traditional approach to marketing fragrance versus an intuitive intelligence-based approach on the Intuitive Compass may be helpful. In Figure 5.2, the Intuitive Compass on the top shows a traditional approach to marketing driven by sales. It shows how creativity is naturally limited when marketing is confined to chasing market share. The Intuitive Compass on the bottom shows the intuitive intelligence-based marketing approach, which is creative and value-based, and which generates many possibilities to engage consumers and create a myriad of opportunities to generate sales because value is brought to the consumer in many authentic and creative ways.

There are a few factors that contributed to the success of the Big Pony Collection of Fragrances. Surely the success of Big Pony shirts

FIGURE 5.2 Conventional Sales-Driven Marketing and Creative Value-Based Marketing

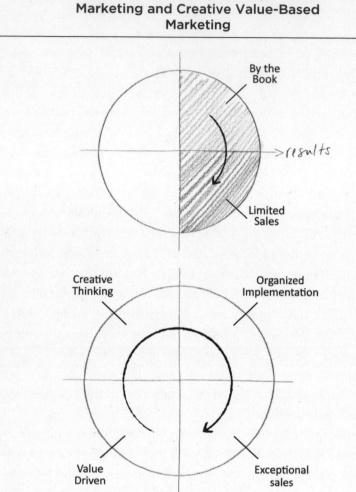

helped greatly, and Guillaume de Lesquen's expertise and more than twenty years of experience in the beauty industry were certainly big factors. But I believe that his genuine openness to a new way of thinking and new marketing approaches was hugely instrumental in reaching a new audience.

BETC AND EVIAN: LEADING WITH HEART AND MIND

Whenever I think about reaching a huge audience in a very competitive, saturated market, one exceptional advertising campaign for mineral water — Evian — and one exceptional advertising executive — Mercedes Erra — come to mind and spur me to new thinking.

In the summer of 2009 Evian, the French bottled water brand, launched an online video campaign as a part of its larger "Live Young" campaign. The video (as of October 2010) had been downloaded over a hundred million times. It was listed in the Guinness Book of World Records as of 2011 as the most watched viral campaign of all time. It also won the Gold Award for Best Visual Effects at the prestigious London International Awards, which honors creativity and new ideas in advertising, design, and digital media.

What on earth caused all this fuss? Babies. On roller skates.

WEB

The video, called "Roller Babies," opens with a graphic that says "Let's observe the effect of Evian on your body," and then shows about a dozen babies roller skating and break-dancing to "Rapper's Delight," a 1979 hip hop song by the Sugar Hill Gang. It is surreal and funny — hilariously funny — and not at all what consumers had come to expect from a brand that has historically taken a more elegant and understated approach in its advertising. Evian had never used viral advertising before, and it took a bit of convincing before Danone, the owner of Evian, would sign off on launching the campaign. But before that it required a lot of tolerance for chaos to even get the video made. As Fabrice Brovelli, head of production at the advertising agency behind the campaign, said, "Nothing happened as planned, the shoot was meant to last four days and it took eleven; the negotiations for the rights to Rapper's Delight, this hit from 1979, turned out to be a real crusade. And the final result seemed just too far out for Evian's image."[12]

The international campaign, directed by Michael Gracey, was the most efficient viral campaign ever. The strategy had been well thought out; teaser videos were sent out a few weeks before the online launch.

The first one showed a baby doing the moonwalk. The second one, which seemed more homemade, showed a baby break-dancing. These were followed by videos of fake interviews with the baby actors. Then, in July 2009, Evian unleashed its viral video on the Web. In addition to an astounding 102 million views, it generated 130,000 comments and 500,000 Facebook fans by April 2010. Ten months after the online release, Evian brought Roller Babies to television in the United States and Europe. Jerome Goure, VP of marketing at Danone—the company that owns Evian—had initially voiced skepticism about launching virally; he had this to say about the transition to television: "While we are expanding into traditional media in order to broaden even further the reach of the 'Live Young' campaign, online remains a major pillar of our strategy."[13] Speaking about the firm's earnings on February 16, 2011, Danone CFO Pierre-Andre Terisse told analysts that its full-year and fourth-quarter results were in line with expectations. The waters division saw sales in the twelve-month period to the end of December climb by 5.3 percent, to 2.87 billion euros (US$3.89 billion).[14] "We are entering 2011 with a healthy face; if you want to understand what the performance evolution of water is, you just have to look at the fourth quarter and our 5.2 percent sales growth," Terisse told analysts. According to Danone official communication, this acceleration is explained in part by the Waters division's ability to promote its brands.[15]

This bold move to choose a viral launch over a television launch is the opposite of the direction most advertising campaigns take. Many popular television advertisements are uploaded to YouTube *after* they have aired on television, and people go online to watch television commercials that they have heard about or to share their favorite television ads with their friends. But this viral strategy—which was promoted by Mercedes Erra, founder and chairwoman of BETC, the advertising agency that created the campaign—was hugely successful.[16]

BETC is the largest advertising agency in France and part of the sixth-largest communication group in the world, Euro-RSCG.[17] It was named the "best creative agency" by CB News in 2009 for the twelfth time in fifteen years and was the most awarded French agency at the Cannes 2010 Advertising Film Festival. The same year, a film produced by BETC for the French cable television Canal + was voted the most creative advertising film worldwide. It was the first time a French advertising film ever reached the number one position globally. Much of its success can be attributed to its leadership. Mercedes Erra, more than any other creative strategist I have met, has mastered the art of bringing southwest thinking to every quadrant of the Intuitive Compass.

Super rigorous in the analysis of brand and communication strategies, Mercedes is equally comfortable with the logic-defying twists and turns of the creative process, which often succeeds only by violating meticulously planned strategies. Besides an enormous capacity for hard work, she nurtures a set of values that together define a powerful, winning culture: collaborative team spirit, generosity, empathy, compassion, intuition, patience, passion, and the interplay between reason and instinct. These values serve to facilitate a synergy between account managers and creative directors who consistently develop successful advertising campaigns. The campaign they did for Evian stands out as an example of how legacy brands can capture the imagination of the younger generation while staying true to their own DNA.

What I also find fascinating about BETC's achievements is that in spite of being an incredibly large agency with a staff of eight hundred people it still retains an uncanny capacity to adapt to the high speed of changing markets. Who would think that the biggest agency in France would be bold enough to launch a completely unique and provocative campaign for mainstream bottled water online before bringing it to television, and to take this risk with one of their largest accounts? This is the kind of challenger's move you would anticipate in an up-and-coming ad agency or a pure player, but not in a well-established agency like BETC. This highlights the remarkable ability of BETC's leading team to rethink every aspect of its business and evolve constantly along with the fast-changing environment of the new economy.

SUCCESSFUL BUSINESS THINKING FOR THE NEW ECONOMY

There are four core aspects of doing business successfully in the new economy: leadership, work culture, marketing, and the business model. The Intuitive Compass and Intuitive Intelligence facilitate a new approach to each, helping clients to understand where they are and what they can do to improve their performance. This approach puts the development of sustainable innovations and long-term value generation at the heart of business thinking.

QTICS METHODOLOGY

The real-world case studies in this chapter demonstrate the power of Intuitive Intelligence in action. Every company I work with—indeed, every company that exists—faces its own set of challenges and operates with the particular strengths and weaknesses of its employees, so the path to innovation is always unique. Solving real-life business challenges entails deep conversations with our consumers, our employees, and ourselves. To start this conversation, I have devised a common framework I call Quadruple Turbo Intuitive Compass Synergy (QTICS). You can use this practical framework in your own organization.

WEB

    I begin by examining any company I work with on four key dimensions—leadership, work culture, marketing/branding, and business innovation—to see how they are performing. Through the lens of the Intuitive Compass, using a questionnaire customized to the company (size, industry challenges at hand, history, market context, and so on), I establish a diagnostic and discuss it with the CEO and sometimes with the executive team. We look for areas for improvement, even if sometimes it means radical change in the company's business approach. Once we've agreed on the objective, I put key stakeholders in the room for a one-and-a-half-day seminar to teach them how to use Intuitive Intelligence and the Intuitive Compass to begin an accelerated path to sustainable growth. It's a highly experiential seminar; I use activities derived from theater techniques, such as the ABC exercise, to get participants to engage with their intuition and more playful nature, and I stage and facilitate creative brainstorming sessions using the model of the Intuitive Compass to bring out all the talents in the room. We identify the key challenges of the company, prioritize them, and put them in perspective in light of the new environment that the new economy has imposed on the company's industry. In an effort to help the company evolve and succeed in its environment, I facilitate a diagnostic of the strengths and weaknesses of the organization, using a long series of questions to see where the company falls on the Intuitive Compass.

The following section presents some of the questions I raise in the course of the seminar in regard to the four key dimensions of a sustainable business strategy. You may find them to be a useful starting place for examination of your own company. We take the answers for the four key dimensions and turn each of them into a profile on the Intuitive Compass, which we then interpret and discuss individually and as a whole.

Leadership

In the new leadership mindset, the conventional view of hierarchical power is replaced by a web of interconnected relationships. It requires a deeper understanding of human nature and takes into account instinct and play. This mindset recognizes the power and promise of intuition and the unconscious. It's important that you have a reasonably objective understanding of your own leadership style before you can effectively change the way you lead your organization. The following questions will help you get a sense of how you lead.

- Is your leadership style about control or influence? Does it embrace the nonlinear aspect of life as SEMCO does, or is it more conventional?
- How do you influence your team members' work? What systems do you have in place?

- Is your leadership style addressing the instinctual and emotional dimension of every relationship, or is it more intellectual?
- Is your leadership really about bringing value to all people around you or simply about getting people to do what you want them to do?
- Do you, as a leader, understand the power of symbols and stage powerful business rituals?
- Do you seek adulation or ego-reinforcing behaviors from your employees, or are you more likely to encourage your employees to be honest and forthright with you, even if their feedback is not positive?
- Do you allow yourself to notice the unusual in order to innovate and stay ahead of the curve in all areas of your business?

Asking yourself these questions will help you get a stronger understanding of your leadership style, where it lies on the Intuitive Compass, and which aspects of intuitive intelligence it embodies as well as which aspects of intuitive intelligence it is not tapping into.

Work Culture

To get the most out of employees in terms of creativity and agility, you need to create a work culture that enables them to explore new ideas freely and fail without fear of reprisal. A work culture that is open to new ideas is key to success over the long term. A work culture that honors autonomy generates unexpected—and often lucrative—new products. A fluid, vibrant work culture resonates with and balances the complexity and unpredictability of today's business landscape. The following are some questions that can reveal the state of your work culture as it stands currently.

- Is your work culture about anticipating your employees' deeper need for meaning?
- Is your work culture hierarchical only? If not, do you have systems in place for informal gatherings, informal exchanges of information, informal participation?

- Do you really care about people being happy, or do you just give it lip service?
- Do you make it explicitly safe for people to try new things and to fail?
- Do you encourage diversity in age, ethnicity, professional background, gender, and sociocultural styles? If so, how?
- Do you allow for and promote play? If so, how?
- How do you inspire employees' creativity?
- How do you create among employees a natural sense of belonging to your organization?

Each question represents one key aspect of a work culture relevant to the new economic environment. Answering these questions should help you understand your current work culture and see ways that you can improve it.

Marketing / Branding

Marketing and branding can no longer be a one-way conversation in which companies dictate to consumers. To achieve top-of-mind status with the new consumers—who are behaving more and more like community members, *prosumers* (professional consumers), and influencers—companies have to get into two-way conversations that begin with a mutual understanding and the delivery of a valuable service, and then move naturally to profitability and strong brand equity. Interaction via social networks and codevelopment of products are two innovative ways that forward-thinking companies are revitalizing their marketing and branding strategies. Answering the following questions can help you understand how your company truly sees its customers.

- Do you focus on consumers simply as profit centers or as valued members of your community?
- Do you approach profit as a function of the value you bring to your community members, or do you relate profit to shareholders' return on investment, or both?

- Are you only following trends, or are you truly innovating—are you able to be disruptively innovative?
- Are you able to create retail experiences in which your employees/sales people are evangelists rather than paid mouthpieces?
- Do you involve the consumer enough in the innovation and value creation of your company?

Answering these questions will guide you to review your relationship with your customers—what is founded on and how it is facilitated. Once you know how your organization views its customers, it will be easier to find ways to improve the relationship you have with them and succeed further in the new economic environment.

Business Model

Whereas the traditional business model was solely about profit, the new business model is about sustainable value creation. In the old economic paradigm, we typically used hierarchical power structures and fear to achieve dominance. In the new economic paradigm, successful businesses leverage collaboration and cooperation into a competition for significance, such as offering value to all the people who are involved, directly or indirectly, with your business activities. When you deliver substantial value to all of your communities and properly manage all four quadrants of the Intuitive Compass, then profitability follows naturally. The following questions will help you understand the focus of your business model.

- Is your business strategy profit-centric or based on sustainable value creation?
- Do you believe that sustainable value is beneficial to all of your stakeholders?
- Are you looking at short-term or long-term sustainable value creation to measure the impact of your decisions?
- Are you spending enough time anticipating where technology is going and how it will affect your business?

- Are you capable of designing totally new product lines tailored to untapped consumer groups, including developed market nonusers and emerging market new consumers?

After you've answered these questions, you should understand whether your business model is focused narrowly on dollars and cents profit, or if it is focused broadly on value creation.

A PATH TO ACCELERATED GROWTH

When a company is able to engage all four aspects of its business from the perspective of the four quadrants of the intuitive compass, then it is bound to reap exceptional results. It creates a powerful synergy between two pairs: leadership and work culture on the one hand, and the marketing and business model on the other hand. As we saw with Unimedia, the media company had to rethink its leadership and corporate culture to get to a new understanding of consumers and the reinvention of its business model, because one feeds the other. In the case of Ralph Lauren, understanding the motivations of a younger generation was critical to envisioning a different relationship to fragrance. This is where the president of Ralph Lauren Fragrances decided to focus the work. But for both Unimedia and Ralph Lauren Fragrances, the Intuitive Compass (and Intuitive Intelligence) helped them to fully embrace the paradoxical nature of business: a need for concrete results and logical steps in a highly unpredictable context with challenges that at times seemed intractable.

When we work with four compasses to address each of the four key aspects of business at the same time, we create a Quadruple Turbo Intuitive Compass Synergy. This configuration shows us powerful results, as in the case of Unimedia and the Big Pony Collection of Fragrances.

Optimizing return on investment makes perfect sense from a logical standpoint, and it makes at least as much sense to also optimize human fulfillment. Decoding the hidden human motivations and values

FIGURE 5.3 Quadruple Turbo Intuitive Compass Synergy

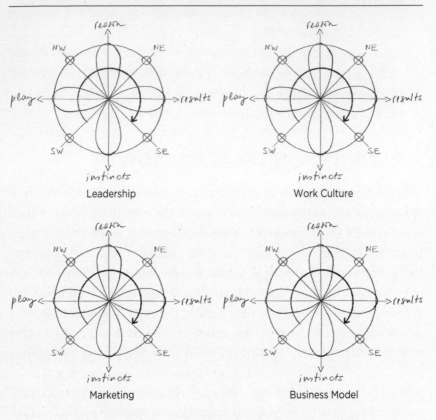

underlying all four core aspects of business and taking the universal quest for meaning and satisfaction into account are always sure roads to sustainable success. The difficulty for some is that these are never rational or conscious routes; this is what makes business innovation so hard but also so interesting. When we accept these truths, business becomes an art form, and the results look magical.

A NEW PATH TO SUCCESS

These examples illustrate a radically new business framework in which creativity is a core staple of leadership, sustainable value is at the heart of the business model, we have a new understanding of consumers and the consumer value proposition, and innovation is a driver of sustainable growth—and all of these things become the fundamental underpinnings of business.

To implement this type of business model in our own organizations, the first thing we need to change is our mindset. As we saw in the case of Unimedia, implementing changes, even when they are positive, can be upsetting to some people. We need to be able to tolerate a period of time in which we aren't where we used to be but we also aren't yet where we would ideally like to be. When we change our mindset and open ourselves to new ways of thinking and behaving, things that didn't seem achievable can be achieved—like turning a failing publishing company from red to black, or the wildly successful launch of a fragrance collection to a previously disengaged consumer group.

The tools that we use to make these changes can range from relatively easy things—like the ritualistic team meetings that BETC hosts to kick off new projects—to more complex undertakings—like the reorganization of long-standing employee organization charts, as was done at Unimedia. Determining which kinds of tools are most needed, and which ones have the most potential to accelerate our company's growth, becomes easier once we understand two things: our personal strengths and weaknesses as leaders, and our company's strengths and weaknesses as a complete system. By asking the types of questions that I ask when offering the Quadruple Turbo Intuitive Compass Synergy methodology to my clients, you can begin this process on your own. The stories in this chapter have shown what Intuitive Intelligence looks like in action. It is sometimes messy and disconcerting, very often nonlinear, but highly valuable for its ability to spur sustainable innovation and return struggling companies to good health.

6

the intuitive compass
in action

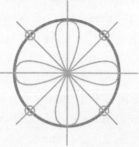

It would be erroneous to assume that intelligence is necessarily
conscious and deliberate. We know more than we can tell.
—Dr. Gerd Gigerenzer

The Intuitive Compass is a tool that helps us innovate, solve problems, and move forward creatively in a highly unpredictable environment where old practices no longer deliver what we need to succeed and achieve sustainable progress. It enables us to reflect on how we (consciously or subconsciously) choose to make decisions or behave in a particular situation. This is crucial, because it gets us to a deeper level of understanding of any given situation. Logic is powerful but rarely deep, because it is dualistic in nature (things are either right or wrong, longer or shorter, before or after, and so on). To go beyond what logic alone can deliver (an objective analysis) and deal with the subjectivity of any decision (which comes along with its share of ambiguity, complexity, and paradox), we necessarily need to go past logic. This is why the Intuitive Compass and Intuitive Intelligence are instrumental. Once we are able to more deeply reflect on our behavior and decisions, we are well positioned to identify the aspects of intuitive intelligence that, if integrated into our daily lives, would help us achieve our business and personal goals.

Completing an Intuitive Compass involves answering a series of questions that reveal your proficiency in each of the four quadrants of the compass. In this chapter we will learn how to use the Intuitive Compass in real life and how to use Intuitive Intelligence to leverage the value of each of the four quadrants. We will also discuss the critical issue of how to manage the creative process, and take a look at how the Intuitive Compass reveals the synergies and tensions that exist between Reason and Instinct (the North-South axis), and Results and Play (the East-West axis). This information shows us how to use the four tenets of Intuitive Intelligence to maximize the impact of our strengths, and effectively overcome our challenges. We will also review practical ways to access and develop skills for the four tenets of Intuitive Intelligence: thinking holistically, thinking paradoxically, listening for the unusual, and leading by influence.

Let's start by looking at two case studies and two Intuitive Compass questionnaires.

CASE STUDY: ALI

Every year I give a seminar called "Intuitive Intelligence and Innovative Leadership" to MBA students at L'Ecole des Hautes Etudes Commerciales (HEC) in Paris, one of the world's most renowned business schools and Europe's leading business education campus. The purpose of the seminar is to teach students a new approach to business leadership to prepare them to succeed in the new economy using the model of the Intuitive Compass. Toward the end of the seminar, after a day and a half spent together, I ask participants to create an Intuitive Compass on how they approached the subject matter. (You took a similar self-assessment at the beginning of this book.) The objective is for them to become more aware of how they react to newness and disruption and to learn more about their personality, their behaviors, and their mode of leadership. Where they fall on the Intuitive Compass usually casts a revealing light on how they deal with the experience of learning a business approach that is radically new and different from what they've learned in more traditional classes (like marketing, law, or finance). It is an experience that can be at times confusing or frustrating.

They first answer a series of questions I created that reveals their competency in each of the four quadrants of the Intuitive Compass, in the context of participating in the seminar. (Note that you can create a questionnaire and draw an Intuitive Compass to chart and evaluate any business situation, challenge, or strategy.)

Next, I guide them in transferring the results to a blank Intuitive Compass in a way that visually represents where their strengths and weaknesses lie.

The following are some of the questions I ask them to answer, rating themselves from 1 to 5 (1 being the lowest and 5 the highest). The questions here include notations of the quadrants they pertain to; however, students are not shown these notations until after they have answered the questionnaire. Note that of the eight questions, there are two pertaining to each of the four quadrants of the Intuitive Compass (northeast, southeast, southwest, and northwest).

1. How open were you to the new ideas presented in the seminar? (Northwest)
2. How organized and meticulous are your notes? (Northeast)
3. How effective have you been in achieving the objectives you set for yourself at the beginning of the class? (Southeast)
4. How easily were you able to bear confusion during the ABC exercise? (Southwest)
5. How comfortable were you going with the flow during the class? (Southwest)
6. How efficiently did you manage time during the individual exercises? (Northeast)
7. How aware were you of the goal of reaching Z during the ABC exercise? (Southeast)
8. How open have you been in reconsidering your ideas about efficiency? (Northwest)

The students then use their answers to calculate their average for each quadrant. As simple and immediate as this is, without fail, they always tell me it reveals something interesting to them about how they chose (consciously or subconsciously) to behave in the class and how they could choose to behave differently in a comparable future situation.

Sometimes people see a similarity between what their Intuitive Compass (IC) shows about how they approach a particular problem or situation and the way they perceive themselves. It is important to remember that the IC depends on a variety of variables: what the subject is (work, vacation, relationships, money), the time of year, or even the time of day. The pattern any IC shows is very specific to the question at hand and the context.

When I work directly with clients or students, I help them gain a deeper understanding of what their Intuitive Compass reveals. I did this with one student of mine, Ali, an American from Los Angeles who was studying in France as part of an exchange program with UCLA. Ali was very young—eight years younger than the average age of his fellow MBA students—but he had already been an entrepreneur. I noticed that although his contributions to the class had been quite astute, he had a *laissez-faire* attitude about it all. In the ABC exercise he was quite playful and relaxed; however, during class I often saw him doodling and staring out the window. I knew he was interested, although he seemed to be more interested in his own thoughts than he was in the rest of the class, and I was curious to see the result of his answers on the Intuitive Compass. Figure 6.1 depicts Ali's Intuitive Compass for attending my seminar.

Ali's Intuitive Compass matched my observation of his attitude. Although he is very open conceptually and pretty "playful" behaviorally (he scores big on northwest and southwest), he was not, strictly speaking, in this class to get results. He reacted to the experiences and information as they came; he did not seem to have an agenda. He was open to new concepts and went along with them, which is far from typical. I have a number of students who simply don't understand the exercises and concepts I share and do not respond at all to the whole philosophy

FIGURE 6.1 Ali's Intuitive Compass:
NE1, SE2, NW4, SW4

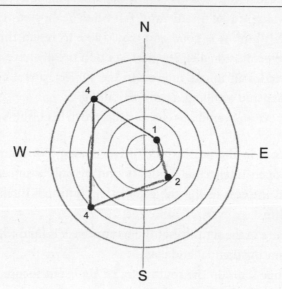

behind the class, at least on the first day. These students are typically very goal-oriented and rather competitive. They have spent sixty thousand euros and have put their careers on hold to attend this two-year program; they are looking for a linear path to greater financial success.

Ali, on the other hand, had a very flexible attitude that contributed to creating an atmosphere of open-mindedness and discovery and a constructive group dynamic in the class. He provided this form of leadership, as far as I can tell, without intent, unconsciously, which explains his low score in the southeast quadrant. The southeast is about achievement through more aggressive actions, and Ali is about achievement through influence.

When I started the seminar I had asked all participants to state their objective for the class. Ali had said, "I don't really have an objective. We hear about the word 'leadership' all the time, but I am not sure of what they mean by leadership. I have been a young entrepreneur in real estate in Los Angeles and want to move on to other business ventures in other industries. When I read the title of your class 'Intuitive Intelligence and Innovative Leadership' and the description of it, I felt interested because in real estate I rely a lot on my intuition when dealing with buyers and sellers. And I think it is good and would like to retain this approach in my future professional endeavors. So I don't really have much of an objective besides an innate interest in the subject, a real curiosity for your approach and a willingness to play along."

The way Ali answered was clearly reflected in his Intuitive Compass:

- High score in the northwest (4): His strategy for taking the class is very open intellectually; it is bound by only a sincere curiosity and real interest in the subject matter: Intuitive Intelligence and leadership.
- High score in the southwest (4): His approach is fluid when it comes to integrating instinct and play.
- Mid-range score in the southeast (2): He is not focused on results nor on any form of preset performance measure.
- Low score in the northeast (1): He is not organized in any formal way (for example, rather than taking notes, he doodles).

I commented to the class that Ali's Intuitive Compass reflected a positive impact and an original contribution to the class process when it came to discovering new behaviors and learning new concepts. This is a characteristic of leadership by influence, which is important when it comes to supporting innovation. Ali agreed that he saw a lot of himself and his approach to the class reflected accurately in his intuitive compass and added that he had a tendency to seek out work environments that supported his way of thinking and behaving. However, he had not realized that his attitude had a leading impact on the class dynamic, which was confirmed by most participants. He did trust his intuition; however, he was less comfortable with his undirected and playful creative nature. He added that he would never have thought that playfulness could be such an important attribute of leadership. This was a significant breakthrough for Ali's professional growth.

CASE STUDY: ANNA

In my consulting, I sometimes work with entrepreneurs, which I find interesting. Although large corporations have their own set of barriers to growth and innovation, some of the same issues are seen in small companies, even very small ones, as was the case with Event, an event planning company.[1] Event was founded in 2005, and by 2010 it had developed into a successful company that served corporate and private clients in Chicago. Its founder, Anna Brown, wanted to expand her business, but felt a bit stuck as to how to move forward. She was also questioning how she could best define her niche and differentiate her company from the competition. She was even wondering if she should specialize in corporate clients only—perhaps the advertising or retail industry—or if she should also include large weddings and parties for affluent private clients. Her goal was to have more clients who are very interested in throwing unique parties that bring the greatest pleasure to guests, but she wasn't sure how to go about identifying and pitching those clients. We decided to focus on the first question, one that many of us have on our minds: how do we expand our business? By answering this first question, we could see if we could help Anna find deeper creative answers to her other questions.

I had Anna complete an Intuitive Compass questionnaire. As with all IC questionnaires, the rating system was a scale of 1 to 5, and the quadrant notations were hidden until after the questionnaire was completed. These were Anna's questions:

1. How much time have you spent reflecting on why the expansion of your business is important to you? (Northwest)
2. How much time have you spent reflecting on what "business expansion" means to you? (Northwest)
3. How clear are you about your vision of business expansion? (Southwest)
4. How extensively have you quantified the expansion of your business (such as billing volume, number of clients, growth rate)? (Southeast)

5. How much of the expansion of your business have you planned? (Northeast)

6. How willing are you to sacrifice time and energy for the sake of your work and its expansion, even without being clear about the direct financial return on your investment of time and energy? (Southwest)

7. How organized are you about your actions to expand your business? (Northeast)

8. How willing are you to do whatever it takes to expand your business (without jeopardizing its integrity)? (Southeast)

9. How systematic are you about the expansion of your business? (Northeast)

10. How much effort have you spent on determining how you will measure the success of your actions to expand your business? (Southeast)

11. How willing are you to let go of your expectations about results while keeping your commitment to add value to your customers? (Southwest)

12. How much time have you spent articulating strategies to achieve your "business expansion"? (Northwest)

After Anna rated herself for each question, we tallied the results for each quadrant and found the average. These were her results:

Northeast (Questions 5, 7, and 9): $3 + 5 + 4 = 12/3 = 4$
Southeast (Questions 4, 8, and 10): $0 + 5 + 2 = 7/3 = 2.3$
Northwest (Questions 1, 2, and 12): $3 + 3 + 4 = 10/3 = 3.3$
Southwest (Questions 3, 6, and 11): $4 + 5 + 2 = 11/3 = 3.6$

Then we placed each result on each axis of each quadrant in the Intuitive Compass (see Figure 6.2).

Looking at the shape of her Intuitive Compass, Anna had a number of immediate reactions:

• The line image within the IC representing how she approached the business expansion was a diamond shape, elongated on the

FIGURE 6.2 Anna's Intuitive Compass

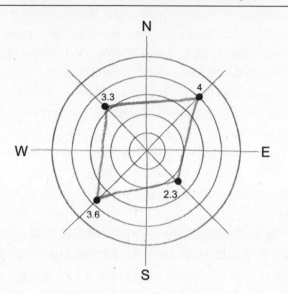

northeast/southwest diagonal and thinner on the north-west/southeast diagonal. She found it strange that she would score high on two such different competencies that she didn't expect to go together: organization and creativity.

- The IC showed that she was detail oriented and would be careful about implementing and administering a business expansion. She agreed that this was true, as she was very conscientious.
- The relatively high southwest result accurately reflected that she is able to let go of results and feel her way through things as they happen.
- Her lower scores in the southeast and northeast quadrants were eye-opening. She believed that with her organizational skills she would be a natural at strategy (northwest). But she realized that this explained why she was having a hard time executing (southeast): she wasn't clear about why and what to execute.
- She believed it was true that although she was on top of her business growth regarding the detail and administration of things

like sending emails, following up with phone calls to prospects, filing information about potential new clients, and the like, she was not proactively initiating targeted growth plans. Instead, she was open to new things and happy to be surprised by new opportunities, and she reacted to them as they came her way.

- There was a certain disconnect between the southwest and southeast quadrants because although she would often have a clear gut feeling for what she wanted to achieve, it was hard to turn these hunches into actionable initiatives.

Indeed, my observation when I looked at Anna's Intuitive Compass and its diamond shape was that she was right — there was some disconnect or imbalance between the two diagonal axes. She was pretty much in touch with what would make her feel good about her business expansion (southwest), but she had not quantified what this business expansion would look like (northeast) and translated it into a strategy (northwest). She also had not explored why she wanted to expand her business. Was it about hiring people and opening an office? Was it about better-quality work? Was it about subcontracting some work and handling other work herself? Having more time for herself? Recognition in the industry? Reaching a critical size among competitors?

The insights that Anna gained through her Intuitive Compass were the first step in her ability to get "unstuck," because they helped her identify the areas where she needed to focus more of her attention. Rather than wasting more energy being unfocused and frustrated, Anna directed her energy toward clarifying her goals and creating a strategic plan. Having this plan for the more specific aspects of her expansion gave her an inner confidence, and she was able to be more strategic in pursuing potential opportunities, rather than simply reacting to those that came her way. She told me later on that she was hopeful that the opportunities she was pursuing would reflect much more closely the strategic direction that she had set up for her business. When I spoke to Anna in early 2011, she had developed and was about to launch a marketing strategy targeting wealthy residents in the greater Chicago area, promoting her expertise in designing one-of-a-kind high-end private parties such as weddings, bar and bat mitzvahs, and anniversary parties. At that time she was continuing to accept and efficiently manage other work that came her way, but she felt much more productive overall since she had begun deploying her organizational strengths in the service of expanding her business in line with her vision for her company. This reallocation of her time and talent was efficient, because beyond a certain point the return on operational efficiency loses its marginal value. That is to say, she created significant potential upside by using her organizational skills to advance her marketing strategy rather than using her organizational skills to refine an already highly organized administration of her existing business, while managing a 20 percent increase in her billing in 2010.

SAMPLE INTUITIVE COMPASS QUESTIONNAIRES

You may want to use the questionnaires in the preceding case studies to create your own Intuitive Compass around learning (Ali) or expanding your business (Anna). In addition, I have created two questionnaires, which follow, for two subjects that come up frequently with my students and clients: corporate culture and team innovation.

Corporate Culture Questionnaire

The following Intuitive Compass questionnaire is suitable both for CEOs trying to get a clearer understanding of how their company culture supports performance and for people in the process of looking for a new job who want to evaluate how well they would fit within the corporate culture of a particular company.

If you are a CEO, it should be easy to get access to the information needed to complete this questionnaire. If you are outside of the company, you can seek interviews with insiders and/or review public documents to complete the questions.

After you have assigned a score of 1 to 5 to each question (1 being the minimum and 5 the maximum), total the score for each quadrant and then divide by 5 for the average score for each quadrant.

Northeast Quadrant Questions:

- How clear are the processes that are in place to administer business?
- How efficient are these processes?
- How well organized is the business?
- How methodical is business management?
- How rationally and logically is business managed?

Southeast Quadrant Questions:

- How highly would you rate your team commitment to achieving results?
- How highly would you rate the efficiency of your company's performance evaluation systems?
- How frequently is performance reviewed and analyzed?
- How robust are your company's performance incentive programs?
- How well defined are your company's parameters and criteria for the measurement of success?

Northwest Quadrant Questions:

- How much emphasis is put on strategic thinking?
- How highly would you evaluate the openness of the culture to new ideas and influences from employees?
- How highly would you evaluate the openness of the culture to new ideas and influences from outside the company?
- How easily does the company tolerate questioning of the status quo and embrace paradox?
- How effectively does the corporate culture encourage play?

Southwest Quadrant Questions:

- How well does the corporate culture support risk-taking?
- How well does the corporate culture tolerate the chaos of the creative process?
- How well does the corporate culture encourage passionate individuals?
- How much of the corporate culture is based on vibrant values and a strong sense of purpose?
- How often do meaningful rituals and symbols play an important role in the corporate culture?

Results in each quadrant provide us with a number of insights:

Northeast

The Northeast quadrant highlights the administrative function. It shows how business is managed and organized. This is obviously an important aspect of business: how can an organization function well when processes are not well managed or are simply absent? Typically, a financial institution or accounting firm would score high in the northeast quadrant, whereas a startup may not be focusing on how to manage a business that is still being shaped. Therefore the important facts here are the nature and maturity of the business. Businesses with analytical functions at their core tend to score high in the northeast quadrant simply because organizational skills are in their DNA. Mature businesses tend to score high in the northeast quadrant because over time it becomes highly likely that systems and procedures have been put in place to ensure smooth operations that support continuation of the status quo. If a business is still young (in my experience, established for less than two years) it is naturally more adaptable; its culture is affected by the nature of the activity but can be influenced more easily because day-to-day activities are less ingrained with habits built over time. It is also important to evaluate the northeast in relationship to other quadrants; a low score in the northeast can sometimes be of lesser importance in a very high-performing culture (indicated by a high score in the southeast) or temporarily out of balance because the company is going through a major phase of reinvention of its business model, which brings more focus on the southwest and northwest.

Southeast

In the southeast quadrant, we have insights into the focus on performance and the measure of performance. A high score would be typical at a sales organization like a network marketing company. A low score would typically be found in a company focused on administration. This quadrant gives you insight into the level of emphasis that is given to results. If you are talented at working with metric objectives, regardless of your function in the company (marketing or sales), you will probably be inclined to seek a company with a high score in southeast, like a sales oriented company. Conversely, if metrics are not your strength or interest, a company with a predominantly southeast culture is unlikely to make you happy or leverage your most valuable talents. In this case you may look for a company that is more about creation (southwest), or about administration (northeast), or about strategic planning or engineering (northwest). Again, the relationship with the other quadrants is key, especially the northwest and southwest quadrants. I know of highly profitable large consulting firms that have no sales objectives and no ongoing measure of the commercial performance; however, because they are very strong in the northwest (strategic planning), they deliver great ideas, and phone calls from new clients continue to come in.

Northwest

In the northwest quadrant we gather information on creative thinking and strategic planning. A higher score is always better, because, as we saw earlier, research shows that openness to new ideas is a factor of longevity. However, a business may be extremely successful a few years in a row simply due to series of great deals (southeast) and bold moves (southwest), without much strategic thinking involved. I've observed that a number of large companies tend to focus more on feeding the pipeline or following the "business as usual" routine strategy to meet sales objectives (southeast). Often companies focus on market opportunities to boost sales, with little thought about sustainable value creation, which leads them to not adapt their business model to today's new market constraints and their marketing strategies to a new type of consumer; a dangerous path in the long run. So it is important to look closely at a northwest score and compare it with the score in the southeast.

Southwest

The southwest quadrant shows how much a company is dedicated to R&D and creation. This quadrant is crucial in the new economy. A high score in the southwest quadrant indicates a buoyant culture that can generate new ideas and creative initiatives and can support an entrepreneurial spirit. What can be problematic, though, is a high score in southwest and low scores in the other three quadrants, as it would indicate a company where leadership and management are not well rounded and business functions are not well integrated. CEOs evaluating their own company should strive for a balance whereby creativity is supported from the perspective of both allowing and funding such activities as well as supporting the marketability of the innovations that are generated by developing strengths in the other three quadrants. Individuals evaluating the possibility of joining a particular company should also look for evidence of this balance.

From these results a number of conclusions can be drawn.

If you're looking for a job, it is important to review the relationship between the culture of the company you are considering joining and your own Intuitive Compass to determine whether it is a compatible match. For instance, if you are more of a southwest type of professional you should really consider whether you're being offered a position in a company that displays a northeast culture, and vice versa. These results are also insightful if you're simply evaluating whether or not you should stay in the company you work for. I have a client, a C-level executive who realized that he would enjoy the southwest culture of a start-up much more than he did the very northeast/southeast culture of the multinational he had been working for since the beginning of his career. He finally decided to leave his job to create his own start-up: a consulting firm with a built-in incubator to launch new digital companies in the new media industry.

If you're the CEO of a company and would like to improve the culture of your organization, analyzing the Intuitive Compass in relation to the culture of your company will lead you to identify areas for improvement in every quadrant where a score is low. You need to put the profile of your Intuitive Compass in perspective with your objectives and also your context at the time of this review: industry, market situation, mission of the company, corporate strategy. Each quadrant with a low score or any imbalance between the four quadrants represents an opportunity for growth. In addition, the Intuitive Compass can help you clarify and articulate to your teams the reason behind the new goals you may set for them.

Team Innovation Questionnaire

If you are part of or are managing a team, you may want to create an Intuitive Compass to evaluate the team in respect to a particular business objective, such as supporting business development, fostering creativity, increasing the efficiency of meetings, improving productivity, or developing more agile teams. Doing so can help you understand your greatest strengths and identify your greatest weaknesses. This knowledge enables you to take actions that will improve your outcomes.

The following is a typical set of questions for the management of innovation. Rate your team from 1 to 5 on each question (1 is lowest and 5 is highest), then for each quadrant's total divide by 5 to get your team's average score by quadrant.

Northeast Quadrant Questions:

- How clearly has innovation been defined: goal, process, expected results?
- How detailed and innovation oriented is your action plan?

- How well defined are the processes you have defined to manage innovation?
- How detailed a plan is in place to monitor the process of innovation?
- How detailed a plan is in place to monitor the output of innovation?

Southeast Quadrant Questions:
- How detailed a plan is in place to monitor the expected output of innovation?
- How well incentivized to perform is the team?
- How detailed a plan is in place to measure the result of innovation?
- Is innovation output actually reviewed and measured?
- How committed is the team to doing whatever it takes to innovate?

Northwest Quadrant Questions:
- How detailed are your plans to qualitatively and creatively analyze the outcome of innovation?
- How well equipped is the team to generate new ideas?
- How effective is the team at seeking new ideas from outside?
- How effective is the team at embracing play as a means to creativity?
- How thoroughly have the potential stumbling blocks to innovation been identified and analyzed?

Southwest Quadrant Questions:
- How effectively are team leaders focusing on leadership by influence?
- How much is chaos encouraged?
- How much is confusion tolerated?
- How much is risk taking encouraged?
- How effectively is innovation explained to the team in engaging and meaningful ways related to the values of the team and the corporate culture?

After completing the questionnaire, you can use the following guidelines to decode the meaning and make adjustments that will improve your team's ability to thrive and innovate.

Northeast

In this quadrant we can see how rational, logical, organized, systematic, and meticulous the team is about getting the results they want from innovation. A high score means there is a high level of organization, detail, and logical thinking involved in the innovation process. Conversely, a low score means that the process of innovation would benefit from a more rational approach and a methodical and detailed action plan with deadlines, a person in charge of the process, or a person accountable for results.

Southeast

In the southeast quadrant, we get feedback on four key elements of innovation: the team's level of commitment to do whatever it takes to innovate successfully while retaining integrity, the team's ability to measure performance, the team's ability to measure the level of success based on well-defined criteria to evaluate performance, and whether the team is financially motivated to achieve results. A low score here is an indication that the team needs to clarify what success means and how it will be measured. It also means that the team needs to reevaluate its level of commitment to achieving that success and management needs to reevaluate how the team will be motivated financially or compensated in whatever way motivates them to get there. Otherwise, the lack of clear incentives means your strategy will not be supported.

Northwest

The northwest quadrant result tells us about the team's openness to new ideas and perspectives about innovation. If the score is low, the team needs to analyze the process of innovation and strategize new and creative paths. This entails defining areas where they need to innovate, such as products and services, management, finances, client relationship management, or marketing and branding. It also means that the team should focus on evaluating how it encourages a culture of innovation (values, behaviors, attitudes supporting play) and supports creative minds.

Southwest

The southwest quadrant results are indicative of the team's capacity to relate to the part of innovation that reaches beyond the bounds of logic. It shows the team's ability to let go of control so that new ideas can manifest and emerge on their own. A low score in the southwest quadrant means that the team should trust the potential of nonlinear, nonlogical paths to innovative solutions more, and consider what more trust could bring along. The team has the potential to see more significant results if members learn how to tolerate confusion, influence behaviors creatively, give more autonomy to individual team members, and allow time for the creative process to unfold more efficiently. This can be taught. The Intuitive Compass is a good tool to show how to trust and how to move through fear and confusion: trust your guts, embrace fear, and use play whenever possible. This can also be supported by an environment in which accepting and rewarding trial and error are communicated as a necessary element of growth and creativity, as well as by a management style that fosters play.

I have used the Intuitive Compass for innovation quite often. It always leads to breakthroughs, as people understand what innovation requires to unfold: an element of chaos, trust in the creative process, a commitment to change, and a focus on implementation that enables people to see concrete results. You can also use it to evaluate whether your team is weak in any particular quadrant, to scrutinize whether your team functions well in the southwest quadrant, and to determine whether you are able to properly manage your team in this same quadrant. The Team Innovation Questionnaire will require a significant investment of time, but the information that you gather can enable your team to create—and follow through on—a far more effective business strategy. The answers you get indicate the ways in which you can apply Intuitive Intelligence to create a more effective business strategy.

THE NEXT STEP: USING INTUITIVE INTELLIGENCE

A completed Intuitive Compass gives us a snapshot of where we are. For example, Ali leads by influence, but he has never considered what that means or how he can leverage it to greater and sustained advantage. And Anna toggles between great explorations in the southwest and vigilance in the northeast, but her lack of strategy—a northwest proficiency—has frustrated her ability to expand her business. Similarly, if you have completed the Corporate Culture or Team Innovation questionnaire, you probably have found areas where you want to make changes and improvements. The next step after completion of an Intuitive Compass is to take action. But how?

This is where Intuitive Intelligence comes into play. Through Intuitive Intelligence, Ali can transform his natural playfulness into a powerful leadership attribute and Anna can transform her rich ideas into actionable strategies and measurable outcomes. Both can work toward an Intuitive Compass that is balanced, in which synergies are activated and tensions are resolved or leveraged.

Working toward a balanced Intuitive Compass requires sharpening your skills in each of the four tenets of Intuitive Intelligence. To show you how, in the following section I'll go through each of the four tenets in detail. For each tenet I've given (1) an example of a company we've discussed that has demonstrated that tenet, (2) an exercise you can use to jump-start Intuitive Intelligence in your own organization, and (3) questions to ask yourself regarding your own organization's relationship to that particular tenet.

Think Holistically

- *Example:* Remember the success Hermès had as a result of balancing exceptional creativity in product development with highly disciplined marketing analysis and sales discipline, and the commercial failure Concorde experienced as a result of inadequate creativity in both product development and marketing strategy. Hermès was able to think holistically and balance all four quadrants, whereas the Concorde's failure was due to a gross imbalance and an obvious lack of holistic thinking. The four quadrants all work together, and none of them can be neglected if you want to keep dynamic balances between reason and instinct, play and result, and among the four quadrants.

- *Exercise:* Approach a new project (such as a new product launch, a move into new offices, a new business plan) from the point of view of the holistic value it brings to your customers' or team members' lives. Instead of focusing primarily on the expected direct material return, think about their personal satisfaction, instinct, the feelings and emotions involved, the personal or group values underpinning the project, and the personal stake as well as the financial return for the company. Then communicate this project management approach to your team. See how people react, their level of energy and inspiration, and their body language. Take note during the project of how people work and how productive they are. You will most likely observe that their level of excitement varies depending on a combination of two factors: which quadrant you're addressing and where you think they probably fall on the Intuitive Compass.

- *Questions to ask yourself:* Am I looking at the situation as a whole, as an interconnected and interrelated system, or am I leaving out any of the four quadrants of the Intuitive Compass? If the latter, which quadrant(s)? And how can I see any neglected quadrant as part of the whole? What does the situation as a whole tell me that a fragmented view would not reveal?

Think Paradoxically

- *Example:* Google and SEMCO both took a unique approach to organizing working hours and employee time management. We generally go by the assumption that the output of our work is a linear function of time, but it is not; human beings are not machines. Although most companies still impose time constraints and a schedule, thinking this is the best way to keep order and to optimize productivity, by doing so they negate the self-organizing principle at the heart of any living system and ignore the paradoxical fact that some of us can be very productive and creative in the morning and not do much in a few hours of applied effort in the afternoon, or vice versa, or not be productive for three days and then come up with a genius idea in a split second at the end of the following day. Google, which has a highly analytical and rigorous corporate culture, is still able to stage work in a very playground-like work environment. Google fully embraces the paradox of a playful environment for a very analytical type of work and gives away 20 percent of office time to its employees so they can manage their schedule and work according to their own idiosyncratic relationship to time.

- *Exercise:* Plan your week to include moments for play—deep play, the way a young child would play, immersed in the moment without caring about other people's judgment or what's going on around you. It can be drawing, reading a comic book, taking a walk in the park to collect leaves, playing with a doll or soldiers—let yourself simply enjoy these playful moments. Then observe what happens to your spirit, level of energy, creativity, and productivity when you go back to work afterward.

- *Questions to ask yourself:* When I plan my playtime, am I applying a learned rational rule (think "common sense")? Would a deeper understanding of the situation, with its intangible dimensions and unconscious dynamics, clearly indicate that another approach would make "better sense"?

Notice the Unusual

- *Example:* Virgin America was able to reinvent the terms of service in domestic flights in an industry where little innovation had been seen, due to low profit margins and high market share competition. By opening up to their feelings and not thinking about services solely through financial analytics, Virgin America was able to win a leadership position in domestic air travel in only a few years.

- *Exercise:* Watch someone on TV or listen to someone who is on the radio or talking to you. First pay attention to the meaning of the words, then switch and pay attention to the sensations you feel as you hear the sound of the voice. What do you notice in your body? Are you aware of any sensorial cues, any feeling? Is an inner voice telling you something? Notice and write it down, even if none of the cues or messages makes sense. Repeat this experience over time and see how much you can develop this ability to notice beyond what makes sense and uncover unusual information.

- *Questions to ask yourself:* What precisely am I looking for? Am I really open to being surprised? Am I open to noticing unusual feelings or information? Am I able to connect with the *feelings* I have while I am making sense of the *logical meaning* of what I see and am being told?

Lead by Influence

- *Example:* When managing his campaign, Barack Obama gave up the hierarchical view of his role as a candidate for the U.S. presidency to enlist more supporters and voters to be part of his success. He put forth the interconnectedness and interdependence of people involved in the campaign displayed in his "We Are One" rhetoric, which matches the yarn ball view of the world. This worldview calls naturally for leadership by influence, as trying to control a group of interconnected people simply does not make sense.

- *Exercise:* Apply this to the way you work with a team when you are looking for new ideas. Have all of your team members sit in a circle around an open space free of clutter or furniture. Establish the rule that people can interact outside of the usual hierarchy and titles in the company. Observe the new dynamics and respective individual contributions. Observe how new ideas get generated.

Do not seek control or try to spot the underlying self-organizing principle that leads the group's dynamic. Observe how you can guide the group process without breaking the natural flow. Let the group brainstorm ideas; simply interject words to give the appropriate directions you deem interesting. Do this as often as necessary and be careful to not dominate the process. Respect the equality represented by the circle. This way you allow people to trust the brainstorming process, and deeper ideas will emerge. The less you do to indicate your role of leadership, the more you get from your team.

- *Question to ask yourself:* Am I willing to give up control over a given situation, see how things naturally evolve, and then decide how to possibly influence the course of actions?

Repeat these exercises regularly. It takes practice, and there is no set rule; it is about a creative exploration of what lies beyond logic, reason, and the conscious part of our minds. However, as we now know, we must respect a number of principles (taking a holistic approach, embracing paradox, being open to the unusual, giving up control) and circumstances (physical environment, playfulness, rituals) in order to allow deeper perception of what is contemplated and a greater level of influence over any process.

Now that we have reviewed and practiced specific situations to hone each tenet of Intuitive Intelligence, we need to address two final questions: how do we access our unconscious and its wealth of original information, and how do we work with our intuition to navigate the unconscious in a productive way?

GETTING TO INTUITIVE INTELLIGENCE THROUGH INTUITION

To tap in the whole of our intelligence, we need to allow mental and emotional space to relate to the intangible and the unconscious, to integrate what is complex, and to accept that our human nature

FIGURE 6.3 How Intuition Facilitates a Synergy Between Reason and Instinct

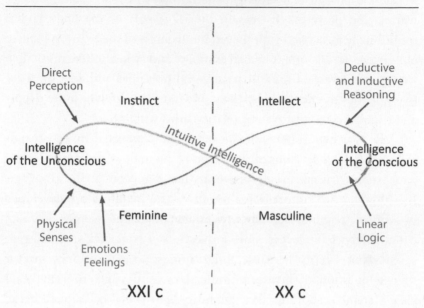

is playful and instinctual. We also need to address our fear of the unknown and our need for control. If we fail to properly manage these, they can easily and even inadvertently turn into obsession, aggression, and destruction. It takes awareness, focus, and discipline to turn the human instinctual force into creative collaboration. Intuition helps us achieve all of this.

Figure 6.3 shows how Intuitive Intelligence facilitates a synergy between our rational mind and our instinctual aptitudes. Our intellect and instinct work together and feed one another: intellect operates from deductive and inductive reasoning, instinct from direct perception. Intuition bridges the gap between the two and receives information from our feelings, emotions, physical sensations, and direct perception.

The diagram shows a feminine quality and a masculine quality on either side of the figure eight. Feminine energy is receptive and creative, empathic, open, welcoming, intuitive, contemplative, and circular, seeking deeper meaning. It lives in the left part of the body and is traditionally associated with the right hemisphere of the brain. Masculine energy is piercing, penetrating, concrete, logical, linear, willful, and powerful. It lives in the right part of the body and is traditionally associated with the left hemisphere of the brain. Whatever our gender, we all partake in dual feminine and masculine energy. When we become aware of these two universal polarities and develop these two qualities of energy, it helps us understand ourselves more deeply and enables us to improve our relationships with others.

WEB

The two hemispheres of the brain are connected by the corpus callosum, which develops earlier in girls than in boys and could explain why young girls are usually more mature than boys at the same age. But although we culturally see intuition as a quality more developed in women, research actually proves that men and women have an equal ability. I think it is more a question of education, societal representations, ability to trust, and readiness to put intuition to use than a question of innate aptitude. Dr. Gerd Gigerenzer makes a clear statement about it: "We still hear that women have much better intuition than men. . . . This distinction sustains an old prejudice. Contrary to common belief, however, men and women share the same adaptive toolbox."[2]

We all have access to intuition. Let's see how to use it.

FIVE WAYS TO TAP INTO YOUR INTUITION

Just as we prepare ourselves for an important interview or set our minds to achieve a challenging goal like running a marathon, we can take steps to invite intuition into our daily experience. The following are a number of ideas to ponder and exercises to do. There is no special order; there is no particular one that is more or less important than the others. Try all of them. Consider adapting them in a way that speaks to you.

Revisit Your Perspective and Perceptions

- Consider the possibility that wherever you are now is the optimal place from which to get where you want to go. A Native American proverb says: *What do you do when you get lost? Stand still. The trees and bushes beside you are not lost.*

- Look at a painting by Monet or Picasso and contemplate your ability to alter your perception of reality and bring forth something completely new and unexpected.
- Pay attention to details—like a word, color, or song that catches your attention or comes to mind for no apparent reason—as elements that have the capacity to reveal the whole. Look around you with a fresh eye to rediscover the environment you're in or all data and aspects of the situation at hand that you would like to resolve

Get Comfortable with the Part of Life That Is Not Logical

- Don't immediately ban an idea because it is paradoxical and appears illogical. Welcome paradoxical data or situations. The word "paradox" comes from the Greek *paradoxos* "opposed to existing notions, from para- + *doxa* opinion"[3]; so something that is paradoxical is something we should all look for because we are looking for new ideas, not what is already known and widespread.
- When you receive information that appears to be out of context, take a moment to notice it. It may appear to be out of context, but it could lead you to a deeper understanding of something that is not obvious.

Accept That *You* Are Not in Control

- Allow yourself to be carried away by energies that appear to be chaotic, like the brother in the Edgar Allen Poe story of the maelstrom. Your acquiescence can help the emergence of a new order that you could not have imagined.
- Try to stay in tune with your emotions, especially in moments of stress or chaos. Emotions are energies that are *all part* of a same circle; if we shut one down, we break the circle, and we close ourselves off from *all* emotions, good or bad. If we can avoid

trying to harshly control emotions that feel uncomfortable, they will pass and we will return to a state of balance. The more we accept our emotions, the faster they evolve and the faster we can move on. This is the intelligence of the brain, body, and nervous system; it functions without our conscious intervention.

Relax and Practice Noticing

- The world-renowned mime Marcel Marceau said, "Our body knows things the mind does not have access to." The best gateway to information from our subconscious mind about the world around us is through a relaxed body. The most efficient way to relax our body is not a five-star vacation, it is breathing. Breathing can dramatically alter our experience in any given moment. You can do this almost anywhere with a simple meditation. Sit quietly with both feet on the floor, hands at rest on your thighs, eyes closed. Don't try to alter your breathing in any way, just pay attention to it. Don't think about anything—not your problems, not even happy things—simply focus on the movement of your breath. Do this for a minute, or five minutes, or as long as you like. Taking this little break, even for just five minutes, may at first make you anxious, but give yourself permission to take five minutes in which you do nothing but breathe. To focus on your breathing, simply notice the movement of your diaphragm—the horizontal muscle that moves up and down in your mid-torso. When your diaphragm goes up, you exhale and your rib cage narrows. When your diaphragm goes down you inhale and your ribcage expands. Becoming mindful of the movements of your diaphragm is enough to largely improve your breathing. When you give yourself this permission, your body will relax and your breath will deepen naturally.
- Pay attention. It is very easy to stop noticing small things, or even large things. Buddhists have a practice of mindfulness in which every movement, whether lifting a cup of tea to one's lips or placing a foot on the ground while walking, is afforded the

greatest attention. Be mindful during a routine event such as eating breakfast; afterward, record the sensations, thoughts, and emotions that arose in that short interval.

Sharpen Your Ability to Notice Through Careful Listening

I am going to teach you an exercise, called The Listening Posture, in which you focus on your ability to listen differently. Listening is very powerful. It is a receptive function, which is a feminine quality. Therefore proper listening can greatly help you access the feminine dimension of your psyche and develop your creative sensitivity. There are many other reasons for putting the emphasis on your auditory sense. Some are scientific;[4] some are related to ancient wisdom[5] and rituals.[6] Professor Alfred Tomatis developed the Listening Posture.[7] Although designed for therapeutic reasons, it is also a great way to sharpen your sensitivity, and access and develop your intuition. You can do it anyplace — in your office, or even in a loud environment such as a waiting room.

Instructions for the Listening Posture:

1. Set your intention: Think about an area in which you would like to get insights. Make your question open ended. Write it down.
2. Sit still in a comfortable chair, feel your seat in the chair.
3. Leave your legs and arms uncrossed and relaxed.
4. Close your eyes and focus on your breathing. Breathe naturally.
5. Relax your diaphragm (allow the muscular "floor" in your abdomen to move up when you exhale and down when you inhale).
6. Relax your neck and shoulders, lower back, middle back, and upper back.
7. Relax your facial muscles and the muscles around your upper lip, and tighten the skin of your face up and out to make it more smooth and even.
8. Pay attention to sounds in the room.

9. Focus on your right ear (unless you have impaired hearing, it is the one that can relay sound to your brain in the quickest way).
10. Focus on all high-pitched sounds.
11. Focus on the harmonics of all sounds (the luminescent part of all sounds, like the crest of a wave).
12. Float in this sonic bath. Let these harmonics energize you as much as they open you to greater awareness.
13. Stay in this state for five minutes.
14. Open your eyes and look around the room.
15. Look at your question. Write all the ideas that come to you.

After you have tried these different exercises, keep practicing the ones that resonate with you. Over time these exercises will help your intuitive abilities get stronger and will make it more likely that they will become a natural part of your daily life. Intuition is a skill not made by either nature alone or nurture alone. We are born with a capability, and we turn it into a capacity by using it over and over again. Once you've identified the exercise or the few exercises that are most natural to you, with regular practice you will improve your ability to reflect about a decision or a situation beyond pure logic. This will greatly enhance your ability to pay attention and notice, to trust the unknown and tolerate the confusion that comes with ambiguity and complexity. You will be more comfortable with your own subjectivity. It will prevent you from too quickly jumping to a logical conclusion, which would not necessarily get you to the most creative answers.

THE INTUITIVE COMPASS IN ACTION

This chapter has taken us on a journey from theory to practice. Through a series of questions that home in on the characteristics of each of the four quadrants of the Intuitive Compass, we can gain clearer insight into our strengths and weaknesses as individuals, as teams, or even as companies. The answers to the questions also enable us to see the larger pattern of our behaviors within the context of the Intuitive

Compass—perhaps an overreliance on one quadrant in particular, or complete neglect of another quadrant. This knowledge puts us in a position to make the adjustments to our behaviors that are necessary to create balance and synergies that support innovations and sustainable business growth. Intuitive intelligence is available to all of us to support this evolution. By tapping into our intuition with greater confidence in its power and purpose, we can come up with new insights that inform our personal and business decisions. The Intuitive Compass is always available to provide a snapshot of where we are, and Intuitive Intelligence gives us a skill set to shape our actions in a way that leads to greater success.

7

the next generation of business: moving from selling to serving to leading

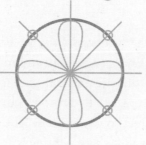

A new scientific truth does not triumph by convincing its opponents
and making them see the light, but rather because its opponents
eventually die, and a new generation grows up that is familiar with it.
—MAX PLANCK

I t is possible to challenge the status quo and, against all odds, bring a unique economic and social value to your community or organization. In fact, many companies and leaders have refuted common business wisdom and done just that. Their extraordinary results prove that ambition, creative imagination, and ideals carried with fortitude, patience, persistence, and intuitive intelligence create silent revolutions. They give us great insight into how to succeed in the new paradigm and how to prepare the new generations of leaders.

Business does not need to be limited to optimizing shareholder value. On the contrary, they can create sustainable value and optimize human capital and ecosystems while generating sound, profitable business. Businesses that know this attract creative employees and loyal customers; they are able to sustain and grow innovation and evolution. Their brands and reputation are icons in their communities because of their influence and positive contribution beyond the bounds of conventional business. These companies have moved from selling to serving to leading their communities. They define the next generation of winning businesses.

SHIFTING GEARS: FROM SELLING TO SERVING TO LEADING

As we have already seen, the new economic context is changing fast. In this complex and rather unpredictable environment, companies tend to become more opportunistic and navigate for short-term wins. The world population is expected to grow by almost 20 percent within the next ten years. A direct consequence will be the emergence of a large new urbanized lower middle class—hungry for upward mobility, and demanding new products and services that they see their more affluent urban neighbors acquire easily. In addition, recent research shows that consumers in developed markets are increasingly demanding of the products they consume, and they are less loyal to brands, further increasing the attractiveness of emerging markets where customers will have—for a while at least—lower expectations because they have less money.[1] So there is a common equation encountered in many different industries, including consumer products, automobiles, chemicals, pharmaceuticals, and financial and insurance services:

more people + more money = more sales opportunities

This straightforward formula is efficient and therefore very appealing, but in the mid- or long term it is probably not serving very well those who use it. It is a purely quantitative approach; it represents an incremental strategy and does not address deeper issues. Experts' research tells us that change will continue to accelerate, and more disruption, more innovation, more commitment, more care to ecosystems, more value, and swifter adaptation are needed. Incremental change is no longer sustainable. The future belongs to those who can deliver exceptional quality products and services in both mature and emerging markets, with a balance between profitability and sustainability. We must focus on exceeding customers' and employees' expectations, and improving their lives and their economic power in the short and long term. This calls for a radically different business philosophy. To thrive in this new world, leaders have to shift gears from selling to serving to leading.

But what does that mean?

In modern conventional terms, a business exists to sell products and services to customers. This is Microsoft at its start. The company came up with a new home computer operating system and marketed it to PC users to make their lives easier. Then Microsoft became bigger and richer and reached a position where it was able to give back, and it did. Today Microsoft gives back to the community; for example, it subsidizes regional public transportation to support the environment.[2]

And then there is the Google model. The company from its inception was born from an ideal. Google's vision has always been to change the world and make it a better place by giving internet users easier access to the plethora of information available online. The difference here comes from the words: "from its inception." Not that there is anything wrong in the way Bill Gates and Paul Allen built their company. They were trying to launch a successful business with their shared skills, which ultimately led to a revolution in the way we work. But this is not what Sergey Brin and Larry Page did with Google.

Google started as a Ph.D. student research project, and both founding students were interested in radical change from the beginning: with "a healthy disregard for the impossible,"[3] they imagined a much better way to search for information on the Internet and empower people's lives, and they succeeded in creating that. They would not put off philanthropy until they became rich. Their vision of the world always encompassed both philanthropy and business. They created a successful business, which gave birth soon after to a successful foundation, using not only donations from Google but also Google's search engine to make critical information available and help with global health issues such as genetic diseases or the flu, preservation of the world's forests via Google Earth, and response to natural disasters via Google Crisis.[4]

Google doesn't just sell advertising to brands and internet users. It serves its communities of users by making its search engine available for social causes, and it also leads by making business decisions such as not being present in the People's Republic of China if that meant censorship imposed on Google by the Chinese government.

Google understands how to do business and do good: Google sells, serves, and leads change, all at once. There are specific differences among these three ways of looking at business.

- *Selling* views business as a transaction: "I sell, you buy." *You deal with your life; I deal with my life.*
- *Serving* views business as a transaction and a means to compensate for inequalities: "I have more than you, and I help you to deal with hardship." It represents a form of solidarity.
- *Leading* views business as a function of life, part of an interconnected web of relationships: "You and I are living together on planet earth, we are interdependent and interconnected, so let's find a way to work together to make it a better place for everyone."

Today connectivity leads to transparency: with all the information available on the Internet, there is no longer a place for businesses to hide. This enables consumers to make more discriminating choices. Therefore companies need to approach consumers as equal members of their community, fully disclosing the values they stand for and what lives behind their brands and business. By the mere fact of technology and the nature of interactions in social media, power relationships between brands, customers, and companies have completely changed. It is obvious that we live in an interconnected world in which attempting to dominate relationships with customers who now have a wide range of product choices, information sources, and huge channels of influence would be simply foolish; it is like sailing against the winds and it is no longer the best way to invest in and build customers' loyalty. Companies that adopt this new philosophy will enjoy a new social and political status. They will be perceived by their consumers, employees, and business associates as political and social change agents: this creates stronger loyalty from and a better reputation with all of these audiences, which is all good for the bottom line. The twentieth-century model of serving, under which major companies would sponsor charity golf events or plant flowers in the local park, is no longer enough. Brands and companies need to position themselves as leaders in their communities and act as such. Community leaders envision the future, take proactive positions toward their vision, and through every decision and action are committed to bringing more value to the community for both short and long-term prosperity.

SEVENTH GENERATION: DOING WELL BY DOING GOOD

Some companies, like the cleaning product brand Seventh Generation, understood a long time ago that taking on a leadership role to bring change in society is an integral part of doing business. And in the process they did very well for themselves and their shareholders. Created in 1987, Seventh Generation, the leading U.S. brand of household products that respect human and environmental health, was for a long time a pioneer in corporate responsibility. Jeffrey Hollender, the founder, owner and CEO of the company up to 2009, said that his objective all along was "to do business in a way that had the most holistic positive impact on society and the planet."[5] He never wavered from his goal. Jeffrey's wife, Sheila Hollender, who was also part of the adventure, told me, "The first fifteen years were difficult because it was a hard sale to convince people that environmental abuse would affect them in all sorts of ways (health, animals, resources shortage, children's future). At the time, people felt they had other problems to deal with."[6]

The Hollenders' efforts paid off. In spite of competing with large companies that were not spending nearly as much, if anything at all, on sustainability (such as choice of supplies, selection of like minded vendors, environmental concerns, raw material extraction, product life cycles, recyclable packaging, and respect for employees), for ten years in a row between 2000 and 2009, Seventh Generation grew by 30 percent every year. And Jeffrey saw his success on another level as well: "It proved that very small companies competing against multibillion-dollar companies could convince consumers to adopt their products for the sake of a greater sense of purpose [and] offer people avenues to express their idealism and their commitment to causes larger than themselves." He added, "The trend toward social responsibility will affect all businesses sooner or later. We can either resist or proactively lead change: those who pretend it's not happening are the ones going out of business in the coming decade."

When Seventh Generation was founded in 1987, "sustainability" was a word rarely heard in business and represented a micro niche in the marketplace. It took courage, imagination, and a sense of moral obligation as much as an entrepreneurial spirit and significant business acumen for the Hollenders to start their company. But it's remarkable to see the actual cultural shift they have been an active part of, as well as the past, present, and future positive impacts of their actions. When they started, environmentally friendly home cleaning products were a rare find in the market. Today many other entrepreneurial brands compete in this market niche. Method, founded in 2001, in San Francisco, focuses on the lower-price-range market of household environmentally friendly products.[7] Caldrea and Mrs. Meyer's Clean Day, specializing in green products made with essential oils meant for high-end and lower-end markets, respectively, were both founded in 1999, in Minneapolis, Minnesota, by Monica Massif, daughter of Mrs. Thelma Meyer.[8] Today even a global company like SC Johnson follows this trend started by inspired entrepreneurs like Jeffrey and Sheila Hollender: the American giant acquired Caldrea Company and Mrs Meyer's Clean Day in 2008.[9] A company like Seventh Generation illustrates perfectly how shifting gears from selling to serving to leading is an effective solution. The approach the Hollenders irrevocably combined business success with a real concern for social (health) and environmental (pollution) issues.

Not only did they sell products and serve by giving back to their consumers via their non-profit organization, but they also lead change. They saw that they could have an impact by doing business, and they grabbed the opportunity.

The Hollenders' view of business is holistic. They decided to review every aspect of their business and make each one as compatible as possible with the sustainability of life: sourcing ingredients, respecting employee legislation, entering into partnerships with companies that would do the same, and so on. They not only focused on generating profit for shareholders and working for the necessary financial health of their company, they also committed to simultaneously producing sustainable value for all. Thanks to imagination, inspiration, and courage, they sold, they served, and they led a silent revolution.

GRAMEEN BANK: REINVENTING LENDING AND TURNING LEAD INTO GOLD

Grameen Bank is another organization that very successfully leads from a sense of purpose and responsibility and has changed the face of the financial world. The founder, Muhammad Yunus, received the Nobel Prize for Peace in 2006 for pioneering a financial institution that provides microcredit (small loans to poor people possessing no collateral) to help its clients establish creditworthiness and financial self-sufficiency.

The success of the Grameen model of microfinancing has inspired similar efforts in a hundred countries throughout the developing world and even in industrialized nations, including the United States. Many, but not all, microcredit projects also retain Grameen's emphasis on lending specifically to women. More than 94 percent of Grameen loans have gone to women, who suffer disproportionately from poverty and who are more likely than men to devote their earnings to their families. As of July 2007, Grameen Bank has issued US$6.38 billion to 7.4 million borrowers.[10] To ensure repayment, the bank uses a system of "solidarity groups." These small informal groups apply together for loans, and its members act as coguarantors of repayment and support one another's efforts at economic self-advancement.

Muhammad Yunus has shown himself to be a leader who managed to translate visions into practical action for the benefit of millions of people, not only in Bangladesh, where he started, but also in many other countries. Prior to the creation of Grameen Bank, loans to poor people without any financial security appeared to be an impossible idea. But from modest beginnings Yunus has proved that it is not only possible, but also lucrative. Ever since Grameen Bank came into being in 1983, it has made a profit every year except in 1983, 1991, and 1992. Grameen Bank made a profit of US$5.38 million in 2009 and declared a 30-percent cash dividend for the year. This is the highest cash dividend declared by any bank in Bangladesh in 2009.[11] And just as important, Yunus has developed microcredit into an important instrument in the struggle against poverty.

These examples may seem paradoxical to a traditional business mind, but they demonstrate that when business is thought of holistically and done holistically, it can be very successful and benefit everyone involved. It takes a real ability to see things differently and notice the unusual to identify new, creative and sensitive approaches, and it requires strong leadership by influence, because trailblazing requires us to give up control and to let an adventurous spirit lead the way. When you are able to not only sell high-quality products and services and give back to the community generously, but also see business as a necessary opportunity to lead change in society because our socioeconomic environment demands it, then magic can happen.

UNILEVER: INCLUDING THOSE LEFT BEHIND, AND DOING WELL IN BUSINESS

This shift from selling to serving to leading doesn't happen only when an organizations starts up, as we've seen with Google and Seventh Generation or in a non-profit organization like Grameen Bank. Some mainstream, for-profit, mature mega-organizations have also shifted gears into more collaborative and inclusive ways of doing business later in their existence. Unilever—the British-Dutch multinational corporation that owns many of the world's consumer product brands in foods, beverages, cleaning agents, and personal care products on sale in more than 170 countries—is a good example.[12] In 2007 Patrick Cescau, then Unilever chief executive, stated that sustainability is "the only game in town" and that the sustainability agenda offers an opportunity to get closer to customers.[13] That same year Unilever became the first tea company to commit to sourcing all its tea in a sustainable manner,[14] a commitment to sustainable agriculture initiated in 1998.[15]

What Unilever did in India is also remarkable. Recognizing both the specific needs and the huge potential of the rural poor market segment in India—estimated at US$4 billion in 2008—Hindustan Unilever Limited (HUL) launched Project Shakti in 2000–2001 as a pilot in fifty villages. The project is an innovative model for connecting with an underserved segment of a market in a deep and meaningful way. With Project Shakti, Unilever managed to improve individual awareness of health and hygiene issues, create income-generating opportunities for an underprivileged segment of the population, and foster the growth of the market for its products. Shakti empowers women in small rural villages across India to become direct-to-consumer distributors of a diverse range of Unilever products, including Lux and Lifebuoy soap, Wheel detergent, Lakme color cosmetics, and Brooke Bond tea.

Much as Avon and Mary Kay did in the United States in the twentieth century, HUL is providing women who haven't traditionally been a part of the workplace the opportunity to step into it and develop new skills as well as income. In addition to providing the women with microcredit for inventory purchases, HUL also provides sales training and, perhaps most important, self-esteem and status. Distributors typically earn between seven hundred and a thousand rupees a month through a combination of a discount on inventory purchases plus a trade margin. This income is a meaningful amount in a country where the majority of people earns less than twenty rupees per day and lives in extreme poverty. The project has grown to reach more than three million households in more than 135,000 Indian villages via the network of 45,000 entrepreneurs. The scope of the project has also expanded to include additional services such as i-Shakti, an internet-based rural information service network providing information on topics such as animal husbandry, hygiene, education, and women's empowerment, and Shakti Vani, a health education initiative. A mobile phone partnership is also under consideration. The success of Shakti has prompted Unilever to export core elements into other markets such as Vietnam, Bangladesh, and Sri Lanka. Project Joyeeta in Bangladesh and Project Saubaghya in Sri Lanka are now empowering Unilever to connect with consumers in rural areas not accessible by traditional mass media or distribution channels. With a large established organization, change can take the shape of pilot programs that, once proven, can easily be scaled to encompass much larger areas.

The business strategy of Unilever India illustrates well how selling can also be about serving people in need and leading change throughout an industry, a region or even multiple countries. So why wait, when some companies already do it and so many causes need to be handled? Businesses have so much power and so much flexibility in how they can use it. Companies are a reservoir of creativity and talent. Companies leading their industry and their communities with a sense of purpose will be the winners in the decades to come.

MATRIX: DOING BUSINESS FOR CHANGE

Matrix, a U.S. professional hair care brand that today belongs to L'Oréal, a world leader in the beauty industry, is also an interesting case of a business shifting gears from selling and serving to a desire to lead for universal change.

Matrix was founded in 1980 by an American husband-and-wife hairdressing team, Arnie and Sydell Miller. They originally set out to provide hairdressers with a comprehensive range of products that would help them take full advantage of their talent and creativity and improve their businesses. Arnie and Sydell created easy-to-understand, easy-to-use products to make hairdressers' lives more creative and productive.

They were all about empowering their peers. Their earnest desire to help was grounded in a strong belief in the power that hairdressers have to make people feel better and, by extension, to influence society positively. Hair is a big part of our inner sense of beauty, and going to the hairdresser involves a set of emotions and feelings around self-image and self-esteem that are deeper than we might think. In the Millers' candid attempt to help by approaching their business with a mindset of serving versus simply one of just selling, they reached a leading position in the U.S. market within ten years. Matrix kept its leadership position for nineteen uninterrupted years. Their approach, based on empowering and serving their customers, clearly worked from a purely financial standpoint.

Unfortunately, at the end of 1992 Arnie Miller passed away and in 1994 the company was sold to Bristol-Myers Squibb (BMS), a major pharmaceutical company headquartered in New York City. As innovative and successful as BMS has always been, they found that the integration of Matrix into their large corporation, which had no experience in the hair care product category, was not easy. In spite of the gradual shift from the original Matrix business strategy—focusing on serving artisanal hairdressers and supporting their craftsmanship—to the more traditional sales-driven strategy at BMS, Matrix managed to retain its leading place in the industry. However, in 2000 BMS sold Matrix to L'Oréal US to focus on its core competence: manufacturing and marketing pharmaceuticals products.

Although it made perfect strategic sense for L'Oréal to acquire Matrix to complement its brand portfolio, Matrix was again integrated into a culture that lived far from its own entrepreneurial origins. L'Oréal's culture is shaped by the pressure of feeding a large pipeline of products and successfully marketing them globally to meet very ambitious sales objectives. L'Oréal has been known for its double-digit growth over twenty-three consecutive years under the leadership of Sir Lindsay Owen Jones.[16] L'Oréal's strong marketing expertise and the power of their distribution kept Matrix afloat for three or four years. However, in 2006 the brand started to experience an ominous double-digit decline in sales. For a number of reasons (questionable management choices and lag time in understanding the DNA of the brand), sales kept plummeting at this same double-digit rate for three years. When Colin Walsh, an executive in his mid-thirties with beauty industry experience, took over in 2009 as president of Matrix in the United States, the brand had just lost its leading position in the U.S. market to Redken Fifth Avenue, another brand of L'Oréal.

To understand Matrix's sales decline, Colin asked himself a number of questions: *Why does Matrix exist? Why do we do what we do? How can we support our partner hairdressers and help the entire industry flourish?* He saw the bad performance of the brand as a clear wake-up call indicating that the departure from Arnie and Sydell's strong belief in and commitment to helping hairstylists was not a good move. He decided to go back to their passion-centric model and move away from the failing sales-driven approach. But, in Colin's own words, it was the "quantum reading of the new worldview" (that is, the yarn ball worldview) that demanded "shifting gears from selling to serving to leading" and reaching for the exchange of true value beyond the usual "costs less" and "lasts longer" promotional taglines. Matrix's business depends directly on a population of craftspeople, the hairdressers, who are driven by a passion for hairstyling rather than the growth of their bottom line alone. In other words, for Colin the goal was to embrace the holistic purpose of creating real value for hairstylists, enabling them to express their creative gifts and share them with their clients and the community at large.

To deepen Matrix's relationship with influential voices in the industry and to empower hairdressers and establish Matrix as a leading change agent of the hairstylists' community, Colin also decided to engage in an industry-wide initiative called Chairs of Change: a non-profit project designed to help hairdressers add value to the world through the magic of their craft. Beauty makes people happy and self-confident, and well-dressed hair is a great part of beauty. In the United States, says Colin, 90 percent of the population goes to a hair salon.[17] Hair salons represent an enormous social crossroads. They are a place for gathering, story telling, idea debating, and fun discussions, all motivated by a shared desire for more beautiful hair. In Colin's own words, "Chairs of Change is an initiative to celebrate the positive change hairdressers bring to our communities all around the country and move beyond the limiting transactional aspect of the business."

Chairs of Change was launched at the end of January 2011. In Colin's estimate, working on this project and involving Matrix partners and counterparts in the design and production of Chairs of Change has already transformed the nature of the relationship Matrix has with hairstylists, distributors, journalists, and anyone involved directly or indirectly with the hair care category. Conversations have deepened and moved from calculating sales and discounts or even discussing products to understanding the beliefs and values of the people behind the work. It has created space for profound alignment and trust, thanks to a deep respect for the passion of hairdressers. Colin sees this unique initiative as a way to provide a much larger and more committed base to the Matrix brand strategy he designed in 2009 and implemented in 2010, the results of which speak for themselves:

Numbers: In 2010 Matrix grew in the United States by 6 percent while the market as a whole declined by 1 percent.[18]

Team: Matrix's U.S. team is strong, highly committed, and energized by focusing on bringing value to the world even more than meeting sales objectives. The organization attracts people who work for value more than for money. They share in the yarn ball view of the world, in which business is not about dominance but about relationship.[19]

Leadership: Colin wakes up in the morning fueled by the idea that he helps hairdressers help their clients who help make the world a better place. Hairdressers inspire him. He enjoys seeing their lives and spending time in salons. "I don't go there to show up as the president of Matrix. I go there to understand their lives," says Colin. Doing so helps him understand how to fill the gaps and needs in their salons and make their lives better. His openness to new ideas and play keeps him equally energized.[20]

Corporate Impact: L'Oréal's leadership team is astute enough to deem Colin's holistic approach worthwhile. Obviously the results help build trust in his process, which is met, in his opinion, "with cautious optimism" yet freed of systematic opposition in the name of a linear financial logic. L'Oréal is well known for its organic and intuitive way of managing talent and projects. As Colin puts it, "I truly enjoy representing the organization with this new paradigm; it is being well understood and well received by senior management. There is definitely a growing awareness of the need for an elevated look at success in business; at L'Oréal that conviction is shared all the way to our most senior management. It really is . . . an exciting journey!"[21]

When I asked Colin about the future of business, his answer was clear.[22] He said he strongly believes that "people — a.k.a. consumers in the old worldview — seek consciously and subconsciously to exchange true value in life. This clearly reaches beyond the usual widgets and promotions, and requires authentic dialogues on which to build value-based relationships. The old transactional business paradigm is fraught with blazing fires burning on all fronts. It is socially, environmentally, culturally, and economically devastating to the world. It simply does not work anymore!"

The buying and selling of Matrix caused the holistic focus to disappear and caused the company to lose its leadership position on the market. L'Oréal had to shift gears to address this challenge. To achieve this, Colin decided to take on an original path, new to L'Oréal. He is not alone in his thinking. When we truly move from selling to serving to leading, we begin to see a multitude of cause-and-effect connections, and then we begin to see ever more ambitious and creative solutions just waiting to be pursued.

SUMMIT SERIES: AMBITION REINVENTED

In addition to these companies shifting gears into a new way of thinking about business, there are organizations that want to accelerate this shift by gathering thought leaders and inspired entrepreneurs to make an even bigger positive impact, using the power of connecting and helping people.

Summit Series is a community of young leaders who come together annually for three days designed to connect, inspire, and empower. The founders are a group of millennial entrepreneurs who gave up consumerism "to build a community of young dreamers." But they also are incredibly busy doers. They produce an annual conference where great minds and creative personalities — Bill Clinton and Ted Turner, among others — share the stage to inspire a group of young movers and shakers. When great minds meet, great things happen.

The group's mantra is "How can I help you?" They created an organization dedicated to helping make the world a better place by allowing people to share ideas that have the potential to be developed into world-changing achievements. There is one caveat, though. Conference attendance is by invitation only. Cofounder Jeff Rosenthal says he wants to curate a community that consists of people who do "truly awesome work" and who are very likeable on a personal level.

Summit Series believes that business is first about people — things done by some people for other people. Because of their truly altruistic spirit, they have infused a great sense of generosity and possibility throughout the conference. And it is supported by the way the conference is set up. Most of the exchange of ideas happens through panels of experts and conference participants who interact with the rest of the participants. There are very few plenary sessions where the speaker talks to the audience without constant interaction. And even during these more formal presentations, they also often open questions to the floor. This creates a great sense of equality. During breaks people connect with one another. It is not about networking in the traditional business sense of the word; it is about cocreating and cofacilitating a global shift. Any person you meet there may have the solution or the connection you need to help your ideas or project move forward. Conversations move fast, ideas fuse, and changes happen, all in a light, friendly, inclusive, and fun atmosphere. Rosenthal notes that a large part of building community is about "creating mutually beneficial connections between Summit Series friends." He takes it upon himself to personally "connect people who can help grow each others businesses, work on projects together, share knowledge, or simply just become good friends."

The Summit Series founders feel that their generation is facing unprecedented challenges, but also that they have more power and influence than ever. They understand that today corporations are more influential than governments. The decisions of the U.S. president directly influences three hundred million people in one region of the world and indirectly many more, but a company like Procter & Gamble, with three hundred brands and a plethora of products and advertising messages, directly touches 3.5 billion individuals in more than 180 countries around the globe.[23] The U.S. president stays in office four or eight years and is constrained by Congress, which can oppose presidential actions and undo previous laws; conversely, for example, Google founders Sergey Brin and Larry Page, in leading Google for more than thirteen years, not only have made life easier for billions of individuals but also have played a significant economic, social, and political role on many levels, from reshaping the advertising industry to influencing regulations on the Internet and expressing public positions in China. This kind of situation is one reason that Summit Series is in close contact with the business world, the non-profit community, and political institutions alike. This puts them in a position to facilitate multiple "mutually beneficial connections"[24] between all these different communities, which otherwise would not necessarily spend the time to exchange ideas and enrich each other.

Their "How can I help you?" philosophy is very efficient. In less than two years they have raised $2,000,000 for non-profits and charities through events for economic and social causes. For instance, in 2009 one event raised $200,000 for the United Nations Foundation in a single night, and in June 2010 an event at the home of hip-hop mogul Russell Simmons raised $265,000 for Clinton's Global Initiative Foundation.[25] More important, Summit Series has connected and keeps connecting the top business minds in the world with some of the best non-profits, helping them operate more effectively, create movements, build websites, and shoot movies about their causes. They've established innumerable connections between inspired and powerful change agents. In 2010 Sean Parker, cofounder of Napster and founding president of Facebook, was introduced to Spotify, a digital music service that gives internet users access to millions of songs. He later decided to make an important investment and joined their board.[26] Qwiki, a video-based type of encyclopedia (a "Wikipedia meets YouTube" digital destination), was founded at Summit Series thanks to crucial meetings facilitated by the Summit Series executive team, which enabled the launch of this digital start-up.[27]

What's interesting is that this group represents the aspirations of a whole generation and a life philosophy shared by many, as the exponential growth of their audience shows. Since its inception in 2008, the number of Summit Series attendees has moved from twenty to approximately a thousand participants in April 2011.[28] What's remarkable is that they've achieved this through word of mouth. No marketing and no social media presence so far. "It is soon!" said Summit Series founder Elliott Bisnow when I asked him whether they had a Facebook page—an interesting position for someone who belongs to a generation said to be about immediacy and instantaneous satisfaction. Elliott and his friends believe in organic growth and random possibilities. Everything in the group is thought out to remove unnecessary hierarchy and regulations. Summit Series has become so financially successful that Elliott felt comfortable in January 2010 leaving the day-to-day operations of his original digital media business to his father and CEO, Ryan Begelman. He then followed his inspiration and dedicated his time to his community of innovators and thought leaders to effect positive change: an inspiration that seems to be shared by an ever-growing number of people in his age group.[29]

THE MILLENNIAL GENERATION: BORN INTO A NONLINEAR WORLD

It is clear that the millennial generation operates with different values than those held by preceding generations. The so-called millennial generation, born between 1978 and 1999, also called Generation Y or the Net Generation, is the first generation to use e-mail, instant messaging (IM), and cell phones and to have access since childhood or adolescence to a world without boundaries or hierarchy that transcends space and time: the Internet.

In the United States alone, millennials number eighty million people. As many millennials have entered the workforce and have come to represent an important share of the market, it is necessary to integrate what motivates them both as customers and employees in marketing and HR strategies. According to experts, these are six of the main characteristics of millennials:

- They are about teamwork and cooperation.
- Their loyalty depends on relationships more than it depends on the name of their employer.
- They say time and flexibility are the most important motivators a company can grant them, the second being benefits and money.
- They are pragmatic idealists seeking to make a difference.
- They value education not for status but for the knowledge that they can leverage to act responsibly and significantly.
- They look for authentic products and experiences.[30]

In addition, the values that are out of touch for them are the values praised in the past decade: high power and dominance, extreme individualism, and conspicuous consumption. This has a direct impact on their purchase habits; how they shop, what they expect from their retail experience, and how they respond to advertising. Their appreciation of teamwork and cooperation is meaningful, as both are underpinnings of the yarn ball worldview. With the high connectivity of the

Internet and the globally focused world they were born into, the millennials have integrated interconnectedness and the interdependence of life and people into their perception of the world.

Experts say that no other generation has ever mentioned time and flexibility among their first three motivators. Millennials' approach to life is more personal and subjective and takes precedence over what we would see as the rule of the game: money. They have reconceptualized money; it is for them just one currency among many that are available to get them the things and experiences that they value. For example, in the preceding list, millennials say that time and flexibility are more important than money when seeking employment. Time and flexibility are currencies to be weighed in the same way as money when they think about compensation for their work. Moreover, their loyalty depends more on the subjectivity of human relationships than on the factual reality of a company; this is a group who can appreciate the intangible and unconscious dynamics of relationships, work, and life. Last but not least, the old worldview of the pyramid is obviously wearing out for them, which is a sign that it has outlived its purpose.

All of this to say that companies, business schools, and corporate training programs should take the characteristics of millennials into close consideration. The western educational system places more value on the old paradigm than on the new expectations and behaviors of this emerging group, even though, as we've seen through countless examples in this book, the old paradigm is no longer the best way to operate, either to engage consumers and employees or to train upcoming executives.

THE FUTURE OF EDUCATION AND BUSINESS

Our socioeconomic context demands new ways of understanding human intelligence and new ways of relating with life and nature. This should be taught from the youngest age, not only in pilot programs and schools for the societal elite but also in large programs offered to all children in the country. With this educational foundation, children will be better prepared to become leaders operating from a framework of influence where the creative process is understood, ecosystems are honored, and businesses missions revolve around a strong sense of purpose to bring about change for the betterment and growth of all.

The director of the Max Planck Institute in Berlin, Gerd Gigerenzer, wrote that "our educational systems place value on everything but the art of intuition." I believe this is bound to change. A former special education pilot program in the United States reveals how Intuitive Intelligence can be fostered from a young age. It was an experiment designed for children with Asperger syndrome, an autism spectrum disorder characterized by widespread abnormalities in social interactions and communication, restricted interests, and repetitive behaviors. The curriculum was a rare initiative developed by a group of psychologists in collaboration with medical doctors from one of the most prestigious universities in the United States.[31] It was designed to help kids with special needs by using an innovative pedagogy, although it was also envisioned from the beginning as a useful model to instigate change in our general education system. Unfortunately, it ended after one year because the main donor to the program withdrew his participation following the September 2008 financial crash.

Kids in the program were taught that they learn not only through rational thinking but also with their five senses, through movement and observation and, equally important, at their own pace. They were offered yoga and theater classes. The teaching environment was comforting, and students could leave the classroom to go to a side room any time they wished to be alone, listen to music on their iPod, or just be silent. No homework was assigned. Students were taught in a way that would increase their capabilities, strengthen their faculties, and lessen their difficulties. Teachers centered their educational approach on individual children's needs. They respected each child's specific learning rhythms, took advantage of their passions, and made the most of their unique creative associations between unrelated subjects. Even though the pilot program lasted only one year, those who did participate got a lot out of it and progressed rapidly. The mother of one student said that her son was "calmer and more balanced." She added, "He has recognized something like a special aptitude in himself and has established contact with parts of himself he never would have without the program."

What is stunning to me is how much the program revolved around an understanding of intelligence that was so inclusive of the requirements of the southwest quadrant of the Intuitive Compass (play, improvisation, an environment conducive of creativity, integrating complexity, leveraging paradox and exceptions) and so close to the concept of Intuitive Intelligence and its four tenets, both in the way they thought out the program and the way they approached kids' intelligence: holistic thinking, paradoxical thinking, noticing the unusual, and leading by influence.

Other schools help the new generation see the world and think about its evolution on very different terms. Competition and ambition are better served by putting energy into collaboration and generosity rather than focusing on the elimination of the weakest. Developing kids' intelligence can be handled in ways that simultaneously foster creativity and adaptability, individuality and autonomy, interdependence and excellence.

One such institution is a private preparatory school called the Centre Madeleine Daniélou in Rueil Malmaison, a city neighboring Paris. The Centre serves students coming out of senior high school who aspire to enter a French business school. The French educational system has a history of elitism and competitiveness unlike any in the rest of Europe. Preparatory schools put a lot of pressure on students aged seventeen to twenty; they are expected to work very hard to get into the business schools. But the Centre is a remarkable exception.

The Centre was born out of the vision of Madeleine Daniélou, a highly educated woman who, at the beginning of the twentieth century, wished to offer young French girls an opportunity to receive a quality education at a time when access to education was still quite limited for everyone, much less for girls. In 1986, following the same humanistic inspiration, the Centre opened a preparatory school where students of both genders study together to enter the best European business schools.

In this school, success is defined as the ability of students to find their own "individual creative impulse" and their ability to socialize with their fellow students just as much as it is about succeeding in entering the business school they wish to attend. Teaching programs focus on transmitting knowledge with the same search for excellence they dedicate to fostering individuals' spiritual and human growth. Although in the end the national examination required for entry to business school is highly competitive by its very nature, the experience that the Centre offers to students as they work toward taking it is anything but competitive. Students work together and are expected to support each other. As with the Three Musketeers, the unlikely motto of the prep school is "All for One, One for All." It is all about self-monitoring and self-discipline to hone a sense of responsibility toward oneself and others. When students reach the final month before the national examination, they work in trios so that there is always one out of the three to pick up the morale of his or her comrades and help keep everyone engaged in their intense study.

The results are exceptional and keep getting better over the years. In fact, the Centre shows the best results of all preparatory schools in France. The director, Mrs. Manuela Rousselot, takes great pride in this, but also notes that while they do strive for excellence, "this should not be confused with the academic success of students. We do not limit the evaluation of our pedagogical work to tangible results. There is more to a human being than what's visible and quantifiable."[32]

The Centre is a perfect example of a high-functioning teaching institution based on a spirit of collaboration and respect for every individual. The Centre does not compete to produce only tangible results, yet it manifests the best of what every student has to offer and discover for himself. It also prepares each student to engage creatively in a world in deep transition and do so with a true disposition toward caring for others and the world in which they live. This great paradox in the world of French educational elitism has been made possible by a holistic approach to education, encompassing the less tangible yet much more potent dimensions of human development.

NURTURING INTELLIGENCE IN ALTERNATIVE WAYS

Although there are very few schools that offer alternative forms of education, the few that do exist are having fantastic results. The good news is that many other innovations in education are well on their way and that our approach to human intelligence has evolved. But we need to keep working at it, especially in the field of business education and corporate training. Business has to be results oriented, but efficiency is still too often understood in linear and isolated financial terms. We need a new approach and a new model of reference to enrich creative problem solving, deepen decision making, and empower a new leadership mindset. Education with a new approach to human intelligence can play a crucial role.

Although Intuitive Intelligence is not a new type of intelligence, it is a different way to organize and use what we already know, what we are already capable of doing and sensing. It makes use of our inherent abilities and aptitudes in the tasks of creative problem solving and decision making. The originality of Intuitive Intelligence, however, comes from a new understanding of the respective roles of instinct in rational decision making, and play in creativity and efficiency. Intuitive Intelligence activates the profound, yet often intangible, interactions between instinct and play represented by the southwest quadrant of the Intuitive Compass. It operates from a different worldview, one that logic alone cannot perceive.

Culturally we focus on the tangible aspects of the world and look at it through a logical and conscious lens. We simplify the world and reduce our experience to make sense of it. This is certainly practical (we can name things, share our experiences, and express ideas through a common language) and reassuring (we can make sense of what we see and what happens to us). But this simplification of perception limits our creative problem-solving capacity and no longer suffices to help us to succeed in the world in which we now live. The world we live in requires collaboration and inclusiveness. It requires us to go past what we see and aim deeper than the material outcome we seek. Today we live in a new economic environment that reflects a new paradigm. It is time to adapt the way we do business and live our lives, if we want to be successful in the new world that is already here.

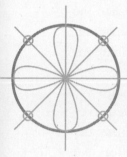 epilogue

The whole idea of compassion is based on a keen awareness of the interdependence of all these living beings, which are all part of one another, and all involved in one another.
—THOMAS MERTON

N ow that we have reached the end of our journey, some of you may ask yourselves *What should I do next? What should I be careful about when applying this new approach to my business?*

My advice to any executive who has decided to take on this accelerated path to innovation and sustainable growth is to resist the temptation to systematically seek immediate financial results and short-term solutions. The Intuitive Compass does deliver very actionable and highly profitable solutions. But to make best use of the Intuitive Compass, to go beyond business as usual, and to reach truly innovative solutions, you need to shift your focus from financial profitability to sustainable value creation. The financial logic is exact but not very conducive to imagination. The concept of sustainable value opens our business reflections and strategies to new horizons. To make deeper and better decisions, you need imagination, patience, an open mind, and tolerance for ambiguity and confusion.

This calls for a new awareness. It requires us to balance our faith in logic with the secular wisdom of instinct. In doing so, we will need to tap into our intuition, an attribute of the feminine part of our psyche. Intuition opens up new possibilities to feed the masculine part in us, which is ruled and often restricted by the logical mind. And that is the message of the Intuitive Compass: anything is possible when the feminine and masculine energies join to cooperate creatively and point our attention to the southwest quadrant, where improbable solutions can come to our rescue.

In our post-modern age we are still not used to the discomfort of the unknown, the demands of the feminine, and the fact that we are not in control. But with determination, courage, and faith we can surrender to another belief system, one that enables us to overcome our fear and escape the deadening impact of our need for control. As is the case with any creative journey, we have no guarantee of success, and no one can show us the way, because the way is unique for each one of us. But we can receive guidance from the part of ourselves that knows better—the intuitive voice of feminine wisdom—and finally find our way out of control mode into a novel clarity and a deeper relationship with life.

Just as it always is for the mythical hero, the path we're facing is filled with challenges and unknown factors. However, we can choose to look at these challenges as parts of a creative process: the process of evolution. And we can rely on the Intuitive Compass to help us with decision making and creative problem solving in these unpredictable times. The southwest quadrant, in careful balance and synergy with the other three quadrants, will provide unexpected creative answers, which will feel like magic to us because we cannot always explain them. In this particular time of many unprecedented challenges we have a unique opportunity to engage and be taught in new ways.

As we have seen in this book, successful real-life examples in the business world prove there is a plausible route beyond conventional logic. This will always require a leap of faith, but the leap can be an edu-cated one. We need to rethink the way we think. We need to reinitialize our thinking program in light of a new scientific understanding of the power of instinct and play and the quantum laws of matter, which show the paradox of our limited individuality within the holistic force of our interdependence and an unlimited number of possibilities. In this new worldview, power has to be reconsidered, money deconstructed and reconstructed into its real purpose: the prosperity of all. We're called to move on. No time to waste. A new generation is already there, and we can all do it. Together we can create a more meaningful, more prosperous, and more balanced world. It requires some adjustments and faith, but it is possible.

The Lakota people have a saying: "It is not about peace on earth but peace with earth." When we observe nature, we see how everything and everyone in nature contributes to the whole; that nothing can exist without the others; that conflict, tension, destruction, complexity, and mystery are also part of it; and that the sum of it all is the most mystifying system we could ever imagine and learn from.

decoding your intuitive compass for decision making

Now that you have learned all about the Intuitive Compass and Intuitive Intelligence, and you understand the powerful outcomes that businesses can accomplish when all four quadrants of the compass are in balance and working synergistically, you are in a good position to evaluate the questionnaire on decision making that you completed at the beginning of this book. If you have not yet completed the questionnaire, now is the time to do it!

Once you have your score for each quadrant of your Intuitive Compass, you can proceed to decode them. Your score for each quadrant will be between 1 and 5. A low score would be 1 or 2, a high score would be 4 or 5. Remember that this Intuitive Compass is specifically about your decision-making skills; if you did an Intuitive Compass on another topic — for example, new business development or product development — your scores might be different. Also, if you were to complete the very same questionnaire on decision making six months from now, your scores might be different. The Intuitive Compass is a snapshot in time; it gives you feedback for exactly where you are in a given moment in regard to a specific topic.

The following explanations for each quadrant should feel familiar by this point. In each I summarize the implications of a high or low score and what the score can tell you about your strengths, as well as indications about areas where you may want to further develop your capabilities and some suggestions for how you might do that.

NORTHEAST QUADRANT

In this quadrant you can see how analytical and methodical you are about making a decision, how focused you are on getting the results you want, how you manage the time you have, and how you organize your environment and your resources to come to the best decision. A high score in the northeast quadrant means there is a high level of logical thinking and organization involved in your decision making; it shows your determination in the decision-making process and how well your organizational skills are mobilized for this. Conversely, a low score means that for you the process of decision making does not follow a logical scheme. When circumstances call for swift, insightful or instinctual ways of making a decision—a capacity very much associated with the southeast quadrant—then little organization makes sense and being methodical is not relevant. But a low score under regular business circumstances means you would benefit from adopting a more rational and methodical approach to optimize your process of decision making. You may want to talk to a friend who makes good business decisions and manages his or her time, environment, data, and thoughts well.

SOUTHEAST QUADRANT

In the southeast quadrant, you get feedback on three aspects of your approach to the decision-making process: your level of commitment to doing whatever it takes to make a decision, regardless of how challenging it may be; your degree of clarity about the possible outcomes of your decision; and finally, your determination to make the best decision possible. A high score indicates a clear sense of about two or three of these aspects. A low score indicates a lack of commitment to making a decision and/or making the best one, and/or a lack of evaluation of the potential outcome of your decision. Depending on what you seek or have to achieve with your decision making you may want to analyze and try to understand why you're not more committed. In your analysis you may want to question whether your approach serves you well in your life; if it does not, consider how you can reframe your approach and empower yourself to be more committed when making decisions. You may also want to spend time reflecting on the potential desired outcome of your decision so that you become more motivated to achieve it. A lack of determination to make a decision may be the result of a desire to avoid dealing with certain feelings: discomfort, pain, fear, and so on. This is why if you have a low southeast score you may want to put it in perspective with your southwest score and look for a correlation between the two low scores as the potential reason for your low score in the southeast quadrant. Compare both scores in the southeast and the southwest. If they are both low it means that whether it is about being efficient and getting results or whether it is about play and free flow it is hard for you to commit beyond what's logical. You may consider looking into your ability to trust and examining whether you have underlying trust issues when making a particular decision or making decisions in general. If it is the first case (trust issue around a particular decision), you may want to review the circumstances around this decision and the consequences of this decision. Try to evaluate whether these are significant enough to justify your low score. If it is the second case (a trust issue around making decisions in general), you may want to either discuss it with a good friend whom you consider grounded and perspicacious or talk about it with a professional coach.

NORTHWEST QUADRANT

The northwest quadrant tells you about your openness to new perspectives and to the various options available to you in the process of making a decision. It also gives feedback on your willingness to analyze and reflect on your expectations about the potential outcome of your decision. If your score is low, chances are it will be difficult for you to evaluate precisely how successful your decision was, how successful it could have been, or what it is that you gained from the fact that you made a decision, because you don't have clear expectations. If, however, you made a decision with a clear strategy, chances are it will be easier for you to accept the outcome of your decision no matter what. Even more important, it will be easier to improve your decision-making process, thereby increasing your satisfaction with the potential outcome. This is because the clearer you are about what you wish to achieve and the path to it, the more flexible and open to improvisation you can be in the process of getting there—and the more prepared you are to accept the outcome of your decision, because it was planned out and thought out rather than random and thoughtless. It is much easier to accept failure after you have strategically thought out a decision than it is when you did not do your homework; in the latter case, playing the victim of circumstances can be an easy copout yet completely disempowering. Moreover, a lack of clarity about making a decision will induce a lack of openness, which in turn will inhibit you from exploring various options for decision making and different motivations to commit to making the decision. A high score in the northwest means that you have clarity about your expectations and an open disposition to new ideas and discoveries about your decision making process, your ideas and your beliefs. A high score in the northwest combined with a high score in the southeast will further optimize your chances of making the best decision.

SOUTHWEST QUADRANT

The southwest quadrant shows your ability to be comfortable while making a decision even when circumstances are uncertain and require you to explore beyond the bounds of logic and let go of mental control over the process. This quadrant is key in approaching creative decisions, as these often require either subjective evaluations or estimations beyond what we know and what is logical. Such questions ask for another type of decision-making process: using our intuition to explore our gut feelings and tolerate the unknown. A high score indicates that you are comfortable making decisions with what many people might consider incomplete data points, or in situations where there are apparently conflicting data. If you have a high score here, you probably can tolerate a high level of ambiguity, and you may very well pursue potential solutions in unusual ways; for example, by looking for inspiration outside of the immediate context of the issue at hand. There's a potential downside to a high score in the southwest: if it is not balanced by high scores in the northwest (where you connect great ideas to actionable strategies and plans) or the southeast (where you put those plans into action and turn them into concrete results), your imaginative, intuitive ideas may never see the light of day or at the least, may not realize their greatest potential. Conversely, a low score indicates that you could benefit from a more experimental approach when you make a decision. It would probably be useful for you to reflect on how you might trust more—within the thresholds of integrity and prudence—when encountering new situations. You may want to improve your tolerance for confusion and try developing a sense of playfulness that will enable you to explore your decisions more easily and enrich the process. If your score in the southwest quadrant is low, you may also want to reflect on how southwest capabilities have become key to making successful decisions in today's economic environment. Of course, you need to consider your southwest score in relationship to your scores in the other three quadrants, as optimum results and the deepest breakthroughs will be gained when the scores in all four quadrants are high and are therefore in balance with one other.

Please visit www.theintuitivecompass.com to try out a longer questionnaire; in it, you'll find results tailored to your combination of results. You can also download on your iPhone, iPodTouch, or iPad the Intuitive Compass app or visit www.facebook.com/intuitivecompass to take a quiz and compare results with friends.

WEB

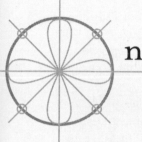

notes

INTRODUCTION

1 Po Bronson and Ashley Merryman, "The Creativity Crisis," *Newsweek*, July 10, 2010, http://www.newsweek.com/2010/07/10/the-creativity-crisis.html

2 MIT Picower Institute for Learning and Memory, *Journal Nature*, February 24 2005.

3 Rochester University, New York, neuroscience research, *Journal Nature*, October 6, 2004.

4 In Stuart Brown, *Play: How It Shapes the Brain, Opens the Imagination and Invigorates the Soul* (New York: Avery-Penguin Books, 2009).

5 Albert Einstein, The Born-Einstein Letters; Correspondence Between Albert Einstein and Max and Hedwig Born from 1916 to 1955 (New York: Walker, 1971).

CHAPTER 1

1 This was the observation of Constantin Stanislavski, who formulated the exercise as part of his renowned system for teaching the dramatic arts

2 George Leonard, *The Silent Pulse: A Search for the Perfect Rhythm That Exists in Each of Us,* rev. ed. (Layton, UT: Gibbs Smith, 2006).

3 Jill Bolte Taylor, "How It Feels to Have a Stroke," TED conference in Long Beach, California, February 2008.

4 Joanna Barsh, Marla M. Capozzi, and Jonathan Davidson, "Leadership and Innovation," January 2008. McKinsey & Company, http://www.mckinsey.com/About_us.aspx

5 Emily Anthes, "6 Ways to Boost Brain Power," *Scientific American Mind*, December 2010.

6 National Institute for Play (NIFP) website, www.NIFplay.org

7 J. Huizinga, *Homo Ludens: A Study of the Play-Element in Culture* (Boston: Beacon Press, 1955).

8 Ibid.

9 Dr. Stuart Brown, www.NIFplay.org

10 Erika Christakis and Nicholas Christakis, "Want to Get Your Kids into College? Let Them Play," special to CNN, December 29, 2010.

11 Marc Bekoff and John Byers, eds., *Animal Play: Evolutionary, Comparative, and Ecological Perspectives* (New York: Cambridge University Press, 1988).

12 Dr. Stuart Brown, www.NIFplay.org

13 Jane McGonigal presentation, Technology, Entertainment, Design (TED), February 2010. TED, which stands for Technology, Entertainment, Design, is a nonprofit organization founded in 1984 that is devoted to "Ideas Worth Spreading."

14 The actual name of this company and certain characteristics have been changed to protect the client's confidentiality.

15 Peter Andrews, "Five Barriers to Innovation: Key Questions and Answers." *Executive Technology Report*, 2006, http://www-935.ibm.com/services/uk/igs/pdf/g510-6342-00-5barriers-etr.pdf

16 Jane McGonigal presentation to TED, 2010.

17 Stuart Brown, *Play* (see introduction, n. 4).

18 2010 IBM Global CEO Study series, http://www-935.ibm.com/services/us/ceo/ceostudy2010/

19 Marian Cleeves Diamond, Response of the Brain to Enrichment, New Horizons for Learning, 2001, http://www.marthalakecov.org/~building/neuro/diamond_brain_response.htm

20 Hayagreeva Rao, Robert Sutton, and Allen P. Webb, "Innovation Lessons from Pixar: An Interview with Oscar-Winning Director Brad Bird." *McKinsey Quarterly*, April 2008, p. 3.

21 Ibid.

22 Amdocs corporate website, http://www.amdocs.com/Vision/AOI/Pages/Amdocs-Open-Innovation.aspx.

23 Paul Sloane, "Inside a Corporate Innovation Camp." *Bloomberg Businessweek*, June 30, 2010, http://www.businessweek.com/innovate/content/jun2010/id20100628_117088.htm

24 Ibid.

CHAPTER 2

1 Such as Columbia University professor William Duggan's book *Strategic Intuition: The Spark in Human Achievement* (New York: Columbia University Press, 2007).

2 All numbers, facts, and statistics in this section are taken from the presentation given by Jean René Fourtou to HEC MBA students at HEC Visions of Leadership on April 15, 2008, which the author attended and contributed to.

3 Fortune 500 final list for 2010.

4 In function, ESP is dissimilar to the ordinary senses; that is, it is independent of the other five senses and such factors as geography, time, intelligence, age, or education. Also, psychical research does support the theory that everyone is born with ESP capability, though some may possess more than others. As found in a survey of Americans published in 1987 by the University of Chicago's National Opinion Research Council, most of the respondents have experienced ESP at least once in their lives (67 percent as adults). However, eleven years earlier the figure was found to be 58 percent (Guiley, 1991), which indicates an increased acceptance of the possibility of ESP among the general public. In Regi Rakshit Negi, "Role of Extra Sensory Perception (ESP) in Managerial Decision Making," *African Journal of Business Management,* November 4, 2010, 4(15), p. 3232–3237, http://www.academicjournals.org/AJBM

5 Douglas Dean and John Mihalasky, *ESP Executive* (New York: Prentice-Hall, 1974).

6 Dean and Mihalasky used a thirty-item test that assesses six information-processing modes and leads to a classification of rational or intuitive.

7 Dean and Mihalasky, *ESP Executive.*

8 Global Management Strategies executive, interview with the author, February 16, 2009.

9 François Dalle, *L'Aventure L'Oréal* (Paris: Editions Odile Jacob, 2001).

10 http://creatingminds.org.

11   The study was conducted by American professor Weston H. Agor, author
     of *The Logic of Intuition: How Top Executives Make Important Decisions*
     (Westport, CT: Quorum Books, 1986).
12   Ibid.
13   Jagdish Parikh, Alden Lank, and Friedrich Neubauer, *Intuition: The New
     Frontier of Management* (Hoboken, NJ: Wiley-Blackwell, 1994).
14   Benedict Carey, "In Battle Hunches Prove to Be Valuable," *New York
     Times* Research section, July 27, 2009.
15   Ibid.
16   C. A. Morgan, S. Wang, S. M. Southwick, A. Rasmusson, G. Hazlett,
     R. L. Hauger, and D. S. Charney, "Plasma neuropeptide-Y concentrations
     in humans exposed to military survival training." U.S. National Library
     of Medicine National Institutes of Health Biology Psychiatry, May 2000.
     From the National Center for PTSD, VA Connecticut Healthcare Systems,
     West Haven, CT.
17   A. R. Damasio, *The Feeling of What Happens: Emotion, Reason and the
     Human Brain* (Cambridge, MA: MIT Press, 1994).
18   Carey, "In Battle Hunches Prove to Be Valuable."
19   "Stuart Brown Says Play Is More Than Fun," May 2008, TED,
     http://www.ted.com/talks/stuart_brown_says_play_is_more_than_fun_
     it_s_vital.html
20   Friedrich A. Hayek, epigraph in Gerd Gigerenzer, *Gut Feelings: The
     Intelligence of the Unconscious* (New York: Penguin Books, 2007), p. 54.
21   The term *reptilian complex* derives from the fact that comparative neu-
     roanatomists once believed that the forebrains of reptiles and birds were
     dominated by the basal ganglia, structures derived from the floor of the
     forebrain during development.
22   Damasio, *The Feeling of What Happens*.
23   Warren Bennis, *On Becoming a Leader: The Leadership Classic*, rev. ed.
     (New York: Basic Books, 2003).
24   Weston H. Agor, *The Logic of Intuitive Decision Making: A Research-Based
     Approach for Top Management* (Westport, CT: Quorum Books, 1986).
25   Dr. Jonas Salk, *Anatomy of Reality: Merging of Intuition and Reason*
     (Westport, CT: Praeger Publishers, 1984).
26   Gigerenzer, *Gut Feelings*.
27   Murray Gell-Mann, winner of the Nobel Prize in Physics, at TED presen-
     tation in March 2007.
28   Carey, "In Battle Hunches Prove to Be Valuable" (see chap. 1, n. 14).
29   PLoS ONE, http://www.plosone.org/home.action
30   Ibid.

31 Ibid. "These results challenge 'the conventional wisdom' that placebo effects require 'intentional ignorance.' [29] Our data suggest that harnessing placebo effects without deception is possible in the context of 1) an accurate description of what is known about placebo effects, 2) encouragement to suspend disbelief, 3) instructions that foster a positive but realistic expectancy, and 4) directions to adhere to the medical ritual of pill taking. It is likely our study also benefited from ongoing media attention giving credence to powerful placebo effects."

32 *Scientific American Frontiers,* PBS, http://www.pbs.org/saf/1307/features/kaptchuk.htm

33 For a definition, visit http://www.businessdictionary.com/definition/emerging-economies.html. For a list of primary and secondary emerging economies, visit http://en.wikipedia.org/wiki/Emerging_economies

34 "In 2006 U.S. gross domestic product (GDP) equaled 13,245 billion US dollars and China's 2,682. In 2010, US GDP become 14,535 and China's 8,133. In 2020, forecast is: 17,978 (US), 12,630 (China). In 2030 the order is said to reverse: 25,610 (China) 22,817(US). Finally BRIC countries cumulative GDP was twice the size of Germany's in 2006 and almost three times in 2010; it is said to be more than four and a half times superior to Germany's in 2020." International Monetary Fund and the CIA World Factbook.

35 IBM Institute for Business Value, "The Future of the Consumer Products Industry," July 2010.

36 National Institute for Play, NIFplay.org

37 http://en.wikipedia.org/wiki/Information_worker

38 Foursquare is a web and mobile application that allows people to upload information about where they are at any particular moment—for example, at a restaurant or a store. These "check-ins" can be reported in Facebook and Twitter accounts.

39 http://ecommerce-news.internetretailer.com/http://isisaccreditation.imrg.org

40 Freer Speckley, Social Audit. Speckley is a consultant and researcher in development and social economy at Beechwood college in the UK.

41 Adam Werbach, *Strategy for Sustainability* (Cambridge, MA: Harvard Business Press, 2009). Werbach is chief sustainability officer of Saatchi and Saatchi.

CHAPTER 3

1 For example, alternative kinds of intelligence are now acknowledged through the work of psychologists including Harvard University professor

Howard Gardener, who offers his theory of multiple intelligence, and *New York Times* science journalist Daniel Goleman, who has written two books on the subject: *Emotional Intelligence* (Bantam, 1997), and *Social Intelligence* (Bantam, 2007).

2 Marius V. Peelen, Li Fei-Fei, and Sabine Kastner, "Neural Mechanisms of Rapid Natural Scene Categorization in Human Visual Cortex," *Nature*, June 7, 2009.

3 This study was referred to in Carey, "In Battle Hunches Prove to Be Valuable" (see ch. 2, n. 14). This section is based on her article.

4 Gerd Gigerenzer, *Gut Feelings: The Intelligence of Our Unconscious* (New York: Penguin Books, 2007), 86.

5 In his book *Gut Feelings*, Dr. Gerd Gigerenzer gives the following as the number of possibilities to choose from: 300×10^{30}, or 30000000000 000000000000000000000000000000000000000000000000000000000000 0000000.

6 David Victoroff, "La Faute de Kerviel," October 13, 2010, www. valeursactuelles.com

7 Kerviel was convicted October 5, 2010 (rfi.fr Radio France Internationale).

8 Arie de Geus, *In the Living Company: Growth, Learning, and Longevity in Business*, rev. ed. (Boston: Nicholas Brealey Publishing, 1999).

9 K. Subhadra, under the direction of S. Dutta, 3M's Organizational Culture, ICFAI Center for Management Research (ICMR), Hyderabad, India, 2003.

10 David A. Vise and Mark Malseed, *The Google Story* (New York: Delacorte Press, 2005), p. 7.

11 Paul Sloane, "Inside a Corporate Innovation Camp," *Bloomberg Businessweek*, June 30, 2010.

12 "Deep Dive," ABC *Nightline*, July 13, 1999.

13 Maud Brottier, head of training, Louis Vuitton, Paris, interview with the author, June 30, 2010.

14 Interview by Arupa Tesolin, http://www.selfgrowth.com/articles/Igniting _the_Creative_Spark_at_Cirque_du_Soleil.html. Lyn Heward is also the author of a recent book *The Spark: Igniting the Creative Fire that Lives Within Us All* (New York: Random House, 2006).

15 Mango 2009 corporate report.

16 In "Mango la Tornade Espagnole" L'Express by Paola Genone, June 16, 2008.

17 In Craig Wilson, "Cirque Ignites Spark," *USA TODAY*, May 9, 2006.

18 Study conducted with 238 employees, interviewed on a daily basis, over a few years, for working on 26 different projects, in 7 different companies and 3 different industries. See *Sean Silverthorne*, "Time Pressure and

Creativity: Why Time Is Not on Your Side: Q&A with: Teresa M. Amabile and Leslie A. Perlow," July 29, 2002, http://hbswk.hbs.edu/item/3030.html

19 Aaron Ricadela, "Apotheker Seeks to Save HP's 'Lost Soul' with Software Growth." *Bloomberg Businessweek*, March 9, 2011, http://www.businessweek.com/technology/content/mar2011/tc2011039_789137.htm

20 Ashlee Vance, "Does HP Need a Dose of Anarchy?" *New York Times*, April 26, 2009.

21 Ricadela, "Apotheker Seeks to Save HP's 'Lost Soul' with Software Growth."

22 In 2008, HP's net revenue increased approximately 13.5 percent from the prior-year period (8.4 percent on a constant currency basis). In 2009, the global slowdown of IT and consumer spending impacted all HP segments, and net revenue decreased 3.2 percent from 2008 (increased 1.3 percent on a constant currency basis). According to HP's 2009 annual report, from 2007 to 2009 research and development group spending evolved as follows (in millions of USD and percentage of group consolidated net revenue): 2007: $3,611 (3.5 percent); 2008: $3,543 (3.0 percent); 2009: $2,819 (2.5 percent).

23 "HP is a technology company that operates in more than 170 countries around the world. We explore how technology and services can help people and companies address their problems and challenges, and realize their possibilities, aspirations and dreams. We apply new thinking and ideas to create more simple, valuable and trusted experiences with technology, continuously improving the way our customers live and work." http://www8.hp.com/us/en/hp-information/about-hp/index.html

24 Ricadela, "Apotheker Seeks to Save HP's 'Lost Soul' with Software Growth."

25 HP.com, official financial data dated February 22, 2011. http://h30261.www3.hp.com/phoenix.zhtml?c=71087&p=irol-newsArticle&ID=1531457&highlight=

26 Ricadela, "Apotheker Seeks to Save HP's 'Lost Soul' with Software Growth."

27 Ibid.

28 Supratim Majumdar and Kumar Satyaki Ray, The Growth Trap: A Case of Maytag Corporation, IBS Case Development Center, 2006. http://www.ibscdc.org/Case_Studies/Strategy/Growthpercent20Strategies/GRS0251K.htm

29 Ibid.

30 Ibid.
31 *Chicago Tribune*, June 5, 2001.
32 Majumdar and Ray, The Growth Trap.
33 Firmenich launched, with the expertise of NPD, a comprehensive study to understand why more and more American consumers have stopped wearing fragrance. For the first time ever, targets never considered in usual fragrance tests were studied—the Non heavy users and Lapsed users. A complex design integrating both quantitative and qualitative studies was built with the NPD 2009 FragranceTrack—a panel of more than eighteen thousand U.S. male and female consumers. Demographics of users was compared and contrasted against Non Heavy and Lapsed Users. Qualitative groups were conducted for in-depth probing. And all findings were then requantified and validated with more than 1,476 consumers of both genders. Armand de Villoutreys, worldwide president of Firmenich Perfumery Division, shared the results of this study at the Women's Wear Daily Beauty CEO Summit in Palm Beach, early May 2010.
34 Majumdar and Ray, The Growth Trap.

CHAPTER 4

1 Paradox comes from greek: *para* = contrary to and *doxa* = common opinion—thus paradox literally means "what goes contrary to common opinion."
2 Hermès website.
3 *"Crash du Concorde: 5 personnes et Continental Airlines en correctionnelle La Depêche – 3 juillet 2008,"* http://www.ladepeche.fr/article/2008/07/03/462591-Crash-du-Concorde-5-personnes-et-Continental-Airlines-en-correctionnelle.html
4 Pareto's principle was devised by business theorist Joseph M. Juran, who named it after Italian economist Vilfredo Pareto.
5 For more information on the importance of the reptilian brain on consumer behaviors, see Clothaire Rapaille, *The Culture Code* (New York: Broadway, 2006).
6 Arie de Geus, *In the Living Company* (see ch. 3, n. 8).
7 In Firmenich and NPD study on fragrance (see ch. 3, n. 33).
8 Michael Rappa, "Managing the Digital Enterprise: Case Study Netflix," http://digitalenterprise.org/cases/netflix.html
9 Mae Anderson, "Blockbuster Bankrupt: Video Chain Files For Bankruptcy Protection," *Huffington Post*, September 23, 2010.

10 "Blockbuster CEO Confused by Fascination with Netflix," *Wired*, August 18, 2008, www.wired.com/epicenter/2008/08/blockbuster-ceo/

11 "Blockbuster Appoints Former 7-Eleven CEO James W. Keyes Chairman and CEO," July 7, 2007, http://investor.blockbuster.com/phoenix.zhtml?c=99383&p=irol-newsArticle&ID=1326678&highlight=

12 Sources: *Los Angeles Times*, August 26, 2010; Bloginity.com, August 27, 2010; Wikipedia.

13 Jay Newton-Small, "Inside Obama's 50-State Fight," *Time*, June 10, 2008, http://www.time.com/time/politics/article/0,8599,1813397,00.html#ixzz1HHNf4sqV

14 "I am asking you to believe, not just in my ability to bring about real change in Washington . . . I'm asking you to believe in yours." This was one of Obama's key campaign slogans. See Organizing for America online, http://abcnews.go.com/images/Politics/obama3.pdf

15 "Mr. Obama led his party in a decisive sweep of Congress, putting Democrats in control of both the House and the Senate—by overwhelming numbers—and the White House for the first time since 1995, when Bill Clinton was president." Adam Nagourney, "Obama Wins Election; McCain Loses as Bush Legacy Is Rejected," *New York Times*, November 4, 2008, http://www.nytimes.com/2008/11/05/us/politics/05campaign.html

CHAPTER 5

1 Kayla Carrick, "U.S. Magazine Ad Sales Drop 8.2 percent, Accelerating Industry Decline," Bloomberg.com, July 2011.

2 The names and distinguishing featues of this client have been changed to protect the client's privacy.

3 Wikipedia (en.wikipedia.org/wiki/Ricardo_Semler) and Lawrence M. Fisher, "Ricardo Semler Won't Take Control," November 29, 2005, http://www.strategy-business.com/article/05408?pg=all—

4 Ricardo Semler, *The Seven-Day Weekend: Changing the Way Work Works* (New York: Portfolio, 2004). In Chapter One, "Any Day," Semler, rejecting "legacies of military hierarchies" in favor of letting employees follow their own intuition, says that his job description is to be a "catalyst . . . broaching weird ideas and asking dumb questions . . . ."

5 Ibid.

6 Reported by Dominique Haijtema, *Ode*, January 2007.

7 "NPD Reports on First Half U.S. Beauty Retail Industry," The NPD Group, Inc., press release, September 1, 2009, http://www.npd.com/press/releases/press_090901.html

8   NPD study conducted in July 2008: over nine thousand respondents between the ages of eighteen and sixty-four participated in the Women's FragranceTrack study. A total of 9,804 adults (eighteen through sixty-four) and 1,941 teens (thirteen through seventeen) participated in the study.

9   Launches of Polo Explorer for men and Notorious for women had not ultimately realized the initial expectations.

10 "Identification and Description of the Leading Edge Values and Life Styles of Generation Y in the US," conducted by Darwin Associates and Intuition, Paris, in February 2009, based on in-depth interviews of ten thought leaders and experts in the field.

11 Companies other than those whose names are on the perfume itself create most fragrances. The leading fragrance manufacturers are Firmenich, Givaudan, and IFF.

12 Fabrice Brovelli, *Le Figaro*, July 10, 2009, http://www.lefigaro.fr/medias/ 2009/07/03/04002-20090703ARTFIG00010-comment-les-bebes-d- evian-se-sont-mis-au-roller-.php

13 Megan O'Neill, "Evian's Roller Babies Viral Campaign Headed for Tele- vision," April 15, 2010, www.socialtimes.com

14 "Danone Waters Enters 2011 with 'Healthy Face,'" February 16, 2011, www.just-drinks.com/ . . . /just-on-call-danone-waters-enters-2011-with -healthy-face_id103099.aspx

15 April 2010, http://www.danone.com/en/brands/business/beverages.html

16 Founder and chairwoman of BETC, executive chairwoman of Euro RSCG Worldwide, managing director of Havas.

17 www.EuroRSCG.com

CHAPTER 6

1   The names and distinguishing features of this client have been changed to protect the client's privacy.

2   Gigerenzer, *Gut Feelings*, p. 73 (see ch. 3, n. 4).

3   Definition of *paradox* from *Collins English Dictionary—Complete & Unabridged 10th Edition* (New York: HarperCollins), http://dictionary .reference.com/browse/paradox

4   Of all the senses a human embryo develops, the ability to listen is first, at just fourteen days after conception. The auditory nerve stem is common to that of the skin. So figuratively we can say that whatever we feel in our skin is deeply connected to what we hear and vice versa. As we saw previously in Chapter Four, through our listening we have the ability to feed our imagination without the filter of the conscious mind. For neurological

reasons our ear is also involved with our sense of balance and vision. This underscores how potent our auditory sense is and how neglected and underexplored it remains to this day.

5 In ancient traditions, vision was symbolized by the arrow of the warrior, a very masculine image. In the action of seeing we organize space in a three-dimensional world, which is a form of appropriation. Conversely, listening was symbolized by the conch shell, the shape of which is traditionally associated with the female genitals. Listening enables us to be in a receptive mode.

6 In Japan during the fifteenth century, people cultivated the art of listening to incense, in a ritual called *Monko* or *Kodo*. By performing this ritual they established a link between their olfactory and auditory senses. This tradition followed a Chinese ritual in which people would listen to tea that had been poured in special bowls that would let the tea sing its melody, linking, in this case, the auditory, olfactory, and gustatory senses.

7 Professor Tomatis was a French ENT medical doctor. He developed the world-renowned Tomatis method, which has helped thousands of children and adults with learning disabilities all around the globe as well as artists and musicians such as the opera singer Maria Callas and the rock star Sting.

CHAPTER 7

1 Guy Blissett, Trevor Davis, Bill Gilmour, Patrick Medley and Mark Yeomans, "The Future of the Consumer Product Industry: The End of the World ... or a World of Opportunity?" by IBM Institute for Business Value, July 2010.

2 Microsoft's main U.S. campus received a silver certification from the Leadership in Energy and Environmental Design (LEED) program in 2008, and it installed over two thousand solar panels on top of its buildings in its Silicon Valley campus, generating approximately 15 percent of the total energy needed by the facilities in April 2005, per Elinor Mills' "Microsoft vs. Google: Who's Greener?" on CNET (CBS interactive on 06–06–2008). Microsoft also makes use of alternative forms of transit. It created one of the worlds largest private bus systems, the "Connector," to transport people from outside the company; for on-campus transportation, the "Shuttle Connect" uses a large fleet of hybrid cars to save fuel.

3 Google founders' motto, in David A. Vise, *The Google Story* (New York: Delacorte Press, 2005).

4 See http://www.google.org

5 Jeffrey Hollender interview with the author, December 20, 2010.

6 Sheila Hollender interview with the author, November 17, 2010.

7 See http://www.hoovers.com/company/Method_Products_Inc/rhhtxti-1.html

8 See http://www.americanprofile.com/articles/mrs-meyers-clean-day-products/

9 See http://www.scjohnson.com/en/press-room/fact-sheets/09–10–2009/Acquisitions-Fact-Sheet.aspx

10 GB at a glance, Muhammad Yunus, Grameen Bank, en.wikipedia.org/wiki/Muhammad_Yunus

11 See http://www.grameen-info.org/index.php?option=com_content&task=view&id=26&Itemid=175

12 See www.unilever.com

13 Unilever's CEO: Social Innovation and Sustainability the Only Game in Town, May 10, 2007, http://www.ethicalcorp.com/content.asp?ContentID=5110

14 Marcy Nicholson, "Unilever to Sell Sustainable Tea," Reuters/*San Diego Times*, May 25, 2007.

15 See http://www.unilever.com/sustainability

16 Sir Lindsay Owen Jones, interview with Simon Hobbs, "Why He's Worth It," *CNBC*, April 2008.

17 According to Matrix General Manager Colin Walsh, in a presentation at Imagination Conference, Palm Springs, California, January 31, 2011.

18 Colin Walsh interview with the author, January 6, 2011.

19 Ibid.

20 Ibid.

21 Ibid.

22 Ibid.

23 March 2010 Personal Care Marketwatch by Data Monitor.

24 Jeff Rosenthal, in a meeting with the author, June 9, 2010.

25 Annie Gowen, "Elliott Bisnow Brings Other Young Entrepreneurs Together in Summit Series," *Washington Post*, January 4, 2010, http://www.washingtonpost.com/wp-dyn/content/article/2010/01/03/AR2010010301686.html?hpid=moreheadlines

26 The amount of Parker's investment in Spotify was kept confidential during an interview with Thayer Walker, who is in charge of Summit Series communication, with the author, January 10, 2011.

27 Thayer Walker interview with the author, January 10, 2011.

28 Ibid.

29 Gowen, "Elliott Bisnow Brings Other Young Entrepreneurs Together in Summit Series."

30 Darwin Associates, New York, and Intuition Consultancy, Paris, France, "The 18–30 Generation: Unique Common Traits and Values," *HR,* May 2007, and Expert's study, March 2009, a proprietary and confidential study commissioned by L'Oréal.

31 The name of the university is kept confidential here as requested by all those interviewed for this section of the book.

32 Manuela Rousselot interview with the author, November 29, 2010.

acknowledgments

This book would not have been born without the intuition and trust of Karen Murphy; I am grateful to her and all on her team for their work and help. I am also very grateful to Kate Lee at ICM for her skillful approach and Jeff Rosenthal from Summit Series for his generosity, both of which led me to Karen. I would like to also thank my friend Dominique Dubois—analyst, artist, and rare human being—for providing ideas, inspiration, and perspectives that greatly enriched this book and the work I do. I also thank all thinkers, authors, and creative minds who preceded this book and were a great source of inspiration; I tried to give justice to their work in quoting my sources, but of course these are not exhaustive. In this respect, I would like to acknowledge the work I am privileged to do with Dr. Mark Kuras in New York and the philosophy of life he represents, as well as my encounter with Tiokasin Ghosthorse and his venerable elders and tradition. Tracy Oats also assisted me in this work and provided support as much as she brought talent and skills to help me write this book. Many thanks also to James Angley, Ethan Bassof, Michael Carlysle, Alain Coblence, Bruno Denis, Naika D'Haiti, Mercedes Erra, Dr. Lynda

Geller, Karen Grant, Janell Hanna, Jeffrey Hollender, Sheila Hollender, Dr. Beverly Hurwitz, Patricia Kamoun, Max Lugavere, Colin Walsh, Guillaume de Lesquen, Mateo Descat, Durek Verrett, Cheryl Heller, Hilary Hinzman, Guillaume Lelong, Manuela Rousselot, Armand de Villoutreys, Thayer Walker, and Bettina Wohlfarth. Finally thank you for all early readers and endorsers for their time and support, which were highly appreciated.

about the author

Francis P. Cholle is a best-selling author and an international business consultant with extensive experience in a variety of industries, from beauty and luxury to pharmaceuticals, communication, media, and information technology. At the age of twenty-four, he became managing director and, shortly thereafter, senior partner of Editions Hazan, a well-known Paris art book publisher, where he engineered and led a turnaround that doubled the company's size and made it the most profitable French publisher in any category.

He is a graduate of the HEC School of Management in Paris, rated in 2010 the best European business school for the fifth year in a row by the *Financial Times*. He is also a graduate of the Creative Problem Solving Institute in Buffalo, New York. He is accredited to offer leadership assessments through the Center for Creative Leadership, the world's largest organization devoted exclusively to leadership research and organization, and he is credentialed to administer the Myers-Briggs Type Indicator.

In addition to his business career, he has studied theater at the Lee Strasberg Theater and Film Institute and music and opera at the Robert Abramson Dalcroze Institute and the Juilliard School. He has directed and assisted in a range of cutting-edge plays, and he has performed the entire repertoire of Mozart's baritone roles. After studying with Sivananda Kutir in Uttarkashi, India, he was credentialed to teach hatha yoga. He is also credentialed in clinical psychology through the Tomatis Center in Paris and New York.

Francis draws on these varied experiences in consulting for and mentoring C-level and senior executives at major, mid-size, and emerging firms around the topics of sustainable innovation and new forms of leadership. His clients include Alcatel Lucent, Bristol-Myers Squibb, SAP Business Objects, Caritas–Secours Catholique, Clarins, Estée Lauder Companies, Firmenich, Hachette Filipacchi Media US, L'Oréal, Louis Vuitton, Matrix, Maybelline, Ralph Lauren, and Siemens.

Since 2008 he has taught a popular course at HEC Paris, "Intuitive Intelligence and Innovative Leadership," following the publication of his best-selling book *L'Intelligence Intuitive* (Eyrolles, 2007) prefaced by his dear friend, advertising guru Mercedes Erra, executive chairman of Euro-RSCG Worldwide and managing director of Havas. Francis has been invited to give lectures on "Intuitive Intelligence and Innovative Leadership" at the University of Pennsylvania Wharton MBA program, Columbia University Graduate School of Business, the Fashion Institute of Technology in New York, Institut d'Etudes Politiques Luxury MBA in Paris, and the ESCP-EAP executive MBA program in Berlin, Milan, London, Paris, and Madrid. He is a frequent speaker, and his conference "A New Intelligence for a New Economy" is also featured on iTunes U, where it hit a record with more than 150,000 downloads.

An active blogger in both English and French, Francis regularly writes articles in the French business press, and he contributed to the 2008 book *L'Art du Management* ("The Art of Management"), edited by Bernard Ramanantsoa, the director general of HEC Group in Paris.

Born and raised in Paris, he has also lived in Germany and Italy and traveled extensively worldwide on all five continents. He studied five languages and enjoys French-American dual citizenship. He divides his time today between Los Angeles, New York, and Paris.

For more information, please visit www.francischolle.com

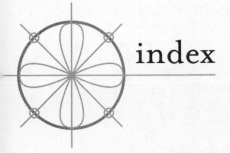

index

Page references followed by *fig* indicates an illustrated figure.